A JOURNEY INTO THE GENIUS MIND

10 THINKERS SHOW US HOW TO THINK

SHAI TUBALI | THERESA BÄUERLEIN

Human Greatness Publishing
Altensteinstraße 48a, 14195, Berlin
www.hg-publishing.com

Cover and internal images:

Friedrich Nietzsche, Leonardo da Vinci, Socrates, Charles Darwin, Giordano Bruno © Shutterstock

Albert Einstein, Barbara McClintock, Sigmund Freud, Hannah Arendt © Science Photo Library

Jiddu Krishnamurti © Imago images

ISBN: 978-3-9822517-0-7
First Edition
Printed in Germany

The chapters on Da Vinci, Socrates, Darwin, and Bruno, were translated from German by David A. Brenner

Edited by Michael Garvey

Cover and inner design by Andy at meadencreative.com

CONTENTS

PREFACE

Everyone knows the mythical stories of moments of sudden revelation in the lives of great discoverers: Archimedes rising from his bath, so deeply impressed by his new discovery that he takes to the streets naked, crying "Eureka!"; Isaac Newton formulating his theory of gravitation upon seeing an apple fall from a tree (or, in the cartoon-like version, after being hit on the head by a falling apple); Albert Einstein witnessing a man drop from a neighboring roof while sitting in his Berlin apartment. Such stories, often distorted and exaggerated, aim to capture the dazzling moments in which the human mind takes its most stupendous leaps. These stories of genius are engraved in our psyches.

However, we tend to neglect a question of great significance: What preceded these sudden leaps? Surely, prior to these moments of profound insight, intense, perhaps unconscious thought processes had taken place in the minds of these discoverers. Something was slowly consolidating in the depths, wordless and elusive. So what were the extraordinary thought processes that enabled these particular discoverers to tap into great cosmic secrets? What unique structures of thinking made it possible for Archimedes to learn so much from his mundane bath and for Newton to deduce a cosmic principle from a falling apple in his garden?

This was the key question that drove us to write this book. We sought to learn about the ways of thinking that yielded such mental accomplishments. In Barbara McClintock's time, there were many other geneticists striving to decode the mysteries of the genome and, in Einstein's time, more than a few physicists and mathematicians came close to discerning the principles of the special and general relativity theory. They looked at the same equations, gathered very similar data, sometimes even shared the same revolutionary thoughts, and yet they could not make that leap. It was our belief that there had to be some factor that propelled thinkers like McClintock and Einstein toward their groundbreaking conclusions.

The enormity of the final discovery is often so dazzling that it is difficult to shift the focus to the hidden mental factor that facilitated it. Thus, we constantly needed to remind ourselves while brainstorming together that our focus had to be the qualities of the discovering mind, rather than the discovery itself. It is so easy to get carried away by Sigmund Freud's intricate models of the subconscious or to become fascinated by the form of the Socratic dialogue that we often ended up straying from the path we had marked out for ourselves. We had set ourselves the task of illuminating the great mind, so although any creation obviously reflects the mind of its creator, it is still the end result of exceptional processes of thinking.

With this guiding question in mind, we did not necessarily choose the most obvious list of geniuses. The Renaissance figure Giordano Bruno, for instance, will clearly never be as well remembered in the history of science as Galileo Galilei; however, it was precisely his ability, as a non-scientist, to realize the infinity and centerlessness of the universe that drew our attention. In addition to choosing well-known figures, like Einstein and Socrates, we allowed ourselves to deviate from the common route in order to explore a few roads that are less traveled by. We were looking not so much for "geniuses" as original and innovative thinkers who were more than simply creative and perceptive within their own field. We sought those rich, complex, and even poetic minds that were characterized by exceptional profundity and insight. Such thinkers seem to possess their own grand vision of the world. Their way of thinking is "larger than life." Consequently, such thinkers often redefine the way humanity as a whole perceives the world in which it lives.

Our criteria make the list of discoverers discussed in this book a rather personal one; although, it must be acknowledged that any selection of the hundreds of great thinkers throughout human history would involve some personal selectivity. We didn't pick anyone who didn't excite us to the root of our being. Delving deeply into someone's mind, especially when that someone is highly intelligent, is so demanding that we felt it would require great passion and curiosity on our part. That is why you will find figures on our list who are less known outside of their particular fields. Jiddu Krishnamurti, for instance, is very famous within spiritual philosophy circles, but hardly known to the general public and Barbara McClintock is far less known than, say, Marie Curie. Yet their unique styles of thinking struck us as well suited to the premise of this book as a whole.

Is it fair that great thinkers like Newton or Michael Faraday, Nikola Tesla or Immanuel Kant, had to be omitted to make room for our less conventional choices? Of course not! We found the decisions about whom to include agonizing—an agony that is experienced, it seems, by all authors who take it upon themselves to create compilations and anthologies. Most probably, we will be haunted by those great figures we omitted for many years, knowing that our list could never really be complete without them.

Our final list contained two biologists—one a naturalist and the other a geneticist—a physicist, a psychologist, and an artist and inventor. The other five people on our list are different kinds of philosophers—one materialist, one spiritual, one scientific, one classical, and one political. Interestingly, and unintentionally, four of them—Freud, Einstein, Friedrich Nietzsche, and Hannah Arendt—came from German-speaking countries. For reasons we will explain below, seven of them have been chosen from either the nineteenth or the twentieth centuries. Only three of them—Socrates, Bruno, and Leonardo da Vinci—lived in more ancient times.

Sometimes it was our wish for variety in terms of fields of research and types of personalities that led us to set aside a particular intellectual giant, as in the case of Newton, who seemed somewhat close in spirit to his "successor" Einstein. But in more than a few cases, we felt compelled to neglect some fascinating figure for the simple reason that not enough biographical materials had been gathered or that not enough of their direct thoughts had survived the vicissitudes of history. That is why you will not find a fair chronological treatment of great minds in this book. For obvious reasons, there is far more documentation regarding the inner worlds of nineteenth- and twentieth-century thinkers. As our intention was to tap into the inner worlds that gave rise to breakthroughs, we had to rely on such documentation.

The lack of documentation was a major problem when it came to great women thinkers. Here, we were faced with one of the saddest aspects of human history: the fact that women were not encouraged to think at all. Learning about courageous women here and there throughout history, like Hypatia or Anne Conway, Émilie du Châtelet or Mary Somerville, who vehemently resisted the status quo and creatively participated in a patriarchal world filled us with admiration. Even in the twentieth century, especially its first half, women had to demonstrate their genius literally against all odds. They were rarely allowed to hold powerful positions and were too often robbed of their discoveries, which were claimed by the men around them. Biographers and historians are toiling to grant these women the historical status they truly deserve. In light of this state of affairs, we chose two twentieth-century female figures, about whom there is richer and more intimate documentation.

Now, we are not biologists or physicists or psychologists. We do not pretend to be among the "twelve people in the world who understand Einstein's relativity theory,"[1] nor do we claim to fathom the intricate developments of twentieth-century genetics (though we certainly went over and above our intellectual limits in our attempts to comprehend both!). Fortunately, the aspiration of this book is not

1 Maurice Timmermans, "Myth: hardly anyone understands the general theory of relativity," *Observant*, January 10, 2018. https://www.observantonline.nl/English/Home/Articles/articleType/ArticleView/articleId/13192/Myth-hardly-anyone-understands-the-general-theory-of-relativity.

to provide a complete understanding of such discoveries. Revealing the structure of thinking that led to them is a very different task: It doesn't necessitate being a specialist in the field, but it does require a more direct understanding of the way in which the person's mind encountered its object of study. This allows for a much more intimate and personal approach, during which we no doubt exhausted our capacities as an investigating journalist who has been observing social and psychological phenomena for years (Theresa) and an independent thinker who has been looking into the human psyche and mind for quite some time (Shai).

How exactly did we accomplish our goal of merging with these great minds? After all, our extensive study of the materials at hand could not directly provide us with the answers we sought. As we have said, ways of thinking tend to hide between the lines, more hinted at or echoed in the biographical material itself than explicitly stated. Over time, we found several ways of cracking their ways of thinking, though this did not spare us occasional frustration:

1. Comparing the figure's way of thinking with the ways of thinking of other brilliant thinkers who were alive at the same time and yet did not manage to make such a breakthrough. What inhibited such realization? And what made it easier for our chosen thinker to succeed where everyone else seemed to have failed? Put more simply: Why Einstein and not Max Planck? Why Bruno and not a real scientist of his time?

2. Attentively reading the descriptions of the inner processes that occurred just before the irruption of insight. This bubbling inner process is usually disclosed in letters that such figures wrote to their friends or colleagues, in private diaries, and in their friends' and colleagues' direct testimonies.

3. Looking for the common ground shared by all of the figure's various discoveries and accomplishments. Some accomplishments seem to be very different from one another, such as da Vinci's *Last Supper*

and his drawings of the flying machine, but they emerged from one mind, one structure of thinking. Finding that subtle connecting thread was of crucial importance to us. This thread also served as a measure against which we later tested the validity of the way of thinking we defined: Did it apply only to some of the discoveries or did it apply to all discoveries?

4. Identifying other hobbies or interests that fascinated the thinker, such as the music he or she loved or how he or she chose to spend free time. Einstein's love of Mozart, for example, and Freud's obsession with artifacts were of great help to us.

5. Sometimes the thinkers themselves were generous enough to provide us with their own direct description of their way of thinking. This was usually encouraged by some keen researcher. When seeking the right words for this unique self-observation, they tended to use metaphors, which have proved so helpful to us that we ultimately decided to use them as titles for all of our chapters.

6. We sometimes tried to look through the eyes of these thinkers in order to see the world as they saw it. In doing so, we used the richness of our imagination (a capacity which many of these figures greatly encouraged) to sense and feel the intimate way in which their mind perceived, and communicated with, life.

Though all ten chapters have the same structure, we consider each one of the chapters a whole journey in itself (only in the epilogue will we present the connections and relations between all the different journeys contained in the chapters). This is how we experienced the writing of this book: Each encounter with a great mind seemed like a trip into a new world without visible horizons. Indeed, such minds are so vast that we couldn't possibly explore all aspects of them within the limitations of one chapter. We could easily write a whole book on the basis of each of these figures' ways of thinking. The profundity and intimacy of our encounters has also made this volume a personal journey. This is yet another reason why there is no biographical commitment in these chapters or any scientific commitment to outline in detail any of the thinkers' discoveries. Everything else serves as a backdrop for the one drama that truly excited us: the extraordinarily original mechanism of thinking that characterized these great minds.

Can we confidently claim that the mental factor we identify is the fundamental reason for the astonishing breakthroughs made by these figures? Most probably not. There seems to be another "secret" factor that makes a genius a genius—some innate reason for this unique structure of thinking. Though highly inspiring, this element does not seem to be something we can replicate or imitate. So, contrary to Simone de Beauvoir's famous statement that "one is not born a genius; one becomes a genius,"[2] and contrary to those books that claim that we can all become geniuses like da Vinci, we find it questionable, with this secret factor in mind, that anyone can become a genius.

However, this book's true hero is not these ten figures. It is, rather, human thinking, yours and ours, and its dormant potential. The book is all about how our thinking, when it operates optimally, can be a source of tremendous creative worlds, innovative discoveries, and breathtaking insights—as well as how, when distorted and flawed, it can entrap us in hopelessly stubborn patterns and habits. In this broader context, the reason we turned to these great thinkers was less about them and more about us. Assuming that, at least in their own fields of study, their minds were functioning at their maximal potential, we were motivated by the hope of extricating secret ways in which minds, in general, can operate better. So, beyond our declared intention to fathom the workings of great minds, this book also aims to study how we, too, can at least partially imitate or copy such structures of thinking.

This latter ambition was at least as important as the former. Otherwise, reading this book would have been akin to looking at some

2 Simone de Beauvoir, *The Second Sex*, trans. and ed. H.M. Parshley (New York: Vintage Books, 1974), 133.

supermodel, half-admiring, half-envying her beauty, and knowing we could never even get close to attaining it ourselves. Rather than merely presenting these original patterns of thinking, we aspired to bring the mind of the genius closer to that of the reader; in other words, to demonstrate that the ways of thinking of such a mind are at least partially acquirable. Most likely, no one among us is expected, in the near future, to revolutionize physics, as Einstein did, but Einstein's way of thinking can certainly illuminate our thinking errors, as well as new pathways to enhanced forms of thinking.

To fulfill our aim, we intentionally distinguished the pattern of thinking from the thinker and gave it a title (like "paradoxical thinking" or "organic thinking"), thereby making it a principle of thinking, independent of the person. We then present it alongside another more conditioned and erroneous principle of thinking (like "either/or thinking" or "detached thinking"). We felt that presenting two opposing principles of thinking would be more conducive to an inner journey during which self-reflection would be possible. We also related these principles of thinking to the wonderful emerging field of research of cognitive errors and biases. In addition, we dedicated a few pages in each chapter to a more direct confrontation with standard patterns of thinking and the way in which the enhanced pattern of thinking reflects our mental errors and, if adopted, can also correct them. Though this is not a practical guidebook, readers may find suggestions for ways of improving their thinking, as well as thought experiments that they can try.

Shai Tubali and Theresa Bauerlein

CHAPTER 1

ALBERT EINSTEIN

Thinking without words, *or* The beetle that managed to see

We are not the first to be possessed by a wish to understand the mind of Albert Einstein. He, whose mere name has become a synonym for the word "genius" even in the minds of children, has been an obvious target for a passionate pursuit of the nature of genius by scientists and thinkers alike. Some even took the idea of inquiring into the nature of Einstein's mind literally: In 1955, after his death, although the rest of his body was cremated and his ashes scattered, Einstein's brain commenced a strange journey as a wandering relic spanning more than four decades.

A pathologist at Princeton Hospital, Thomas Harvey, had secretly decided to embalm the brain and keep it. In response to the complaints of the horrified Einstein family, Harvey insisted that there could be scientific value in studying Einstein's brain. Unsure what to do, the family did nothing and so Harvey became the sole possessor of the brain and would occasionally send off slides or chunks of the brain to random researchers, as he saw fit.

Only three of the dozens of scientists who enjoyed the privilege of investigating Einstein's brain published significant studies. The first study was by a Berkeley team, which found that part of Einstein's brain, located in the parietal cortex, had a higher ratio of glial cells to neurons.

This could indicate that "the neurons used and needed more energy."[3] However, there were no other genius brains available to help determine whether the findings fit a pattern. Moreover, this may have been the effect of exercising certain parts of the brain for so many years rather than the cause of Einstein's greater intelligence.

A second research study, published in 1996, suggested that the cerebral cortex was thinner than in an ordinary brain and that the density of the neurons was greater. The third and latest research study, written in 1999, has become the most cited. Compared with regular brains, Einstein's seemed to have a much shorter groove in one area of his inferior parietal lobe, supposedly the key to mathematical and spatial thinking, in addition to which this region of his brain was wider. The researchers speculated that such traits could produce richer and more integrated brain circuits in the region.

However, as Einstein's most recent biographer Walter Isaacson wisely writes, "any true understanding of Einstein's imagination and intuition will not come from poking around at his patterns of glia and grooves."[4] The truly relevant question, he concludes, is how his mind worked, not his brain.

Einstein himself generously attempted to fathom the workings of his own mind, often with the encouragement of other thinkers and researchers. Perhaps one of his most colorful and vivid explanations was given in answer to his younger son, Eduard, who wondered why his father had become so famous: "When a blind beetle crawls over the surface of a curved branch, it doesn't notice that the track it has covered is indeed curved. I was lucky enough to notice what the beetle didn't notice."[5] As puzzling as this may sound, this simple metaphor will prove

3 Marian C. Diamond, Arnold B. Scheibel, Greer M. Murphy Jr, and Thomas Harvey, "On the brain of a scientist: Albert Einstein," *Experimental neurology* 88, no. 1 (1985), 198–204.

4 Walter Isaacson, *Einstein: His Life and Universe* (New York: Simon & Schuster Paperbacks, 2017), 548.

5 David Glickenstein, "A Bug's Eye View: The Riemannian Exponential Map on Polyhedral Surfaces," *The Mathematical Intelligencer* 40, no. 2 (2018), 1.

to be a significant key to the secret of Einstein's mind throughout this chapter. So, let us follow this blind beetle's track and try to see through its own eyes what exactly it managed to see and why.

The two faces of the light

In 1900, Max Planck was struggling to formulate an equation that would describe the curve of radiation wavelengths at different temperatures. This peculiar equation seemed to necessitate an odd feature: A "constant" had to be included for it to come out right. In years to come, this would be called Planck's constant, one of the fundamental constants of nature.

Perhaps Planck scratched his head out of intellectual embarrassment. What was this mysterious factor that forced itself into his equation? Did it have any physical meaning at all? It *could* be an indication that the light behaves, at least under certain conditions, not as waves but as something quite different.

Planck was a superb scientist. One can imagine consequences and implications rushing through his mind. If this abnormality revealed something about the fundamental nature of the light, it would cause an earthquake in the field of physics. It would probably bring about the total collapse of classical physics, which he so admired. Ah, good old nineteenth-century physics and its notions of the perfectly continuous behavior of light!

Now, what should he do with this amazing piece of evidence, which showed beyond doubt that light, in its encounters with matter, demonstrates discontinuous, particle-like behavior?

Even if he did feel the earth shaking underneath his feet, he could not accept the contradiction implicit in his discovery. He resettled himself in his chair and closed the matter by determining that his constant was a mere calculational contrivance that explained the particular process of emitting or absorbing light; in other words, this was a special condition in which the light was involved and not its nature.

Who could have known that this disturbing revelation would one day turn into quantum mechanics, one of the greatest revolutions in physics? Planck most certainly didn't. Enamored as he was of the idea of "continuous matter," he truly *preferred to think* of those newfound "vibrating molecules" or "harmonic oscillators," which appeared only in the form of discrete packets, as a phenomenon that had nothing to do with physical reality.

What prevented Planck from taking this giant leap is no great mystery. Clearly, it was not simply a matter of wanting to hold on to his respectable position in the university. Like many other great scientists, he loved the old structures of thought, which felt stable and secure. Newton and the nineteenth-century physicists that followed him had left as their legacy a mechanical universe that was supremely reasonable. In theory, everything in such a safe and steady world could be explained, determined, and predicted. Going against such a conception of the world would mean groping in the dark, with fear and astonishment, and dragging the entire human race toward a new conception of the world that was far less comprehensible and controllable.

Far from the cozy embrace of the academic world, a clerk at the Bern patent office would make the leap that Planck hadn't been able to make. Einstein quickly realized the implications: "All of this was quite clear to me shortly after the appearance of Planck's fundamental work. All of my attempts to adapt the theoretical foundation of physics to this knowledge failed completely. It was as if the ground had been pulled from under us, with no firm foundation to be seen anywhere."[6] In an article published in 1905, Einstein took the mathematical quirk discovered by Planck, interpreted it literally, and analyzed light as if it

6 Isaacson, *Einstein*, 177.

really were made up of light quanta. Thus, he blew on Planck's embers, turning them into the flame that would consume classical physics—and, unintentionally, turning Planck into a reluctant revolutionary. Planck actually resisted his own revelation for the rest of his life. Just before he died, he reflected: "My futile attempts to fit the elementary quantum of action somehow into classical theory continued for a number of years and cost me a great deal of effort. Many of my colleagues saw in this something bordering on a tragedy."[7]

Planck wanted with all his heart to fit the new knowledge into the old structures of thought, whereas Einstein was far more willing to accept that the old structures needed to come apart. Einstein, too, admired the Newtonian universe, but it seems that one of the most elementary characteristics of geniuses is the ability to disengage from the glorious knowledge of the past. The discoveries of geniuses demand a willingness to prefer higher truth to the comfort of existing knowledge. Pursuing such truth necessitates leaping into a new, uncharted territory, which is always frightening. But for geniuses, whatever affords safety becomes a limitation that hinders bolder revelations. Through their eyes, the old knowledge is regarded as we would usually regard our parents: We are grateful for everything they did for us, but also wish to leave behind the familiar nest they created and go on our own journey of exploration.

Although Einstein was not alone in making his revelations and breakthroughs, he was always the one who took the step that everyone else was too hesitant to take. The first reason for this was that he was willing to break the old structures, to admit that they could no longer contain reality. When reality cannot be contained by your structures of thought, what do you do? Squeeze it with all your might to make it fit your worldview or allow this surge of overwhelming confusion to wash over you? For Einstein, there was no choice. Ironically, Henri Poincaré, the man who himself almost came up with the special theory

7 Marco Mamone Capria, *Physics before and after Einstein* (Amsterdam: IOS Press, 2005), 184.

of relativity, yet could not embrace its implications, said of Einstein: "What I admire in him is the facility with which he adapts himself to new concepts. He does not remain attached to classical principles, and, when presented with a problem in physics, is prompt to envision all the possibilities."[8] Freeman Dyson, a theoretical physicist in Princeton, further explained: "When Poincaré looked for a new theory of electromagnetism, he tried to preserve as much as he could of the old ... Einstein, on the other hand, saw the old framework as cumbersome and unnecessary and was delighted to be rid of it."[9]

There was much more to it though: Planck and Poincaré preferred to hold onto their old patterns of their thinking because they thought in a one-dimensional and linear way. They could think only about one route at a time, since their minds weren't flexible enough to move in "wilder" directions. It is like Planck's belief in "continuous matter" and light as an uninterrupted wave: Reality could flow only in one steady direction, without contradiction, and any contradiction would need to be strongly dealt with, excused, or simply overlooked.

Here, they were surpassed by Einstein, whose mind had a unique and rare trait: His way of thinking was multi-dimensional and simultaneous and so he didn't balk at paradoxes and contradictions. On the contrary, for him, a paradox was just a catalyst on the path to some greater and more complex reality. What, to Planck, sounded like two instruments playing different melodies sounded to Einstein like one harmonious melody. For this reason, in the face of the question that had troubled even the ancient Greeks whether the universe was made of particles or an uninterrupted continuum—he was able to answer that the universe was made of *both*. Only a holistic and simultaneous way of thinking could turn such a contradiction into a miraculous dual reality.

Ordinary minds don't like contradictions, since they don't like confusion. They force new and uncomfortable data into old structures,

8 Isaacson, Einstein, 177.
9 Ibid., 134.

simply because they think only in terms of "this *or* that." This is "either/or" thinking, the most common type of thinking, and it is based on sharp and rigid distinctions that refuse to yield even in the face of an overwhelmingly clear reality. When "either/or" thinking encounters a contradiction, it inevitably becomes dazed and confused. Then it denies what it saw.

Einstein could not tolerate "either/or" thinking. He thought in harmonies, unities, and simplicities. In his mind, there could be no contradictions in reality, only wholeness, so any such seeming contradictions only called for a new conception of an even greater, unimaginable wholeness. We can find evidence of this behind any of his discoveries. Whenever the old system of thought became too rigid and dualistic, complicated and conflictual, he sought that perfect melody, a higher form of musicality that beautifully contained two forces as one. After giving a speech at the Salzburg conference in 1909, with the worried Planck in the audience, he merrily wrote in a letter: "Is it possible to combine energy quanta and the wave principles of radiation? Appearances are against it, but the Almighty—it seems—managed the trick."[10] His colleagues, however, did not accept this dual nature of light so merrily. As Banesh Hoffmann humorously wrote: "They could but make the best of it, and went around with woebegone faces sadly complaining that on Mondays, Wednesdays, and Fridays they must look upon light as a wave; on Tuesdays, Thursdays and Saturdays, as a particle. On Sundays they simply prayed."[11]

Since "either/or" thinking can only perceive one part of reality at a time, other physicists were overwhelmed by the new simultaneity. Einstein, on the other hand, was quickly adapting to the more complex worldview. His mind, it seemed, was far more flexible. Instead of resisting the complexity, his mind simply grew more until it could accommodate such complexity. Whereas ordinary rigid thinking

---

10 Isaacson, *Einstein*, 157.
11 Ibid., 38.

understands only static systems and truths, his flexible way of thinking allowed for the paradoxical movement of life and the cosmos. Outside of the realms of "either/or" thinking, a wild cosmic dance unfolded before his eyes: one total movement in which all the different forces are woven together, so dynamic, alive, and vibrant that it can make those bound to ordinary thinking shrink in horror. The difference is akin to that between sharp, cold, metal architectural structures and rounded or curved structures that, though man-made, preserve the flow of nature and seem to emerge directly from the earth. "Either/or" thinking requires that every element be in its proper place: here is "time" and there is "space"; here is the "electromagnetic field" and there is "gravity." Things don't dance; they *function*. This type of thinking is characterized by structure, one-dimensionality, and frozen systems, in contrast to simultaneous thinking, which is distinguished by its ability to allow the destruction of old structures, to contain, without getting confused, paradoxes and contradictions, and to accept dynamic realities.

A dancing universe

From the time of his revolutionary understanding of light onwards, Einstein's extraordinary flexibility of mind threatened to devour any other physical contradiction in our known universe. As Isaacson writes, "He retained the ability to hold two thoughts in his mind simultaneously, to be puzzled when they conflicted, and to marvel when he could smell an underlying unity."[12] He simply couldn't bear when two unrelated theories explained the same phenomenon and he wouldn't accept theories that were limited only to special cases and conditions. Every possible element had to be sucked into this cosmic, unified dance that the exhilarated Einstein saw in his mind's eye.

In 1905, while struggling with his special relativity, Einstein was on the verge of despair. He started feeling that "there appears to be

12 Isaacson, *Einstein*, 157.

nothing else to do than to abandon the principle of relativity."[13] By that time, he had become convinced of two apparently contradictory realities: one was the principle of relativity and the second was the "light postulate." The easiest way to grasp the agonizing contradiction that the "light postulate" introduced into his relativity principle is by using the imagination, as Einstein did. Imagine a ray of light that is sent along the embankment of a railway track. If a person standing by the tracks measured the speed of the ray of light as it passed, they would find that it was traveling at 186,000 miles per second. We would assume that if a person riding on the train moving at 2,000 miles per second were to measure the speed of the ray of light, they would find that it was traveling at 184,000 miles per second. This would mean that the velocity of propagation of a ray of light relative to the carriage comes out *smaller*. "But this result," Einstein complained, "comes into conflict with the principle of relativity." The law of the transmission of light must be the same, whether it is measured from the train or the embankment. How could he have both? This confusion resulted in him spending almost a year in fruitless thought.

Then he had a delightful experience. While walking with a friend and talking about his dilemma, he suddenly got it: *Both are possible*, if we understand that time cannot be absolutely defined. Two events that seem to one person to be occurring at the same time will not seem to be occurring at the same time to another person who is moving rapidly—and it cannot be said that either one of these people is truly correct. Suppose lightning bolts strike the embankment in two distant places, A and B. We would define the two strikes as simultaneous only if we were located at the midpoint between them and the light from both reached us at precisely the same time. But if a train is moving to the right relative to the embankment, the observer inside will be rushing closer to place B and so he or she will assert that the lightning hit at B

13 Albert Einstein, "The Apparent Incompatibility of the Law of Propagation of Light with the Principle of Relativity," in *Relativity: The Special and the General Theory – 100th Anniversary Edition* (Princeton, NJ: Princeton University Press, 2015).

before it hit at A.

Einstein used his lively intuition rather than getting stuck in formulations and concepts: He simply got that the root of the problem was that we think there is an absolute time. The concept of absolute time—time that exists in "reality"—was one of Newton's legacies. In light of Einstein's new insight, that there is no way of knowing that any two events are "absolutely" or "really" simultaneous, Einstein finally made the concept of absolute time collapse. Time became part of the dance: relative, undefined, alive.

Einstein took an even bolder step when he threw the stubborn scientific dogma of the "ether" into the dustbin of history: Ether was posited to be an all-pervading, infinitely elastic, yet utterly elusive substance in which all time and space existed. While the other physicists of his time were frantically and obsessively searching for ether out of a sense of traditional duty, he made Newton's ether disappear along with absolute space and time. In his mind, everything had to move as one, like a whirlpool that consumes every independently existing thing. In his dynamic and living universe, all things constantly pulled and influenced each other.

It was no wonder, then, that after the dazzling success of special relativity, he vigorously moved toward the composition of an even greater cosmic symphony: general relativity. Just listen to the melody of general relativity as it is described by physicist Brian Greene:

> Space and time become players in the evolving cosmos. They come alive. Matter here causes space to warp there, which causes matter over here to move, which causes space way over there to warp even more, and so on. General relativity provides the choreography for an entwined cosmic dance of space, time, matter, and energy.[14]

This was a whole new way of looking at reality. Newton had left behind a universe in which time had an absolute existence and tick-tocked

14 Isaacson, *Einstein*, 220.

along, independent of objects and observers; a universe in which space had an absolute existence and gravity was a force that masses exerted on one another. Then came Einstein, who robbed space and time of their independent existences and showed how they formed the fabric of *spacetime*. This fabric was not merely a container for objects and events; it had its own dynamics that were determined by, and in turn helped determine, the motion of everything within it. Gravity was the curving and rippling fabric of spacetime. Inertia was simply the interaction between masses and not an effect in which "space" itself was involved. How glorious it is to see the moving and living cosmos captured within mathematical equations!

In 1917, Einstein demonstrated the paradox-embracing nature of his mind again when he started developing a "somewhat crazy idea." It was an idea that initially struck him as so wacky that he told his friend, it "exposes me to the danger of being confined to a mad-house."[15] His new theory was his answer to the question of whether the universe is infinite or finite. He claimed that an absolutely infinite universe was not plausible, since there would be an infinite amount of gravity tugging at every point and an infinite amount of light shining from every direction. So what about a finite universe floating in some random location in space? That was also inconceivable: What would keep the stars and energy from escaping and depleting the universe? Einstein conceived of a *third* option: a finite universe without boundaries, a system that is closed but that has no end or edge to it.

In the third and last part of his life, he attempted to attain the ultimate goal: a unified field theory that would tie together electricity *and* magnetism *and* gravity *and* quantum mechanics. "The mind striving after unification cannot be satisfied that two fields should exist which, by their nature, are quite independent," he explained in his Nobel Prize acceptance speech.[16] It had always been his greatest ambition to unify the duality of natural laws. His dream was to discover that the

15 M. Bartusiak, *The day we found the universe* (New York: Vintage Books, 2010), 141.
16 Isaacson, *Einstein*, 337.

force that moves electrons in their ellipses around the nuclei of atoms is the same force that moves our Earth in its annual course around the sun. But it was even more ambitious than that. He was actually hoping to do away with the very concept of matter:

> There is no sense in regarding matter and field as two qualities quite different from each other ... Could we not reject the concept of matter and build a pure field physics? We would regard matter as the regions in space where the field is extremely strong.[17]

How beautiful and utterly simple that would be! However, over time, new forces and elements were discovered, making the picture ever more complex, and Einstein was accused by his colleagues of becoming too philosophical and dogmatic, for he turned his back on the new evidence. He didn't manage to achieve his dream, but he died trying with all his might, even in the last hours of his life. Ultimately, he left for others his dream of a "theory of everything."

Einstein's most basic equation

In the simplest way possible, which was Einstein's favorite way of operating, we can describe his simultaneous mind using this primitive equation:

$$1+1=1$$

"Either/or" thinking leads scientists (and us, quite often) to mistakenly conclude that there are things that simply cannot be reconciled with each other. When faced with the contradictions of life, we believe we can only choose one side of the coin. Such thinking traps us in the world of polarity. Einstein always perceived a dual reality as two sides of the same coin (just think of his most famous equation, $E = mc^2$. It simply

17 Ibid., 463.

states that mass and energy are different manifestations of the *same thing*). It was as if he could see in three dimensions, whereas ordinary thinking can only conceive of one dimension.

For Einstein, two elements always formed one greater element. Add one more element to that greater element and *it will still be one*. How can that be? In "either/or" thinking, every element increases the sum total and so things become more and more complicated with every new thing that enters its system. That's why such thinking tends to automatically reject new ideas and information.

The secret behind Einstein's formula is simplicity. You would expect the greatest genius of the twentieth century to advocate highly sophisticated thinking, but the very opposite was true. The number of Einstein quotations praising the simple mind is astonishing. Whenever Einstein celebrated the emergence of one of his glorious equations, he took pride in its being "simple." He strongly believed that "when the solution is simple, God is answering"—the same God that made nature "according to the simplest conceivable mathematical ideas."[18]

Obviously, Einstein did not praise the simplicity of a caveman hunting for his food. His simplicity wasn't a more primitive level of thinking, but rather a *higher* state of the mind—higher than thinking in terms of distinctions and concepts. Indeed, simplicity was, for him, another kind of intelligence.

"Either/or" thinking would always consider simplicity to be the opposite of complexity. This is yet another duality that needs to be overcome. Simplicity opposes complication, not complexity. We can hold complex ideas in our mind without falling into complication, just as Einstein did, since complexity is simply a state of mind that contains many elements in perfect harmony. We actually need this simple mind to handle complexity and resolve it. The simple can handle the complex,

18 Don A. Howard and Marco Giovanelli, "Einstein's Philosophy of Science," *The Stanford Encyclopedia of Philosophy* (Fall 2019 Edition), ed. Edward N. Zalta, https://plato.stanford.edu/archives/fall2019/entries/einstein-philscience/.

whereas the complicated turns complexity into chaos by making everything appear more contradictory and conflicting than it really is.

In short, we can only really grasp complex ideas with a simple mind. The more complex ideas are, the simpler our mind should be.

In this sense, any pair of opposites we might think of represents a failure in our thinking: We are missing the wholeness and totality that contain them both. The simple mind allows all opposites to fall into place to form one complete picture of reality. Everything that is added only enhances the picture. The simple mind can let new elements in, using them to grow rather than trying to squeeze them into the old box.

Just think for a moment of a few opposites in our lives:

Being in partnership / Being alone

Individuality / Dependency

Wild instincts / Self-discipline

Animalistic urges / Sublime urges

Material / Spiritual

Religious / Scientific

Tension / Relaxation

Friction / Peace

Emotion / Intellect

Intuition / Logic

Egoism / Altruism

Free will / Determinism

"Either/or" thinking is so rigid that it can never contain such opposites as part of one natural flow. Even when it accepts a certain pair of opposites as two legitimate expressions in life, it is able to stick to only one at a time. That is why Einstein, loyal to his simultaneous thinking in his personal life too, confused and agitated so many by defining himself as a "deeply religious nonbeliever—this is a somewhat new kind of religion."[19]

Life is a set of paradoxes. For ordinary thinking, paradoxes represent logical failures, but here is a thought experiment that might challenge that perception: Can we imagine a reality that allows both opposites at the same time? Can we think of such contradictions and search for a place in our minds in which they are completely contained in harmony? Is there a place in our thought in which we can see with dazzling simplicity that relaxation, for example, is not in contradiction with tension, that these two can co-exist as one?

If one looks deeply into one's own mind, it may become apparent that the mind is constrained by rigid and sharp distinctions and the notion that it must always choose one and neglect the other. Knowing that we can have them both may come as a relief; it's as if we are creating a vaster space within that can contain all the forces of life. Really, these are complementary opposites that dance and move together. Neither exists without the other. So they can either cancel each other out or come together to form a greater whole. For Einstein, such thinking was closest to God's reality: a totally complex system that operates and flows as inseparable unity and can never be understood through complication or contradiction. Only a very simple mind could get into God's head.

However, our journey with the blind beetle has not yet come to an end. After all, the question remains: How could Einstein perceive these simple/complex patterns of reality?

Thinking without thinking

19 R. Dawkins and L. Ward, *The God Delusion* (Boston, MA: Houghton Mifflin Company, 2006), 36.

The house was a mess. Mileva, Einstein's first wife, was lying down in the bedroom, still exhausted after Eduard's difficult birth three months ago. The newborn was crying with all his might while Mileva was gently trying to comfort him. His older brother, 6-year-old Hans, tried to get his father's attention so he would play with him. "Wait a minute. I've nearly finished," Albert said mindlessly while scribbling what, to Hans, looked like strange figures and forms on a torn piece of paper. A second later, his father moaned, "Oh! This doesn't work! Where is it?" Hans knew that he was referring to his violin. Albert ran into his study and closed the door. Shortly thereafter, beautiful harmonies filled the house with heavenly beauty. Carried away by the melody, Hans could no longer play. Even tiny Eduard stopped crying. Fifteen minutes later, a joyful voice announced: "There, now I've got it!"

This was a typical afternoon in the Einstein family's house in Zurich in the year 1910. But the violin also proved very useful during those years when Einstein lived alone in Berlin and wrestled with the general relativity theory. He would often play the instrument in the kitchen, late at night, improvising melodies while he pondered complicated problems. Then, in the midst of playing, he would excitedly declare, "I've got it!"

Einstein was considered a talented violinist and touched the hearts of his listeners even in his adolescent years. But playing music did not serve as an enjoyable distraction or as a hobby, like playing golf or mountain-climbing. It encouraged his mind to come up with some new, far more creative answer. The violin and the piano were actually tools of insight that helped transfer his mind to the heart of the cosmos, where God's perfect melodies, so he felt, were played and waiting to be turned into either equations *or* symphonies.

On the wall in his study, he hung pictures of his three greatest sources of inspiration—the English scientist Michael Faraday, the Scottish physicist James Clerk Maxwell, and the English mathematician Isaac Newton—but a portrait of another figure that had just as powerful an influence on his science was conspicuously absent: that of Wolfgang Amadeus Mozart. In Einstein's mind, Mozart's music seemed "deterministic," as if plucked from the universe rather than composed. He felt that Mozart's creations were so pure that it was like they had always been present in the universe. For Einstein, playing music—Mozart's, in particular—was a significant way of grasping the hidden musicality of physics.

If there were a subfield in physics called "musical physics," Einstein could be considered its forefather. In fact, sometimes it seems like Einstein was just as much of a musician as he was a physicist. He even said, "If I were not a physicist, I would probably be a musician. I often think in music. I live my daydreams in music. I see my life in terms of music."[20] When trying to trace the hidden forces that enabled him to make the giant leap of relativity, he said, "The theory of relativity occurred to me by intuition, and music is the driving force behind this intuition. My parents had me study the violin from the time I was six. My new discovery is the result of musical perception."[21]

Terms like "musical perception" and "thinking in music" are far from typical descriptions of scientific thought. Einstein told researchers that he often thought in terms of musical architectures. According to the engineer-composer Robert Mueller, Einstein's friend Alexander Mozskowski "says that Einstein recognized an unexplainable connection between music and his science, and notes that Einstein's mentor Ernst Mach had indicated that music and the aural experience were the organ to describe space."[22] This is also how he judged the truthfulness of his colleagues' theories: not through intellectual assessment, but through attentive listening. Celebrating Niels Bohr's model for the structure of

20 Jude Treder-Wolff, *Possible Futures: Creative Thinking for the Speed of Life* (Smithtown, NY: Lifestage Productions, 2008), 121.

21 Robert Scott Root-Bernstein, and Michele Root-Bernstein, *Sparks of Genius: The 13 Thinking Tools of the World's Most Creative People* (Boston, MA: Houghton-Mifflin, 1999), 61.

22 M. Root-Bernstein and R. Root-Bernstein, "Einstein on creative thinking: Music and the intuitive art of scientific imagination," *Psychology Today* 42 (2010), 1–7.

the atom, he declared: “This is the highest form of musicality in the sphere of thought.”[23]

Could music, Mueller wondered, have allowed Einstein to make a connection between time and space through its architectonic, or structural, nature, combined with its spatial and temporal aspects? Mueller’s own feeling was that Einstein’s “disposition to architectonic logics of abstraction was formulated by his early musical experiences, and even enlarged by a constant struggle for musical experiences which helped him build a rich mental perceptual fabric of space and time in which to perform his scientific theorizing.”[24]

For Einstein, the barrier separating the arts from physics was very thin, since it was not the content of an idea that determined whether it was art or science, but rather *how* the idea was expressed. “If what is seen and experienced is portrayed in the language of logic,” he explained, “then it is science. If it is communicated through forms whose constructions are not accessible to the conscious mind but are recognized intuitively, then it is art.”[25] That is to say that he approached physics as an artist—specifically, as a musician. He would listen to the harmony beneath the dualities and polarities of physical forces, using musical architectures to communicate with a reality that existed outside the rigid concepts and divisions of ordinary thinking. In other words, he looked for his equations outside the mental realm, in a place that contained no words, only melodies.

---

23 Richard Brenner, *Lepton and Photon Interactions at High Energies: Proceedings of the XXII International Symposium, Sweden 30 June-5 July 2005* (Hackensack, NJ: World Scientific, 2006), 448.

24 R. Root-Bernstein, “Multiple giftedness in adults: the case of polymaths,” in *International handbook on giftedness (*New York: Springer, 2009), 856.

25 D.S. Cunningham, Vocation across the academy: *A new vocabulary for higher education* (Oxford: Oxford University Press, 2017), 126.

This was Einstein's secret: He used non-verbal thinking, thinking without thinking.

All other scientists were stuck with verbal thinking. Words and concepts were made to create distinctions and divisions: "this *or* that." Just think of this chapter's journey: With words, we have created divisions between "either/or" thinking and simultaneous thinking and now between "verbal thinking" and "non-verbal thinking." Our mind forms these two opposing concepts. Words are based on comparisons between things: "This is me and this is the sofa I'm sitting on." In words, "night" is the opposite of "day," whereas in reality it is really one flow, and "death" is the opposite of "life," whereas in reality death is an integral part of life's movement. This means that when we use words, *we inevitably create contradictions*, since "this" cannot be "that" and vice versa. Thus, it follows that words are great organizers—they put everything in its place and establish order—but they cannot really help us solve contradictions.

Verbal thinking creates different categories of reality and then gets trapped in them, forgetting that it created them in the first place. It's a slave to its own rigid concepts. Definitions help differentiate things, but these things then start moving further away from each other until we can no longer reconcile them. That's why verbal thinking finds it difficult to conceive of light as both waves and particles. It is so used to such distinctions that it cannot accept the simultaneous reality. It sees duality, even when in reality there is only singularity. In this way, verbal thinking becomes disconnected from simple and direct wholeness. If we rely solely on such thinking, we eventually lose touch with living reality.

"Either/or" thinking *is*, therefore, verbal thinking. If one wants to solve contradictions and get in touch with the wholeness of life, rather than one's ideas of life, one needs to look to other kinds of thinking. We know of at least one person who understood how to bypass verbal thinking and managed to solve conceptual contradictions through a totally different system of thought: Albert Einstein.

Solutions from another world

So what exactly was Einstein's way of thinking? It is astounding to realize that, actually, he didn't really think! At least not in the conventional way.

Einstein's dominant way of thinking was non-verbal. By "non-verbal," we mean that he would consider and inquire into a problem or a question using non-verbal means, such as musical structures, mystical or cosmic meditation, imagination and visualization, and intuition. This rare form of inquiry seemed to allow him to proceed where verbal thinking got completely stuck and entangled in its own contradictions. While all other physicists struggled with verbal thinking, Einstein continuously discovered solutions in "another world," solutions that were not derived from the existing order. Perhaps this is what we mean when we intuitively advise someone to "think outside the box" in the face of a problem that needs to be solved creatively: Drawing on something from the "outside" can result in unusual solutions, since "inside" we no longer have access to any creative breakthroughs. Isn't that precisely what Einstein meant when he said, "We cannot solve our problems with the same thinking we used when we created them"?[26] It seems as if the solutions of non-verbal thinking appear from nowhere, just like quantum particles, and somehow rearrange everything, turning the chaos of verbal thinking into a higher form of order.

Words and concepts are laden with the memories of everything that we, as human beings, have attached to them throughout history. They are based on accumulated knowledge, on the collective agreements that we all make, and so they necessarily limit our view. It's very hard to see anything new with this burden of memory, since verbal thinking doesn't leave much room for unknown possibilities or uncertainties. We see our world through mental constructs and cannot separate the two. The word "sunset" arises when we view the sunset, or even a second before, so do we really watch the sunset or do we just think we watch it?

26 David Suzuki and Ian Hanington, *Everything under the Sun: Toward a Brighter Future on a Small Blue Planet* (Vancouver: Greystone Books, 2012), 2.

The question is whether the brain can move from verbal thinking to non-verbal thinking. Obviously we need words and concepts—Einstein used these too—but perhaps they could be a secondary activity of the mind, with its center kept free from the bondage of words and concepts. For Einstein, this was his natural reality from childhood.

Here, we enter a mysterious part of Einstein's mind. Einstein only employed words and even mathematical symbols in what he explicitly called a secondary translation step—*after* he had solved his problems through the formal manipulation of internal images, feelings, and architectures. "I very rarely think in words at all. A thought comes, and I may try to express it in words *afterwards*," he wrote.[27] Einstein expanded on this theme in a letter to the French mathematician Jacques Hadamard, who had approached him with questions regarding the nature of his thought processes. Einstein wrote:

> the words of the language, as they are written or spoken, do not seem to play any role in my mechanism of thought. The psychical entities which seem to serve as elements in thought are certain signs and more or less clear images which can be "voluntarily" reproduced and combined ... The above mentioned elements are, in my case, of visual and some of a muscular type ... Conventional words or other signs [presumably mathematical ones] have to be sought for laboriously only in a secondary stage, when the associative play already referred to is sufficiently established and can be reproduced at will.[28]

Einstein's autobiographical notes reflect the same thought: "I have no doubt that our thinking goes on for the most part without the use of symbols, and, furthermore, largely unconsciously."[29]

---

27 P. Galison, G.J. Holton, and S.S. Schweber, *Einstein for the 21st century: His legacy in science, art, and modern culture* (Princeton, NJ: Princeton University Press, 2018), 42.

28 Arnold H. Modell, *Imagination and the Meaningful Brain* (Cambridge, MA: MIT Press, 2006), 29.

29 Galison, Holton, and Schweber, *Einstein for the 21st Century*, 42.

Thus, verbal thinking was, for Einstein, merely the humble servant of intuition. It was employed after the intuitive insight to order and translate everything that had been revealed.

There seem to be at least four non-verbal means that Einstein used extensively. The first one was, as we have seen, *music*. The second was *imagination and visualization*: He didn't probe intellectually into physical problems, but saw them as three-dimensional, living, and elastic realities. In the words of one of his first students: "Behind a formula, he immediately saw the physical content, while for us it only remained an abstract formula."[30] Just think of our little beetle or the way he solved special relativity by imagining watching lightning strikes from a moving train or the way he broke through his general relativity difficulties by considering the experience of gravity while inside a falling elevator in space. He always seemed to be able to escape the rigidity of verbal and mathematical formulations through such visualizations.

The two other means he employed were *meditation* and *intuition*. His form of meditation involved looking directly into the wonder and mystery of the physical universe, most probably with open eyes. He could do that for hours: Whenever he would sail his wooden boat *Tinef*, for example, he could go all day long, just drifting around and meditating (often getting lost and needing to be rescued). At such times, he would experience an overwhelming "cosmic religious feeling," a feeling of "utter humility toward the unattainable secrets of the harmony of the cosmos."[31]

Intuition seemed to be the outcome of these meditations. "At times," he said, "I feel certain I am right while not knowing the reason."[32] This is why he usually didn't start forming a theory using empirical data; on the contrary, *first* the general principle was wrested from nature and only

30 Isaacson, *Einstein*, 549.

31 Ibid., 389.

32 L. Zhang, R.J. Sternberg, and S. Rayner, *Handbook of intellectual styles: Preferences in cognition, learning, and thinking* (New York: Springer, 2012), 360.

then would empirical evidence follow. Remember that he described his thought processes to Hadamard as "visual and some of a muscular type." This was a remarkable response, as Hadamard was, by that time, already dividing mathematical scientists into two mental domains: algebraic and geometric. What is this strange muscular intuition then? Cosmologist Brian Swimme described it as "a birth that permeated him whole, his mind, his muscles, his viscera ... He was not contemplating something apart from himself. He was absorbed in the experience of the feelings in his body ... that were caused by the causes permeating the universe."[33]

Could we consider something in the same way, transcending our familiar languages, words, and concepts? Perhaps using non-verbal thinking as a way of creatively solving problems in our lives would be a good starting point. While contemplating a problem, we could listen to great music, paint, focus on a piece of great art, walk silently in nature, or meditate. These activities could inspire us through their deep connection with an underlying harmony. Using visualizations instead of words when thinking about a problem could also serve as a creative bypass, providing us with a sense of elasticity and flow. Solutions to problems need not necessarily be "logical." Solutions could be connected to the feelings in one's body, as when the body responds with excitement to something it recognizes as "true" or when possible solutions sound either inharmonious and discordant or melodious. Perhaps we, too, could hear Einstein's beautiful violin playing during moments when we face seemingly insurmountable obstacles to our thinking.

33 Swimme, *Hidden Heart*, 117–118.

CHAPTER 2

FRIEDRICH NIETZSCHE

Thinking that seeks no comfort, *or* Sailing the stormy sea of doubt

On January 3, 1889, Friedrich Nietzsche left his lodgings in Turin, Italy, probably for one of his famous long walks. Upon seeing a cabman beating his horse at the cab rank in the Piazza Carlo Alberto, he cried out, ran to the animal and embraced it before falling unconscious, drawing the attention of passers-by, who crowded around. Attracted to the scene, Nietzsche's landlord recognized his lodger and had him carried back to his room. When the 45-year-old philosopher finally came to, he seemed to be a changed man. He started making such a ruckus shouting and singing and playing the piano that his landlord almost called the police. After calming down, Nietzsche set about writing a series of epistles to public figures and his friends, announcing that he was Dionysus and the Crucified. To the Danish critic and literary historian Georg Brandes, who was among the first to recognize and publicize Nietzsche's work, he wrote: "After you had discovered me it was not difficult to find me: the difficulty now is to lose me … The Crucified."[34]

---

34 R.J. Hollingdale, *Nietzsche: The Man and his Philosophy* (New York: Cambridge University Press, 1999), 238.

For some reason, before Nietzsche was discovered by Brandes in 1888—the last year of his active and "conscious" life—he had been *very* difficult to find. During his prolific career as a writer, his writings had been met with chill indifference. At best, he had managed to raise a few eyebrows. So, for nearly 16 years, he had been motivated solely by self-belief. "If I were unable to draw strength from myself," he wrote to a friend, "if I had to wait for applause, encouragement, consolation, where would I be? What would I be?"[35] Some might say this was a compensatory megalomania and others might think this reflected profound intuition; nevertheless, during all those years he had clearly been kept alive by a growing sense of purpose. He had been driven by the inner conviction that his works belonged to the "very few, perhaps none of them is even living yet," that, "only the day after tomorrow," would appreciate their importance and so he was writing for "future millennia."[36]

When, in 1888, he finally started to receive attention, he responded with great excitement. However, the tragic irony of his story persisted even then. As Brandes wrote, "To all that was tragic in Nietzsche's life was added this—that, after thirsting for recognition to the point of morbidity, he attained it in an altogether fantastic degree when, though still living, he was shut out from life."[37] Diagnosed with "general paralysis of the insane" (caused by late-stage syphilis), he did not know that he was becoming famous—nor did he know that his fame was based on a complete distortion of almost everything he had taught.

It took Nietzsche 11 years to die. In that time, he became a legendary, almost mythical, figure. To those who now flocked to see him, he seemed to exist in a world beyond human reach. "A man

35 Jennifer Ratner-Rosenhagen, "American Nietzsche," *Nochrisis*, November 26, 2020. https://nochrisis.blog/american-nietzsche/#:~:text=Nietzsche%20never%20tired%20of%20contemplating,consolation%2C%20where%20would%20I%20be%3F.
36 Friedrich Nietzsche, "The Anti-Christ, Ecce Homo, Twilight of the Idols, and Other Writings – Edited by Aaron Ridley and Judith Norman." Cambridge University Press. http://assets.cambridge.org/052181/6599/excerpt/0521816599_excerpt.htm.
37 Hollingdale, "Nietzsche," 195.

without qualities upon whom any characteristics might be put," his insanity was perceived by the strange cult that gathered around him as an "ascent into the mystic." Surprisingly, Nietzsche himself had foreseen this when he wrote, "I have a terrible fear that one day I shall be pronounced 'holy.'"[38] The man who had dedicated his entire being to liberating humans from the metaphysical world was now becoming what he most detested.

Worse, he came to be identified with the ultimate heirs of the movement against which he had, from the first, opposed—anti-Semitic, race- and state-worshipping, anti-rationalist Nazism. Strangely, even this had been "prophesized" in his writings. He had written he would be misunderstood and for a long time thought "an ally of powers he abhors."[39] Those who were living in the hope and expectation of a "New Reich" were looking for its heralds and they thought they recognized one in Nietzsche. The Nazis, who enjoyed the fact that the mentally broken philosopher could no longer object, built a museum at Weimar to glorify his name and his "philosophy of power." They efficiently explained away the numerous places in his writings where he had not only expressed enmity toward the Reich, but also warned against its rise. To Nietzsche, the Reich represented what he dreaded the most: the rise of nihilism in a godless world, ruled by nothing more than Darwin's brutal "survival of the fittest."

Only gradually did researchers and biographers clear Nietzsche's image and writing of anti-Semitic suspicion and establish him as a strikingly individual philosopher whose philosophy continues to present a highly relevant challenge to the post-modern secular and rational culture of the twenty-first century. "The difficulty now is to lose me," Nietzsche wrote to Brandes. Indeed, these words, though obviously

---

38 Maria Popova, "Friedrich Nietzsche on Why a Fulfilling Life Requires Embracing Rather than Running from Difficulty," Brainpickings, November 26, 2020. https://www.brainpickings.org/2014/10/15/nietzsche-on-difficulty/#:~:text=I%20have%20a%20terrible%20fear,anyone%20can%20confer%20upon%20himself.

39 Hollingdale, *Nietzsche*, 104.

written in a mentally distorted state, echo the philosopher's enduring relevance and perhaps explain why books that seek to elucidate his philosophy are constantly being published.

Undoubtedly, Nietzsche's unique structure of thinking led him to make a series of fascinating discoveries in the depths of human psyche and the foundations of human culture, discoveries that profoundly undermined many taboos and convictions. It is time, then, to wonder about the nature of his groundbreaking way of thinking.

Truth or happiness?

By the year 1862, when the young Friedrich Nietzsche was only 18 years old, he had already begun to seriously question the religious spirit he had inherited from his family. His father and grandfathers had been pastors and everyone expected that he, too, would pursue this traditional profession. However, Nietzsche's restless spirit would not comply. In the framework of the literary and musical society "Germania," which he formed with two of his friends, he wrote essays that defied not only Christianity or religion, but also the very way of thinking that could give rise to any such belief system.

In his essay "Fate and History," he advocated a condition of permanent doubt. He called philosophical inquiry a *Versuch*—an attempt or experiment. He even employed the imagery of a stormy sea to describe the state of unconviction in which the true inquirer lives, in much the same way he would employ it in his most famous text, *Thus Spoke Zarathustra*, 21 years later: "To dare to launch out on the sea of doubt without compass or steersman is death and destruction for undeveloped heads; most are struck down by storms, very few discover new countries. From the midst of this immeasurable ocean of ideas one will often long to be back on firm land."[40]

40 Hollingdale, *Nietzsche*, 25.

Three years later, at the age of 21, Nietzsche abandoned the study of theology, thus breaking with his father's lineage for good. During his Easter vacation in 1865, he refused to go to church with his mother and then informed her, without much tact, that he was finished with Christianity. His sister Elizabeth, a devout believer, was even more strongly shaken by his apostasy than their mother and when Nietzsche went back to Bonn, she sent him an earnest letter defending the Christian faith. More than any of his many publications, his reply to her provides the key to understanding his structure of thinking:

> Concerning your basic principle, that truth is always to be found on the side of the more difficult, I agree in part ... On the other hand, is it really so difficult simply to accept as true everything we have been taught, and which has gradually taken firm root in us and is thought true by the circle of our relations and by many good people, and which moreover really does comfort and elevate men? Is that more difficult than to venture on new paths, in conflict with custom, in the insecurity that attends independence, experiencing many waverings of courage and even of conscience, often disconsolate, but always with the true, the beautiful and the good as our goal? Is it the most important thing to arrive at that particular view of God, world and reconciliation that makes us feel most comfortable? Is not the true inquirer totally indifferent to what the results of his inquiries may be? For, when we inquire, are we seeking for rest, peace, happiness? No, only for truth, even though it be in the highest degree ugly and repellent. Still one final question: if we had believed from our youth onwards that all salvation issued from someone other than Jesus, from Mahomet for instance, is it not certain that we should have experienced the same blessings? It is the faith that makes blessed, and not the objective reality that stands behind the faith ... Every true faith is infallible, it accomplishes what the person holding the faith hopes to find in it, but it does not offer the slightest support for

> a proof of objective truth. Here the ways of men divide: if you wish to strive for peace of soul and happiness, then believe; if you wish to be a disciple of truth, then inquire.[41]

In this surprisingly mature letter, Nietzsche distinguishes between two types of thinking: comforting thinking and truth-seeking thinking. Although comforting thinking often claims to possess the "truth," any "truth" it may possess is only comfort and reassurance in disguise. Comforting thinking is motivated by the wish to find peace of mind, a "truth" that can bestow on the thinker complete restfulness, so this type of thinking can never truly inquire. The results of the inquiry are predetermined: With comforting thinking, you can only find what you were hoping to find.

On the other hand, truth-seeking thinking is a genuine mode of inquiry. In this mode, the inquirer is unconditionally prepared for any kind of truth. The inquirer is, in fact, indifferent to the results of the inquiry. After all, why should "truth" be lovely and blissful? Why wouldn't it be "ugly and repellent"? If truth is to be "true," it should have the capacity to shake one's entire structure of thought and life, sometimes leaving one "disconsolate" and compelled to confront a painful, even harsh reality. Before investigation, the true inquirer must vehemently remove any unconscious hope for peace of mind—any part of him or her that would rather settle for some comforting belief that exchanges truth for something cheaper, but emotionally more satisfying.

"There is no preordained correspondence between truth and happiness, between what is true and what is pleasing," writes one of Nietzsche's prominent biographers, R.J. Hollingdale.[42] If happiness is what one seeks, one should not embark upon the dangerous path that leads to truths, which are just as likely to be ugly as wonderful. Accordingly, Nietzsche's mother consoled herself over her son's

---

41 Julian Young, *Friedrich Nietzsche: A Philosophical Biography* (New York: Cambridge University Press, 2010), 59.

42 Hollingdale, *Nietzsche*, 32.

defection from religion with the thought that since God directs all of our actions, he must have directed her son's action too and so she resigned herself to accepting His will. Nietzsche, on the other hand, took the dangerous path of truth-seeking thinking.

One should not underestimate the allure of comforting thinking. In time, Nietzsche would point his stinging arrow at the greatest philosophers of human history, from Plato onwards, declaring that they, too, had been tempted to associate "truth" with that which elevates the spirit of man. Just think of Plato's three "ideas": the Good, the True and the Beautiful. Nietzsche was suspicious of the notion that the three should go together as one and felt that this association between them was motivated more by human wishes and needs than by fierce investigation. If you need to feel that truth is, for example, divine love, because that would give rise to great positive emotions in you, then that is exactly what you'll get. Yet Nietzsche could not let his own mode of thinking be influenced by such narcotics, since he could clearly see that this would lead him to self-deception.

The letter to his sister Elizabeth was the starting pistol that announced the beginning of a lonesome journey toward truth at all costs. During this journey, he would feel compelled to jettison any type of "convenient truth" and to reject any "compassion" toward himself. This is the first and most crucial step of truth-seeking thinking: It's not so much about hoping to realize the complete and final "Truth"—with a capital "T"—as it is about discarding any illusions or thinking errors. What does one stand to gain from this, one might ask? Total freedom of the spirit, Nietzsche would answer. You forgo comfort, but, along with it, you can only lose that which is not worth keeping. Even if you end up hanging in space, naked and empty-handed, at least you know you have stripped your thought of all mental projections and distortions and get to keep your two eyes wide open, free to see everything just the way it is.

As early as the age of 15, Nietzsche composed a poem in which he acknowledged the condition and cost of such freedom of spirit.

"Whoever knows me calls me: the homeless man," he wrote, yet, being without a home, he is free "as an eagle."[43] Home is a refuge, somewhere one can rest one's head, but the truth-seeking inquirer cannot afford to have a home. Any inquiry is like going on a journey during which you cannot look back—when you look back, you rely on your own preconceptions, which are really just your hopes that certain things are "true." Nor can you look ahead in anticipation of finally reaching a place of relaxation. The true inquirer must renounce any longing for a static state, since truth is, in a way, the very freedom to inquire, question, doubt, destroy, and rebuild. "Convictions," Nietzsche declared, "are more dangerous enemies of truth than lies."[44] Thus, the goal of inquiry is not attaining some conviction—when we wish for convictions, we are, in fact, longing for the comfort of absolute and decisive knowledge.

For Nietzsche, philosophical thinking is an ongoing experiment. Classical philosophers, in a way, "played it safe." For example, they believed in God and so they determined to "prove logically" the existence of God; the existence of God was not the result of their inquiry, but rather its very beginning. Nietzsche felt that in order to truly and freely inquire, one should "live dangerously"—or, more accurately, think dangerously. Experimenting with "explosive" thoughts that are unbearable to the comfort-seeking mind is essential in truth-seeking thinking. "A thing might be true although it were harmful and dangerous in the highest degree," Nietzsche writes. "Indeed, the basic constitution of existence might be such that one would be destroyed by a complete knowledge of it—so that the strength of a mind might be measured by how much 'truth' it could endure."[45]

---

43 The Nietzsche Channel, "Nietzsche Poems," Nietzsche Channel, November 26, 2020. http://www.thenietzschechannel.com/poetry/poetry-dual.htm.

44 Philosiblog, "Convictions are more dangerous foes of truth than lies," Philosiblog, May 20, 2013. https://philosiblog.com/2013/05/20/convictions-are-more-dangerous-foes-of-truth-than-lies/#:~:text=%E2%80%93%20Nietzsche,what%20a%20fight%20it%20was!.

45 Friedrich Nietzsche, *Beyond Good and Evil*, trans. Helen Zimmern. Marxists.org, 2003. https://www.marxists.org/reference/archive/nietzsche/1886/beyond-good-evil/index.htm

This was precisely what impressed Nietzsche so much about his spiritual mentor, the German philosopher Arthur Schopenhauer. Although he ultimately severed all connections with Schopenhauer's philosophy, he maintained his reverence for Schopenhauer as a person, as he was struck by his willingness to endure the pain and discomfort inherent in hard truths. The authentic inquirer modeled by Schopenhauer would "voluntarily take upon himself the suffering involved in being truthful,"[46] indifferent to his own shaky feelings, desperate hopes, and fragile needs. Truth-seeking thinking is neither emotional nor sentimental: Emotions distort the search for truth because they compel the inquirer to long for pleasurable feelings and to avoid pain at all costs.

The happy death of hope

It was this truth-seeking thinking that made it possible for Nietzsche to succeed in his greatest philosophical endeavor: demolishing metaphysics once and for all. It enabled him to strip the human world, culture, philosophy, and psyche of even the subtlest forms of metaphysical dependency. While he was certainly not the first to declare secularism, he was probably the most thorough secular thinker of all. He ensured that all remnants of the old belief system were removed in order to free man at last. "It is a war," he declared, "but a war without powder and smoke ... One error after another is calmly laid on ice ... Here for example ... 'the saint' freezes ... at last 'faith,' so-called 'conviction,' freezes; 'pity' also grows considerably cooler—almost everywhere the 'thing-in-itself' freezes."[47]

Metaphysics basically holds that at the core of the phenomenal world there exists a "being" that remains forever unaffected. While everything

46 Hollingdale, *Nietzsche*, 104.
47 Rebekah S. Peery, *Nietzsche for the 21st Century* (New York: Algora Publishing, 2010), 57.

in the phenomenal world is moving, it remains still; it exists separately and independently. Thus, we can include in metaphysics religious belief, mystical experience, and metaphysical philosophical logic. The "thing-in-itself," or the noumenon (the opposite of phenomenon), was famously employed by Kant to suggest a world that can never be fully known to humans, as it is beyond reason.

According to Nietzsche, it was human beings, with their comforting thinking, who invented the metaphysical world. In this indifferent world of struggle, human thinking would rather have some "other world," which is, unsurprisingly, the very opposite of this world. If, in this world, there is no obvious justice, the other world should be just and fair. If, in this world, we're mortal beings, we are "souls" who cannot die in the other world. Knowing that God is on your side, and so every step you make is wisely guided, soothes the acute sense of uncertainty and fear of the future. Knowing that if you act correctly now you will be rewarded equips you with a guide map and a sense of meaning. Through the conception of the metaphysical world, the human being is no longer alone: There is an external logic and reason behind seemingly arbitrary and random events.

Nietzsche fought to destroy this "other world," which had previously been taken for granted not only in religious and mystical circles, but also in philosophical thought. He was not interested in the question of whether or not there is such a world—he claimed that all of our ideas or beliefs arise within the phenomenal world and since we cannot escape this world, it is not possible to look beyond it to know the "Truth." Instead, he had two "truth-seeking" questions to which he subjected any metaphysical assertion:

1. *Why does the thinker want to think this is true?* Is it possible that the thinker is attempting to avoid pain or flee from some difficult life situation? Is it possible that the thinker wishes to feel pleasant feelings, to feel more secure, or even to feel more powerful? Moreover, is this "truth" what the thinker was hoping to discover

in the first place? In examining each metaphysical claim, Nietzsche was more interested in the psychological need that made a person cling to this "truth"—the hidden benefit to the inquirer. If the claim was revealed to be no more than a comforting concept, it would represent self-deception and bondage and should be dispassionately disposed of at once. Take, for example, the statement, "God is good," a presupposition of any religion, mystical school, or metaphysical philosophy. How can we know that God is really good? When we state that, aren't we at least a little motivated by the wish that God is good? Is this goodness a plain fact or a mere wish?

2. *Is this "truth" really necessary to complete one's essential knowledge?* With this question, Nietzsche obviated the need to determine whether the metaphysical world exists at all—not only can't we know; we can live without it. Actually, living without the metaphysical world would improve the lot of humankind: We would become more responsible for ourselves, determine our own future, and no longer wait for consolation or support. This question helps us dismiss any thought that hinders our capacity for self-reliance and self-growth. If a "truth" is superfluous, it's harmful. It's even worse when this "truth" is limiting.

To assess the truthfulness of a statement, it is not sufficient to examine it only in itself. There is a whole psychological world that gives rise to the adoption of a certain truth. The motivation behind the thought is as important as the thought itself. Here, psychology, the science of the psyche, and philosophy, the science of thinking, become one and the same, so, in this sense, Nietzsche was a psychologist of philosophy. That is probably why Freud praised him for having "more penetrating knowledge of himself than any man who ever lived or was likely to live."[48]

48 Walter Kaufmann, *Freud, Adler, and Jung* (Piscataway, NJ: Transaction Publishers, 2009), 266.

Psychology was, for Nietzsche, a way of explaining the world that did not rely on metaphysical concepts, a way of seeing human behavior just as it is. Through penetrating psychological insight, one could expose the underlying forces behind human behavior without angels and demons, sin and punishment. Such insight was "the axe which is laid at the root of the 'metaphysical need' of man."[49] Indeed, with this unusual philosophical tool of investigation, Nietzsche managed to make unprecedented breakthroughs in the field of psychology that anticipated Freud's subconscious. When one seeks truth rather than comfort, one gains the ability to see through superficial human behavior—often characterized by noble sentiments and high moral values—to the "ugly truth" of the hidden motivation. An apparently selfless deed may, on a deeper level, be motivated by a desire to satisfy an egoistical wish.

Nietzsche identified the hidden motivation, which he named the "will to power," beneath many noble emotions and gestures. Love, the so-called unegoistic passion, was understood by him as the desire to exercise the greatest degree of power over the loved one and sex was, for him, the most unconstrained expression of egoism, as the lover really wants sole possession of the person he or she desires. In philosophy, Nietzsche discerned the tyrannical impulse of the spirit, a wish to subject the whole world to one's own vision. While philosophers always claimed that their philosophy described reality as it was, they were more like artists who created the world in their own image. They did not expose a "Truth"; they merely invented one, driven by their passionate desire that their perspective would become absolute and would overpower all other perspectives. Thus, the German philosopher bombarded the Greek myth of Olympus, the Buddha's concept of "emptiness," and Christian salvation. According to him, the Greek "knew and felt the terrors and horrors of existence: in order to be able to live at all he had to set before it the glittering dream-image of the Olympians."[50] The Christians' idea of the salvation of the weak was another prime example of comforting

49 Hollingdale, *Nietzsche*, 120.
50 Hollingdale, *Nietzsche*, 83.

thinking. This was, he said, no more than a reaction to life and a flight from the real world, in which the powerful ruled.

Nietzsche's truth-seeking thinking led him to discard the metaphysical world, both because it was "created" to provide comfort and because it was not necessary for human growth. He denounced the emotional need for a peaceful and unchanging center at the heart of the world. He held that there was no place of peace and retirement from the world of change. Only this Darwinian world of struggle existed, without even laws of nature to organize the chaos.

In this sense, he was perhaps the only thinker who fully realized the implications of Darwin's world in the context of the human experience. He felt that his contemporaries, the rationalists of the nineteenth century, were maniacally celebrating their newfound freedom from God without understanding that the consequence of this was that they must confront the dangers of such a new world. When one finally faced this godless reality of utter loneliness, would there be any point or meaning left to fill up the terrible vacuum that had been created?

"God is dead" is not a superficial formula, some arrogant declaration of independence. It is intended to imply the death of all that ever has been or ever could be subsumed under the name of "God," including all other worlds, ultimate realities, and all God-given moral codes. The famous parable, "The Madman," illustrates how seriously Nietzsche took this new human situation:

> Have you not heard of that madman who … ran to the market place and cried incessantly: "I am looking for God! I am looking for God! … Where has God gone? … I shall tell you. We have killed him—you and I … But how have we done this? … Who gave us the sponge to wipe away the entire horizon? What did we do when we unchained this earth from its sun? Whither it is moving now? … Are we not perpetually falling? … Do we not feel the breath of empty space? … How shall we, the murderers

of all murderers, console ourselves?[51]

Nietzsche sensed that the death of the metaphysical world had not yet been realized or accepted. People still thought in a way that would be appropriate only if God were still a reality. People still thought, for example, that morality, the evaluation of what is "good" and what is "bad," could still exist in such a world. Nietzsche knew that it couldn't; notions of "good" and "bad" were revealed to be social conventions under the guise of "truth."

This is the great advantage of truth-seeking thinking: It doesn't evade the pains of reality, so the thinker becomes far more capable of facing reality. In contrast, comforting thinking could be compared to certain narcotics, which can be emotionally gratifying, while at the same time putting you to sleep. The very purpose of comforting thinking is to obviate the need for the thinker to confront reality. Such thinking is naturally drawn to concepts that seem to offer some hope of an alternative reality. Yet, in truth-seeking thinking, hope is a distraction from self-responsibility and self-reliance. So although the end of hope would, to most people, seem like a tragic state, for the truth-seeking thinker it is an empowering state.

Truth-seeking thinking allowed Nietzsche to strip reality of all metaphysics *and* to face the uncomfortable and demanding consequences. He was not hoping to evade the burdens of reality, nor was he relying on faith in some external reality to save him the trouble of finding his own solution. On the contrary, "freedom" meant relieving oneself of one burden to take on a heavier one in its place: In the absence of any metaphysical meaning, one was now obliged to create one's own meaning.

Comforting thinking is not exclusive to religious hopes. It is the mode of thinking that helps us live in a secular universe, in which there

51 Emrys Westacott, "What Does Nietzsche Mean When He Says That God Is Dead?" ThoughtCo., January 8, 2018. https://www.thoughtco.com/nietzsche-god-is-dead-2670670.

seems to be no higher being, humans are essentially continuous with the animals, and death is the end, without having to confront this difficult reality on a deep level. In this sense, it is a distracting mechanism that makes everything easier than it really is. If God is dead, Nietzsche reasoned, the world has lost its value and all ethical, metaphysical, and logical worlds lie in ruin. From this, it followed that there was nothing in all existence that man can rely on other than himself. This meant that man could no longer remain his old self. The death of hope and comfort should give rise to a totally new human being.

The comfort bias

Though our comforting thinking, which dislikes painful realities, would not like us to admit it, our thinking tends to suffer from a comfort bias. This means that we have an instinctive resistance to any truth that can make us feel uncomfortable. When given the choice, we would rather embrace a more soothing "truth," a description of reality that would make us feel more comfortable and at ease. Exchanging the painful and demanding reality for reassuring and effortless thought is part of the pleasure-seeking tendency of the brain.

In his work, Daniel Kahneman has shown that human thinking is essentially lazy and instinctually biased toward "cognitive ease."[52] Cognitive ease is associated with repeated experience and familiarity; convenient familiarity and safety are not easily distinguished from truth. Cognitive ease determines whether something is true if it "feels true," "feels good," and "feels effortless." This implies that *what feels good also feels true.*

Truth-seeking thinking, in its sincere wish to attain truth, is an effortful process that tends to yield results that are difficult to grasp. That is why we are much more likely to avoid such thinking and take the easy

52 Daniel Kahneman, Thinking, Fast and Slow (London: Penguin Books, 2012), 59–70.

path: contenting ourselves with partial truths or, worse, embracing a truth substitute, a "nerve-relaxer," that provides a soothing affirmation. This is dangerous, since our thinking will seek only a "truth" that is the humble servant of a desired emotional state and is therefore likely to make enormous errors in judgment and prediction. This was Nietzsche's suspicion about human evaluation and it is confirmed by Kahneman's research: When we pretend to judge something, we start with the conclusion and then the arguments follow. Moreover, if you *want* to believe that a conclusion is true—and you will want to believe it if it makes you feel good—you will also tend to believe any argument that appears to support it, even when the argument is unsound.

It is our instinctual bias toward comfort that makes us hold onto pleasant images and ideals even if reality proves us wrong again and again. Indeed, comforting thinking endows the thinker with a remarkable capacity to deny reality and subject it to the softening effect of the ideal. We would naturally prefer to think of weddings and marriages as extremely happy and romantic events, efficiently "forgetting" the outrageous divorce rate in Western society (53 percent in the United States, 49 percent in Germany). When we get married or attend the weddings of friends or family, we rarely take the trouble to look into the future and think of all the horrible quarrels, nights of deadly tension, and betrayals. Even though most, if not all, men could never live up to the ideal of "real men"—confident but loving, ambitious but emotional—the notion of the perfect "Prince Charming" still lurks somewhere in the back of many women's minds (eventually resulting in harsh criticism of the failing men). All the difficult, even terrible, crises and intense frustrations are wiped from memory. We still think of vacations and holidays as wonderfully rejuvenating and magical, even though they often end in depleted energy and disappointment. Many consider their youth sentimentally, as if it were a period of great promise, even if it is necessary to disregard many memories and feelings from that time in order to do so. People's self-image is usually one of selflessness and goodness that does not take into account all of the jealousy, vengefulness, and pettiness that run through their minds daily. Comforting thinking is also the cause of the well-researched cognitive bias that causes us to overestimate our chances of success and luck—we simply ignore statistics and think of ourselves as exceptional.

Evaluating things by comparison with ideals—that is, what we hope and want to think they could be—can be thought of as a form of "positive thinking." It is likely that at the back of our minds we know we're deceiving ourselves, yet we choose not to move to the other side—that of "cognitive effort" and experiencing pain. Truth often causes discomfort, since acknowledging it necessitates rearranging one's perception of reality, as well as losing the stable structures one has worked so hard to build in life. Truth is also frequently followed by pain. Sometimes pain is even an indication of truthfulness, since it results from the discrepancy between our mental image, our ideal, and reality. When reality doesn't align with our ideal, it is the ideal that needs to go, but who would willingly let go of a comfortable illusion? After all, *since it is the brain's instinct to avoid pain, it is the brain's instinct to avoid truth.*

These illusions seem to work like protective shields that keep reality out of our exhausted awareness. Comforting thinking helps us avoid effortful confrontation unless it is necessary. It helps us escape reality and compensate for whatever is missing from that reality through our thoughts. When we must confront the hard truth, it helps us come to terms with its harshness through all kinds of pain-relieving concepts.

However, truth-seeking thinking, as Nietzsche demonstrated, is a better tool for handling reality, because it does not seek to escape, nor does it rely on hope. Therefore, the energy of the thinker is far more concentrated on dealing with what is happening. It also results in a greater sense of self-responsibility. Consequently, this mode of thinking does not waver even in harsh conditions. The biggest problem with comforting thinking is that it eventually results in fragility of mind. It is a thought process that is not at all used to facing reality, so when it does, it is deeply shocked and shaken.

Many cling to ideals about their family relations and friendships, for example, that these relationships cannot fail them. When these ideals shatter—the romantic partner betrays or stops loving them or their mother behaves in a way that is at variance with how a mother "should" behave—people are shaken to the core. In reality, it is only false images that shatter and an existing truth that is revealed. It's just that we had previously been overly protected by our own comforting thinking.

Comforting thinking also makes us far more prone to making erroneous decisions. It is easy to see why this is the case when the only truth is the truth we want to hear. It is almost impossible to distinguish the right from the wrong when one holds some "preferred" truth dear. We often attempt to solve a problem or find an answer to a question while holding onto hidden assumptions. It is important to keep in mind that our brain will tend to "find" the answer that best suits its "cognitive ease" inclination. It will usually opt for that which is familiar, cozy, safe, effortless, and self-accepting—anything that evokes a good mood. Other possibilities, which may strike the brain as effortful, unfamiliar, destabilizing, and stressful, will often be deemed not the "right thing for us" and rejected—for the wrong reasons. Whatever causes warm, positive feelings and emotions will seem truer—again, for the wrong reasons. This is true not only in the case of decisions, but also in relation to our adoption of concepts and mottos. Since our cognitive biases toward comfort work against us, before making any decision, it would be wise to ask: What is my preferred "truth"? What is my hidden inclination? And why is this my immediate inclination? Putting such preferences and inclinations aside as much as possible might allow us to engage in more truth-seeking decision-making.

How Nietzsche overcame his need for peace

There was nothing comforting about living inside Nietzsche's body. By his twenties, the young philologist was already engaged in a daily battle with ill health. He was beset by migraines, which would attack overnight and sometimes persist for three days, during which time he would be incapable of eating. If he ate, he would find it impossible not to vomit. Such attacks left him so utterly exhausted that he soon became an easy target for other ailments. Any attempt to understand his behavior during his adult years must take this daily struggle into account. We can imagine the process of his tireless writing: Almost blind, tormented by a severe migraine, exhausted, he would gather all his mental forces to write his passionate aphorisms. Indeed, his resistance was tremendous and, thus, he lived up to his own ideal of constant self-overcoming. Again and again, he seemed to be done for and, again and again, he recovered. Ultimately, he summed up his experience in the well-known epigram: "What does not kill me makes me stronger."

One might expect that such anguish would creep into his writing, making it at least somewhat bitter and pessimistic, but his suffering had the opposite effect: "It was during the years of my lowest vitality that I ceased to be a pessimist," he wrote, "The instinct for self-recovery *forbade* to me a philosophy of indigence and discouragement."[53] It was during his most physically tormented years that he started to develop what was, to him, the ultimate renunciation of comforting thinking. This was his most "dangerous" thought experiment, which would elicit from his innermost being the final "yes" to life just the way it is.

The concept, or rather the vision, of "eternal recurrence" was the "edge" of Nietzsche's thought. It was his way of measuring his strength and freedom of mind and, even more so, his love of life. Put simply, "eternal recurrence" held that, with no higher or external reality, material life as we know it goes on forever like a closed circle. Since this is an unbreakable circle, life would inevitably repeat the same forms and experiences over and over again—which implies that we would have to repeat the life that we're living right now countless times. "This life, as you live it now and have lived it," Nietzsche explains, "and there will be

53 Hollingdale, Nietzsche, 107.

nothing new in it, but every pain and every joy and every thought and sigh and all the unspeakably small and great in your life must return to you … The eternal hour-glass of existence will be turned again and again."[54]

For Nietzsche, this powerful question—"Do you want this again and again, times without number?"—was the end of all escape and consolation. A clear "yes" response would mean the removal of the subtlest barrier of resistance between him and life. That is why he considered it "the extremest formula of affirmation that can ever be attained."[55] It was also the culmination of his philosophical endeavor to put an end to all metaphysics. Now the only reality left was material life, without any horizon, final destination, or purpose. Man was left with this moment alone and only he could give it meaning.

Agreeing to repeat this life over and over again also means the end of man's endless pursuit of pleasure and avoidance of pain: Just as the joys of life will be repeated endlessly, so too will the pain be eternally relived. This implies that we should wholeheartedly embrace our most terrible moments without ever seeking refuge in pain-relieving thoughts. Such a mind would be extraordinarily strong, since it would no longer fear pain. It would love life, but not because life is beautiful or because life will one day become beautiful here or somewhere else. This love would fill life with divinity, the same divinity that the "other world" robbed long ago. It is in the total absence of hope and comfort that such a mind could find a new kind of happiness, meaning, beauty, and grace.

The idea of eternal repetition could only arise from a form of thinking that had ceased to wish for peace of mind. Strikingly, the idea reflects Nietzsche's deepest structure of thought: a constant restless

54 Emrys Westacott, "Nietzsche's Idea of Eternal Recurrence," ThoughtCo., February 12, 2020. https://www.thoughtco.com/nietzsches-idea-of-the-eternal-recurrence-2670659.
55 Hollingdale, *Nietzsche*, 147.

state of passion and inner fire. Whereas restlessness of mind is usually perceived as a negative state, Nietzsche believed that it was very similar to the real and healthy rhythm of life itself. In this sense, his thinking was not separate from the dynamic of natural evolution—forever fighting to overcome and grow out of a ceaseless struggle between destructive and constructive forces. There seems to be no end to this natural process, no rest and no peace, and Nietzsche's thinking replicated this as if it were the mental expression of evolution.

One could go so far as to say that if life had a mind, this is probably what it would look like. Nietzsche's mind was like a force of nature, like volcanoes, thunder, and earthquakes. This is not nature as the European Romantics, the Greek stoics, and other philosophers who sought peace of mind and comfort had wanted to see it. This is the nature that Darwin revealed: the heated arena of clashes between forces, each striving to expand and rise to new heights. Certain thinkers had sought to lead the human mind to a state of total peace through the abolition of will and all conflicting forces. For Nietzsche, the human mind was not meant to be at peace. Strife, he believed, was the perpetual food of the soul. His mind was driven by an innate compulsion to evolve, to flow dynamically as part of the creative stream of life, and to remain forever active—since active meant awake and alive.

"Yes, I know whence I have sprung!" Nietzsche exclaimed in a poem. "Insatiable as a flame I burn and consume myself! Whatever I seize hold on becomes light, whatever I leave, ashes; certainly I am a flame."[56] Such passionate thinking could make it easier to abandon one of the greatest human hopes: the hope for retirement from the tireless process. That's why most people are divided: One part of them is the endless stream of thoughts—wanting and struggling—while the other part fantasizes about complete peace and relaxation. Nietzsche's thinking was not divided in this way. For him, peace of mind meant accepting that life offered no respite and his unique mind could somehow relax

56 Hollingdale, *Nietzsche*, 77.

into this unrelaxing stream. Not only was there no respite in life; the mind, too, was in a state of constant activity. Thus, the mind could never achieve some final developmental goal, a state of perfect knowledge and conviction upon the achievement of which it could let passion wither away. On the contrary, like life, it would abandon any fixed and over-satisfied position and destroy its own habits and old formulas to creatively rebuild itself in an endless cycle.

To emulate this type of mind, try to detect your own comforting beliefs and escape fantasies, which are keeping you from experiencing life as it is. These beliefs and fantasies only seem to be empowering; in truth, they weaken your strength of mind and your ability to cope with real life challenges. Examine your beliefs to determine whether you hold them not because they are true, but because they give you comfort. Consider the ways in which your thoughts attempt to escape reality. Do you have an escape fantasy? Do you harbor some dream of retirement from life, the achievement of a state of final rest? Then give this a try: Let go of it, just as an experiment. If you are inclined to think, "I can't bear this stressful life; there are too many things to do; I wish I could go on vacation instead," perhaps "relaxing" into the stress and accepting it as a part of life could make your thinking in response to the stress much clearer and more effective. What would happen to your thinking if you let go of all fantasies, comforting beliefs, and hopes of relaxation? It is not a coincidence that our thinking naturally flows, like a stream that cannot be stopped. Essentially, this flow is very similar to the rhythm of life itself. So what happens when your thinking does not resist this rhythm? It is possible that when you stop resisting, you will be able to tap into the stream of passion and ecstasy to which Nietzsche had access.

CHAPTER 3

BARBARA McCLINTOCK

Organic thinking, *or* The different kernel on the corn cob

When, during the 1950s, renowned molecular biologist Joshua Lederberg returned from a visit to Barbara McClintock's lab, he remarked: "By God, that woman is either crazy or a genius."[57] Although it is now clear that McClintock will be remembered in the history of science as a genius—for she was the geneticist directly responsible for one of the greatest revolutions of twentieth-century biology—as we learn more about McClintock's extraordinary personality and way of thinking, we will come to see why Lederberg wasn't sure.

Barbara McClintock, it seems, gave new meaning to the term "outsider." She was "outside" in every sense of the word: She was outside her body, her gender, any form of personal relationship or family unit, as well as any scientific framework and accepted method. She was so unusual that when biographer Evelyn Fox Keller approached her for help turning her inspiring story into a biography, she did not see how her life could possibly be of interest to the world. She was too different, too anomalous, too much of a "maverick," she said, to set an example for others.

57 "Colleagues: Barbara McClintock," *Esther M. Zimmer Lederberg Memorial Website,* retrieved March 2, 2013. http://www.estherlederberg.com/EImages/Cold%20Spring%20Harbor/McClintockB.html.

Since she was a little child, she shied away from anything feminine. Very early, she realized she was a "girl doing the kinds of things that girls were not supposed to do."[58] She refused to adapt to the limitations imposed on her sex and vehemently demanded the same freedom men had to pursue their individual passions. She quickly began to dress in an androgynous manner, remained forever loyal to her shingled hairstyle, and had no interest in personal attachments to boys or, later, men. She never felt the necessity for emotional and physical attachment and so could never understand the idea of marriage. In general, she never pursued any of the goals that were considered conventional for women. However, anyone who thought she dreamed of being a man couldn't have been further from the truth. McClintock rejected the idea of her being a "lady scientist," so she was bewildered when feminists tried to make her an icon of a woman struggling in a man's world (though she did encounter the limitations put on her gender from time to time). She wished to transcend gender altogether. When a person gets to know you well, she said, they forget you're a woman; the matter of gender drops away.

It wasn't just femininity that she wished to do away with. What she really strove for was freedom from the very sense of having a body. "The body was something you dragged around," she once explained. "I always wished that I could be an objective observer, and not be what is known as 'me' to the other people."[59] Anything that separated her from her scientific passion, anything that compromised her capacity as a pure observer, needed to be removed, as if it were a lens that clouded the direct sight of the mind's eye. Even her name was external to her, something that belonged to others, who saw her from the outside. That's why she forgot it every now and then. As a junior in college, she had

58 Evelyn Fox Keller, *A Feeling for the Organism* (New York: Owl Books, 1983), 25.
59 Alan Soble, "Keller on Gender, Science, and McClintock," in Cassandra L. Pinnick, Noretta Koertge, and Robert F. Almeder, eds., *Scrutinizing Feminist Epistemology: An Examination of Gender in Science* (New Brunswick, NJ: Rutgers University Press, 2003), 65–101.

to take her final in geology, a subject she loved. She couldn't wait. The examiners gave out the books to write the answers in and requested that everyone write their names on the front page. While most did this first, McClintock couldn't be bothered and instead started writing with great delight. When she did finally turn to writing her name, she couldn't remember it and was too embarrassed to ask anybody what it was. It took her about 20 nervous minutes to remember it.

Her gender, body, and name were a nuisance, obscuring her direct and immediate contact with her object of observation. She derived true happiness only from immersing herself in her passionate pursuit. When she joined a jazz improvisation group and played at a dance, she was convinced she had slept through a whole number. At the end, she "woke up" and asked the saxophonist if she had fallen asleep; he answered that she had been doing just fine. Such unconscious states of complete immersion would recur over and over again during her scientific work.

Her capacity to be alone in a state of self-dissolution, focusing only on the object of her passion, was remarkable. As a child, she scared her mother whenever she occupied herself in her favorite way: sitting alone, intensely absorbed, just thinking about things. Later, when she began to pursue her scientific work, this absorption continued to be her sole motivation. McClintock never engaged in the kind of deliberate planning that characterizes most people's choice of a career. She claimed she had never thought about her career. She was simply doing what she wanted to do and never felt that she was required to continue something or that she was dedicated to some particular endeavor. Her path was uncharted and she had no professional aspirations—consequently, every once in a while, she did find herself jobless and uncommitted to any framework. Once, after having been cautioned about driving on some long and hazardous road, her only concern during her journey was that if she were killed, she would never get the solve to the problem she was working on at that time. "I was just so interested in what I was doing I could hardly wait to get up in the morning and get at it," she said when describing her childlike capacity for absorption.[60]

McClintock spent most of her life alone—physically, emotionally, and intellectually. Autonomy, with its attendant indifference to conventional expectations, became her trademark. Her originality made her a free spirit. She followed stern rules of her own rather than conforming to imposed rules. This allowed her to remain detached from scientific trends and enabled her to simply follow what was "obvious" to her, almost independent of the responses of her peers. She was still the girl who had, in high school, insisted on solving problems in ways her instructors had never expected. It was the process of finding an answer in her own way that gave her pleasure and it was to this, and only this, that she was committed.

Interestingly, it was this very lightness of mind—this freedom from any defined name, body, gender, attachment, career, or method—that gave rise to the series of stunning leaps she made in the field of genetics.

My friends, the chromosomes

McClintock's personal story is completely intertwined with the story of genetics as it emerged as a new area of study at the beginning of the twentieth century. McClintock's involvement with genetics began early enough for her to take part in, and indeed help create, this initially inchoate science. It's hard to imagine that at the beginning of the twentieth century, genetics, which is now considered a well-established and indispensable science, was no more than an abstract vision of heredity. Although the nineteenth-century work of Gregor Mendel had been rediscovered in 1900, the term "genetics" was not coined until 1905 and "gene" did not become a recognized word until 1909. Even then, "gene" was a word that could not be attached to a material reality

---

60 Todayinsci, "Science Quotes by Barbara McClintock," November 27, 2020. https://todayinsci.com/M/McClintock_Barbara/McClintockBarbara-Quotations.htm.

inside the organism. At best, it was an abstraction invoked to make sense of the rules according to which inherited traits are transmitted from one generation to another.

Genetics, when the young and enthusiastic McClintock first encountered it, was scarcely older than she was herself. When she was an adolescent, her particular field of expertise came into being. A series of chromosomal and genetic studies on the fruit fly, *Drosophila*, would finally confirm the relationship between genes and chromosomes. With these results, geneticists could at last confidently postulate a physical basis for Mendelian genetics. The outcome was the birth of cytogenetics: the science that links the study of the visible structure of chromosomes and genetics.

It was into this exciting and dynamic area that McClintock was drawn. During her twenties and thirties, she managed to far surpass her own educators and to make discoveries unparalleled in the history of cytogenetics. Her first breakthrough occurred when she discovered a way to identify maize chromosomes—that is, to distinguish the individual members of the set of chromosomes within each cell. She completed the task within two or three days, much to the dismay of her employer, who had been working on the problem for a long time. She improved the technique she had devised until she could observe individual chromosomes throughout the course of their cycles of division and replication. Previously, chromosomes could be seen and counted, but they had been simply "the chromosomes" and could not be further differentiated or individualized. McClintock found that she could give each chromosome an identity. Each acquired a label and could be followed throughout the course of its life. Every chromosome, she discovered, had a distinctive morphology—a length, shape, and structure of its own. These special features would become crucial landmarks in the exploration of unmapped genetic terrain. The genetic information of maize became detectable using a microscope and McClintock established herself as the foremost investigator of cytogenetics.

In 1927, when McClintock, who was not quite 25 years old, received her Ph.D., she felt driven to show how sets of genes that are inherited together are carried by specific chromosomes. Surprisingly, although it was, at the time, clearly necessary to demonstrate the relationship between chromosomes and genetic systems, her endeavor was completely original. However, hers was not an easy task and she needed help—or at least so it seemed. At that time, there were two kinds of geneticists: the breeders, who did nothing but breeding, and the people who worked with chromosomes. They never came together; they even worked in separate places. McClintock shocked those around her when she insisted on being both kinds of geneticist in one. Unstoppable, she seemed keen to individualize and personalize her subject of study. Just as she was looking for individual chromosomes, so she was determined to encounter individual maize plants in their natural environment: the field. Corn genetics is hard work. Labor begins early in the morning, before it gets too hot, and continues throughout the day. Nevertheless, McClintock felt compelled to unite direct observation with the naked eye and her discoveries under the microscope—that is, to understand the connections between the organism as a whole and its tiniest particles.

Her fame reached a peak in 1931, when she succeeded in determining the chromosomal basis of genetics. Her experiment would later be considered the final link in the chain of classical genetics. However, her unique style of thinking was most evident in the way she pursued abnormalities that others preferred to push aside; she recognized such abnormalities intuitively as hints of more general laws. One day, as she was moving through the field, she noticed plants that were variegated, that is, expressing both dominant and recessive traits. That fall, she received a copy of an article in which variegation was described. A small chromosome seemed to cause a genetic fragment to "get lost." Immediately, she intuited that this must be a "ring chromosome." Neither McClintock nor her colleagues knew, at that time, of the existence of such a chromosome, but she was so sure of its existence that she sat and wrote to the other geneticists about it at once and quickly began to cultivate a new set of similar plants. When the first plant was ready, her hand shook as she opened it up to extract the material to be examined. In the lab, she discovered that it did have rings and so did every other plant that she had assumed would. She was excited, but also relieved. Why had she been so sure of a phenomenon of which she had had no knowledge? To her, as she says, the "logic" was compelling: "The logic made itself … What's compelling in these cases is that the problem … is not something that's ordinary, but it fits into the whole picture, and you begin to look at it as a whole … It isn't just a stage of this or that. It's what goes on in the whole cycle. So you get a feeling for the whole situation of which this is only a component part."[61]

McClintock's ability to get a feeling for the organism as a whole by delving into one "abnormal" component was exceptional. Geneticist and friend Marcus Rhoades once told her, "I've often marveled that you can look at a cell under the microscope and can see so much!" She responded, "When I look at a cell, I get down in that cell and look around."[62] Without being able to say quite what it was she was seeing, she seemed to be able to arrive at a functional description even in the total absence of biochemical terminology. It was as if she was in direct communication with the living and complete dynamic of the cell.

In many respects, McClintock was an old-fashioned naturalist at a time when the whole world of biology had already transitioned from the observational to the experimental. That's why her theories were often ridiculed by colleagues as "non-scientific." The stories she tells to illustrate the meaning of her "understandings" recall the naturalist tradition. Vehemently resisting the trend of isolating components of life, she thought of chromosomes and genes as properties belonging to the organism. Always maintaining her philosophical and methodological independence, she tended to shift between what she saw under the

---

61 Keller, *A Feeling for the Organism*, 67.
62 Ibid., 69.

microscope and her experience of the "living" thing. Her view of what was important was at variance with the views of those around her. She was skeptical of those who thought they were going to solve the genome, since she believed that it wasn't solvable; the genome was a mere symbol, like those used by a physicist. She rejected the geneticists' zeal for quantitative analysis. They were so intent on making everything numerical, she complained, that they frequently missed seeing that which was there to be seen. Her own method was based on seeing one kernel of corn that was different and making that understandable. She felt that her colleagues, in their enthusiasm for counting, too often overlooked that single aberrant kernel.

This was a powerful element of what we might call McClintock's organic thinking: She maintained direct communication with her object of study and therefore would never overlook its "aberrations." Indeed, there was no aberration; what we think of as abnormal behavior for an organism, a deviation from the "norm," was, for her, a hint of a higher and more complex order that we had not yet fully grasped. An "abberation" was like a message, given to her by the plant itself, informing her of the presence of a deeper dynamic secret. For McClintock, it was the smallest detail that provided the key to the larger whole; the individual case held within it the more complete truth or law. When one deeply considers a disturbing fact that doesn't fit into one's existing model, the fact could eventually result in the model being integrated into a new way of seeing the world. There are good reasons why things don't fit into our models. Organic thinking is always willing to forgo the theory to accommodate the reality.

On the other hand, detached thinking, which observes things from the outside, seeing them through numbers and statistics, general laws, and theoretical models, doesn't like to trouble itself with exceptions. It overlooks these deviations, sometimes dismissing them as "mistakes" or "accidents." It likes its models of reality too much to abandon them for the sake of an individual exception. McClintock's vision, however, was so organic that it allowed her to develop astonishing insight. By simply going through the field, looking at the plants themselves, she knew what the microscopic inspection of the cells' nuclei would later reveal. She would make her guess for every plant and was never mistaken. All she was conscious of doing was looking at the fine stripes of recessive tissue on the plant and her "subconscious mind" did the rest. She understood all of the plants directly, without needing to use conscious and rational thinking. Her organic thinking sought intimate and total knowledge of each and every plant—it was, as one of her colleagues put it, as if she could write the biography of each individual plant. The "answers" she was looking for always came directly from the organism. Only after attaining answers did she outline the intricate logical series of steps that led to them.

McClintock's organic thinking was strikingly evident when she was asked to identify and analyze the tiny chromosomes of *Neurospora* (a red mold on bread). These chromosomes had hitherto eluded all attempts at identification. In two months, she managed to make marvelous leaps, but it is the story of her difficulty along the way that should interest us. After about three days, she found she was getting nowhere. Feeling totally lost, she realized she had to "do something" with herself, so she went for a walk. She sat tearfully beneath giant eucalyptus trees and yielded to her "subconscious thinking." After half an hour, she jumped up with the answer in mind and ran back to the lab. In her own words, under the trees, she had brought about a change in herself that enabled her to see without obstruction. Where before she had only seen disorder, now she could easily distinguish between the chromosomes: "I found out that the more I worked with them, the bigger and bigger they got, and when I was really working with them I wasn't outside, I was down there. I was part of the system … I even was able to see the internal parts of the chromosomes … It surprised me because I actually felt as if I were right down there and these were my friends."[63] When

63 Juliet Mitchell, "Introduction to Melanie Klein," in *Reading Melanie Klein*, eds. Lyndsey Stonebridge and John Phillips (New York: Routledge, 1998), 29.

her mind was in the right position, her physical eye was able to see so much more—or, better yet, to serve as a perfect reflector.

Scientists often pride themselves on their capacity to distance their subjective selves from the object of study. The greater the distance between them, the more "scientific" the mind. For McClintock, many of her original breakthroughs resulted from turning object into subject. She herself put it simply: "I'm not there!" The self-conscious "I" simply disappeared, so there was no seer to interfere with the process of seeing; a direct communication between mind and plant could then take place. It was as if the mind could thus tune into the language of the plant, rather than its own conditioned language. Here again, we find evidence of McClintock's incessant drive to put aside any distinct "observer" defined by name, gender, or body. Forgetting herself made her mind transparent, so it was capable of reflecting the reality of the thing. For this reason, the art of "seeing" was, to her, the center of her scientific experience: If one couldn't see, it was only because one was standing in one's own way.

Organic thinking is like listening to living systems. It is primarily guided by the wish for intimate knowledge and only later does it seek logical, or more objective, knowledge. That's why it considers nothing to be a disturbance, as when one enters into a new relationship and is willing to get to know the other person as a whole, including his or her imperfections. This type of thinking is not concerned with theories and dogmas, since it considers these to be interferences to the dynamic process of seeing. When a mind engaged in such thinking wants to learn something, it "lends" its own eyes to the object of study. It lets discovery arise from the object itself, as if the mind was but a continuation of it. The eye and the mind become extensions of the thing that is being perceived.

This is very different to the usual way of thinking. Indeed, the very concept of "thinking" seems to be the opposite of intimacy. Intimacy should remain in the world of emotions, whereas thinking is the act of considering something—the way one observes, examines, categorizes, and interprets. When thinking, the observer forces him- or herself on the observed: He or she has his or her own agenda and wants the living thing to fit a concept that obeys, under all circumstances, his or her own definitions and generalizations. It is for this reason that detached thinking is not fond of aberrations and exceptions. It wants to feel in control and hates when small details suddenly appear and interrupt the all-inclusive generalization that it has finally managed to achieve.

The unique form of organic thinking that led to McClintock's achievements and recognition would result, over time, in an unbridgeable gap that would isolate her from the scientific community for more than 30 years. The same ability to "listen" to the material, outside of any methodological framework or accepted model, and pay attention to aberrations rather than general laws would result in her becoming an aberrant and overlooked kernel on a corn cob for a very long time.

A corn that speaks

In 1944, McClintock began to detect a remarkable tendency in her maize plants: a stable pattern of instability. Each seedling, she realized, exhibited a characteristic rate of mutation that was unchanging over the life cycle of a given plant. A plant that started out with only a few mutating cells would maintain that level of mutation throughout its life. Mutations did not strike capriciously; they were set off by a constant factor. Something in the plant, she deduced, was controlling the rate of mutation. If these mutations were followed, they could lead to a history of cell differentiation that was not random at all. The implication of all of this was that genes were controlled by yet another unknown element.

Moreover, occasionally, sectors of variegated tissue demonstrated a rate of mutation that was different to that of the plant as a whole. How could that be, if these distinct sectors arose from an individual cell? And why would two sister cells give rise to two adjacent sectors that followed different patterns? McClintock sensed that this was the clue she needed and immediately dropped everything else to pursue this line of study. She couldn't get the idea out of her head that one cell gained what the other cell lost. She began looking for a point in the plant's cell history that led to the differentiation of two cells and that could explain the presence of different tissues in one organism. Underlying this entire inquiry was a major question regarding the way each organism arrives at its own form. For two years, McClintock worked without knowing what she would discover. Yet her organic thinking kept her joyful and she just let the material tell her where to go—"and it tells you at every step what the next has to be."[64]

This patient inquiry, which involved inner vision and the study of detectable patterns, eventually led to her greatest breakthrough: the discovery of transposition. Transposition occurs when a chromosomal element shifts from its original position and is inserted into a new position. Again, McClintock stumbled across this phenomenon thanks to her willingness to observe the unruly behavior of her individual plants. On one plant, kernels that "should have been" colorless contained well-defined sectors of pigmentation. Mysteriously, the dominant genetic factor responsible for the inhibition of color "got lost." The frequency of its loss seemed to be regular. Now McClintock could look for the genetic source of this regulation, though this was no easy feat: She was attempting to locate an element whose existence was only suspected. Even if it did exist, it expressed itself only through the loss of other genetic factors.

McClintock called this mutation-controlling element Ac. With this factor, she finally had an answer to what it might have been that "one

64 Keller, *A Feeling for the Organism*, 125.

cell gained and the other one lost." It was a unit of Ac that shifted from one chromosomal strand to another. This was undreamed of—that one could detect the original position of the Ac and then find it somewhere else—yet the hypothesis of transposition seemed to work wonders. Everything began to fall into a relatively simple scheme.

When McClintock presented transposition in 1950, she was sufficiently aware of the disparity between her own thinking and that of her colleagues. She probably hoped that her list of past achievements would at least give her some credibility. It did not. Her talk was met with stony silence, then mumbling, some snickering, and, eventually, outright complaints. She tried again and again to illustrate the veracity of her claims to no avail. Indeed, things only got worse: She was ridiculed, considered mad, and was no longer invited to talk. Understanding how a fully explained model supported by strong evidence could be so easily rejected could allow us to better comprehend McClintock's thinking.

The first obvious explanation is that McClintock was attempting to describe a system she had lived and worked with for over six years, in a plant she had worked with for almost 30 years, all under special isolated conditions. She had a far more intimate knowledge of maize than anyone in the audience. A biologist who was not in ongoing direct communication with the corn field, as she was, could not follow her vision. This was compounded by the language she used, which seemed to contain extra-rational elements, derived from some inner perception of a panoramic view of the cell. It was as if she could see what was actually happening to the chromosomes as they developed in a fourth dimension.

But there was an even more serious factor behind the rejection of her model. A major paradigm shift was taking place precisely at that time: Biology was moving away from both observational and experimental science toward a brand-new era of molecular mechanics. The living organism would be replaced with the tiniest physico-chemical parts. Old-timers like McClintock, who remained committed to the inherent complexity and mystery of life, were expected to step aside.

The success of molecular biology introduced a vision of unprecedented order into biology. In this vision, which placed great emphasis on the power of simple models to account for the complexity of living things, there was little room for phenomena like transposition that defied such accountability. A simple model without exceptions was what everyone strove for and indeed, at least for some time, it seemed as if few basic questions had been left unanswered and as if the secret of life, at least in principle, had been revealed. In 1944, the revolutionary paper by Oswald Avery, Colin Macleod, and Maclyn McCarty, demonstrating that DNA provided the material basis for inheritance, was published, presenting a different model of scientific explanation. This model recalled the perfectly mechanistic picture of Newton's universe. Accordingly, it was all-embracing: It should be valid for the simplest and smallest organisms, as well as the most complex organisms. As always with science, however, the satisfaction biologists felt over the exhaustion of their subject was premature. Vexing and disturbing observations began to accrue and the simple model became increasingly complicated.

McClintock was doing her work during this excited new era, in a different biological world, and her discovery was far too early a sign of the failure inherent in the simple model that had been proposed and enthusiastically embraced. It presented a serious challenge to the static central dogma of the model. The dogma asserted that information originated in the DNA and that it was not then subject to modification; in other words, that the DNA was the ultimate cipher that sent orders to the cell and therefore determined the development of the entire organism. None of McClintock's fellow biologists were ready to accept that the cell's DNA could rearrange itself under certain conditions. The very notion was upsetting: It would necessarily mean that the genes, too, were dependent on other factors and that information could also flow backward to them. Biologists were hoping for a far more static DNA, like simple units laid out in a fixed, linear sequence. McClintock's disturbing work, however, clearly demonstrated the existence of a living and unpredictable system. It was not only the DNA that affected the cell; elements in the cell affected the DNA. Instead of an unchanging string of genes, her genetic elements could spontaneously move from one site to another, even from one chromosome to another, carrying new instructions to the cell and rearranging its genetic organization. Here, we see again how McClintock's organic thinking allowed her to follow the wildest aberrations of the material itself and thus see the failures of the theoretical model.

Even when, in the second half of the twentieth century, this vision of the genes as fixed units strung along chromosomes like beads on a thread was being questioned, McClintock's transposition was still rejected. One might expect that a proof that genetic elements changed their function according to their changing location would immediately be embraced in this bewildered atmosphere, but it wasn't. Why? According to McClintock, it was the biologists' desire to cling to the dogma that prevented them from having any feeling for the organism and caused them to impose the answer they wanted to hear on it. "Organisms," she says, "can do all types of things. They do fantastic things. They do everything we do, and they do it better, more efficiently, more marvelously … It turns out that any mechanism you can think of, you will find—even if it's the most bizarre kind of thinking … So if the material tells you, 'it may be this,' allow that. Don't turn it aside and call it an exception, an aberration, a contaminant."[65]

If you looked hard enough and carefully enough, a single organism would reveal its secrets. It would tell you not just of one, but of many mechanisms it had evolved to regulate the expression of genes—mechanisms that enabled its cells to produce exactly what was needed, when it was needed. Other biologists, McClintock felt, simply would not allow the results of the experiments to speak for themselves. They knew what they wanted the material to tell them and they could not recognize anything else it might be telling them. An implicit adherence

65 Keller, *A Feeling for the Organism*, 199–200.

to models prevented them from looking at data with a fresh mind. Tacit assumptions imposed unconscious boundaries around what was thinkable and what was not; the unfamiliar became increasingly unthinkable and people forgot that theories and models come and go.

McClintock's own work was teaching her, over and over again, that the genetic apparatus is more labile and flexible than the central dogma allowed. In time, she discovered yet another entirely new system in the nucleus that controlled gene action. The genome was revealing itself to her as much more than a series of blueprints: It contained a "secret" program that enabled it to express only a certain part of its inherent potential. McClintock's immense discoveries would not be recognized until the mid-1960s, by which time molecular biology had grown vastly more complex and was capable of identifying the patterns she had seen in her corn kernels. It was only when molecular biologists began to lose their confidence in the stability of the genome that they were suddenly able to see how the genome undergoes rearrangement under a wide range of circumstances.

Inspecting a certain chromosomal aberration in *E. coli*, biologists located a small group of segments of DNA that were displaced from elsewhere on the bacterial chromosome. It became clear that these segments could turn genes on and off. Not long thereafter, an even more dramatic instance of genetic mobility was found in *Salmonella*, in which genes seemed to move at will. Even though it had hardly been conceivable only a few years earlier, it now seemed only logical that bacteria would evolve such a mechanism to greatly increase their adaptability. Great excitement was aroused by these movable genetic elements, which were called the "jumping genes," and the question of whether transposition occurs in higher organisms was immediately raised.

This was the moment of redemption for McClintock's disregarded and ridiculed work. It was revealed that the controlling elements she had discovered in maize, which were even capable of regulating the precise timing of genetic function, were not abnormal, but were, rather, part of normal development processes. What had been considered abnormal proved to be a key to a previously misunderstood higher order: Genetic mobility was simply another form of evolutionary adaptability. Indeed, ever since transposition was shown in mammals, its implications for genetic organization, development, and evolution remain the subject of debate. McClintock herself believed that genetic modification is never random, but is a capacity of the organism to re-program itself in response to environmental pressures.

In 1983, McClintock was awarded the Nobel Prize for physiology or medicine and her place in the history of modern biology was thereby secured. Transposition, once a bizarre thought that occurred to one solitary scientist, is now a crucial element of an emerging biology of development and evolution.

Our disturbance-free judgments

In many respects, we are all theorists. A theorist is a person who looks at a particular phenomenon through the lenses of generalizations, fixed categorizations, distinct evaluations, and models. When a theorist encounters aberrations that seem to contradict his or her theory, he or she tends to make the new information fit into the theory, rather than forming a new theory on the basis of the aberration. Any additional information that fits perfectly into the theory is welcomed. Is that not what we do all the time?

Any new information that seems to contradict our fixed way of thinking is considered a "disturbance" by our brain. Our automatic thinking becomes extremely uncomfortable when our generalization is threatened. What are we meant to do with this new information? Why bother to rearrange a whole worldview that has been created on the basis of years of experience and acquired wisdom? Rather, we unconsciously try to ensure that our judgments and worldviews remain undisturbed. Any new information is skillfully modified to confirm our theory or simply rejected as unreliable, unfounded, and unproven.

Indeed, it is not part of our "plan" to have our well-crafted opinion about something or our fully controlled lifestyle and habits suddenly overturned by an invasive new detail. We prefer to hold onto the judgments that seem to work for us. Openly listening to a compelling individual story from a country we consider an "enemy" could undermine our political evaluation and force us to rethink the whole situation. Hearing a fresh and convincing perspective that completely opposes our own and perhaps calls for a radical change in our lifestyles leaves us in a dangerous state of confusion. These are all "real-life disturbances" that lead us to doubt our models of reality. They tell us that our model is stagnant and partial, but in those critical moments, we tend to choose "our truth" over the facts. Facts become relevant to our brain only when they serve our impeccable truth.

Information disturbances are especially hostile to our generalizations. One well-researched cognitive error appears to highlight this habit of our mind to "jump to conclusions": hasty generalization (or faulty generalization). Hasty generalizations occur whenever we develop a "theory" or a "model" based on only a few instances of a certain phenomenon. We draw a conclusion that doesn't consider all variables, but pretends to encompass the entire phenomenon. The temptation to do this is great, for example, when it comes to statistics based on a small sample group: The researcher may wish to draw from these statistics comprehensive conclusions about entire populations. On a more personal level, when we hear about a couple of corrupt politicians, we complain that "politicians are corrupt." When we are betrayed by two good friends over a period of two years, we might conclude that "there are no real friendships in this world." And when we read about a few instances of violence or local wars in the newspapers, we judge that the human world is a "cruel place." This tendency is also referred to as the "fallacy of the lonely fact." Faulty generalizations may lead to further incorrect conclusions. For example, we might conclude that citizens of a certain country are genetically inferior or that poverty is generally the fault of the poor. After the over-generalized conclusion is made, any further evidence that might interfere with it is intentionally disregarded.

Generalizations impress us, since they seem like confident statements. Special and individual cases, on the other hand, cannot be turned into clear opinions; they seem to demand much greater mental strain and attention. As we do not have the time or energy to pay such dedicated attention, we hastily form opinions and every opinion—whether a political view or an evaluation of another person's act—is, in a way, a hasty generalization. An opinion represents the wish to ignore countless disturbing details in order to consolidate some unwavering judgment. It is for this reason that opinions are only polite on the surface; on a deeper level, they regard any new piece of information as a potential enemy. We don't want to let the smaller and more complex details trouble us. We want to believe that we know how things should be. Just think for a moment of how we ignore unwelcome details in order to put to rest some matter that we are too tired or too uninterested to reconsider. Is there anything more tiring than reservations and second thoughts?

Ideally, small and disturbing details that we become aware of after we have reached a conclusion should be welcomed for they have the potential to make us smarter. The more details we take into account, the fuller the picture becomes and the more our judgment has to rely on. However, seeing the wisdom of this necessitates changing our style of thinking radically. When we learn about special cases, we must refrain from instantly classifying them as part of some general law to which we want to cling, instead patiently considering them and thinking how they might affect our laws. This may be difficult as statistical thinking often rules our culture. Many people see any homosexual as a representation of the gay community and any single mother as a reflection of the problems of single-motherhood. But just as one rock can hold within it the entire history of the cosmos and one brain can reveal the secrets of the human subconscious and one human being can carry the history of all mankind, this consideration of the special case, too, may be a step toward a microscopic world that telescopic thinking can never reach.

Statistical thinking is a significant aspect of detached thinking. Although obviously helpful, it also poses the danger of distancing us, the observers, from the actual and concrete problems of living. One clear example is when a government proudly announces impressive economic growth rates while, behind the numbers, citizens are experiencing poverty and struggle. Do we look, then, at the numbers or at what people are actually experiencing? Our brains are increasingly being trained to see reality through the lenses of statistical rates and predictions, yet clearly reality is not a number. Life is far more complex and contains far more individual ingredients than statistics can take into account. So although there is a necessity for such models of reality, perhaps it would be wise to make sure that they don't ultimately entrap us in one-dimensional, static, theoretical views of life. When we find ourselves trying to fit data from reality into statistics, we are out of touch. McClintock's story illustrates that statistical aberration can teach us more about life than statistical accuracy.

In so many ways, our mental habit of generalization prevents us from observing the world as it really is: an inconceivably complex, living phenomenon. It seems like our thinking prefers to conceive of the world as a clear and immovable picture. Thus, when we look at phenomena, we mainly see our own opinions reflected back at us. To demonstrate this insight, we can call to mind one of our more conclusive generalizations and then think of a possible special case that might invalidate this generalization or at least challenge it: for instance, confronting the opinion that "spiritual people are hazy, dreamy, and unrealistic" with powerful examples of spiritual people who are deeply realistic and grounded, such as the Dalai Lama; or challenging the notion that "philosophy is not a real or serious occupation" with extremely successful philosophers who are engaged and influential in our culture; or re-examining the notion that "environmentalists only care about the environment, not about people," in light of highly humanistic environmentalists (such as Henry David Thoreau); or challenging the belief that "feminists only try to be like men and lose their femininity" with illuminating examples of feminists who praise "feminine" qualities.

We can also practice acute awareness whenever we experience "disturbances"—real-life aberrations that interrupt the way things "should be," such as a sudden illness that disrupts our future plans. As soon as we find ourselves rejecting the aberration, we can ask ourselves instead: What is missing from my perception that makes me see this as a disturbance? Perhaps by waiting anxiously to recover from the annoying illness so one can return to one's normal lifestyle, one misses the whole point. Perhaps the illness is an indication that certain aspects of one's lifestyle should be thoroughly looked into, omitted, or rearranged.

Additionally, we can try to observe a certain phenomenon without seeking the immediate satisfaction of "opinion" and instead looking at it from all possible angles. Thus, we might come to find that it is not possible to come to an "opinion" and that it is preferable to deal with reality just as it is. By delaying forming opinions, it becomes possible for us to see the unpredictable and the unexpected. Instead of seeing only what we want to see, only that which confirms our models of reality, we exit the "hall of mirrors," in which all we see is our own reflection, and learn how to reflect something other than ourselves and our own opinions. We learn how to observe without our preferences and hidden assumptions unconsciously defining what we are able to see and what we can never see. The results may not be perfect, since we are always bound to some degree of subjectivity but one's perspective could certainly be considerably widened by such a practice.

Plants are *not* plastic bags

McClintock's "pure seeing" seems to correspond to the famous problem of the "observer effect" in physics. The observer effect demonstrates how the very act of observation causes changes in the observed phenomenon. This coincides, to a degree, with McClintock's intuition that the more one fills the role of observer, the less one can truly see. Rather than serving as an immaculate mirror that clearly reflects the observed reality, the observer distorts the reflection. In other words, one cannot reveal the laws of the universe when one holds onto rules of one's own.

To avoid experiencing these problems, McClintock explains, one must have the time to look, the patience to "hear what the material has to say to you," and the openness to "let it come to you." In contrast to the rat race of science nowadays, McClintock believed that one had to proceed very slowly, respectful of the hidden complexity that lurks in even the most straightforward-seeming systems. Although she herself worked with an inherently slow organism—it was not possible to grow more than two maize crops a year—she felt that even this rhythm was too fast. If she was really to analyze all that there was to see, one crop was all she could handle.

McClintock stated, "An organism isn't just a piece of plastic." Rather, organisms are ever-changing living things, with an order of their own. This order can only be partially fathomed by scientists; no human-made model could fully do justice to the prodigious creativity of organisms. To study a living thing means not only to grasp its mechanism, but to be driven by a deeper longing to embrace the world in all its complexity and mystery. An organism functions and communicates as a whole, so it is not possible to grasp its totality by dissecting it and learning about some part or other. If one aspires to communicate with the complete organism, one's mind needs to become utterly transparent; otherwise, it cannot be filled by this totality. Only such seeing, according to McClintock, can yield surprising revelations. The experience of surprises in research indicates that the researcher is truly open to being struck by the endless inventiveness of life.

Only a mind that was free from the burden of being the observer could notice, and communicate with, the richness of life, which becomes far more accessible. McClintock never lost sight of the fact that plants are alive, whereas we tend to see them as inanimate. She noticed their sensitivities, their responses to touch, their myriad signs of life, which a casual eye would miss. "In the summertime," she wrote poetically, "when you walk down the road, you'll see that the tulip leaves, if it's a little warm, turn themselves around so their backs are towards the sun ... Within the restricted areas in which they live, they move around a great deal."[66] That is why, she adds, every time she walks on grass, she feels sorry because she knows the grass is screaming at her.

She held that the scientific mind, which sought to study objects as accurately as possible, was incapable of embracing the aliveness that was so vital to the complete understanding of life. In her mind, her objects of study were subjects in their own right. "Organism" was a code word—not simply a plant or animal—but the name of a living form. Indeed, McClintock's inquiry into the world of biology was guided by a sense of underlying oneness of nature: "There was no way in which you draw a line between things."[67] In that sense, she perceived her own mind and her objects of study as being made of the same materials and viewed the mind as an apparatus of nature designed to investigate itself.

While many believe that science gradually leads us toward the complete "truth," McClintock believed that the scientific method alone cannot give us "real understanding." On the contrary, if we rely on it too much, we limit our capacity to discover, since the world is more wonderful than the scientific method allows us to appreciate. For example, as science neglects the oneness of things, it can only give us

66 Keller, *A Feeling for the Organism*, 200.
67 Ibid., 204.

"nature-in-pieces." Accordingly, its solutions to problems solve certain aspects, but never the complete problem. Technology, a clear example of science's partial solution to man's relationship with nature, spoils the environment, but we tell ourselves that this is acceptable because we are using the techniques of science.

Perhaps we could come to embrace this slowness of observation and study as part of the way we reach conclusions. Instead of succumbing to the well-known cognitive bias of jumping to conclusions, delaying the instant gratification of hasty conclusions could lead us to a far more mature form of wisdom. When we think more slowly, patiently holding a question in our inquiring mind and letting all aspects of the problem gradually gather, the solution to the problem may well present itself to us.

CHAPTER 4

SIGMUND FREUD

The excavator, *or* The forgotten secret of the burnt pudding

Whether we recognize it or not, we all speak "Freudian." We casually refer to repression, projection, neuroses, ambivalence, and sibling rivalry. When a historian refers to our time as "an age of narcissism," everyone understands what is meant. Popular culture loves speaking this language too. In TV dramas, sitcoms, and documentaries, Freudian terms are frequently used. In the more professional realm, as Professor of Psychology Susan Krauss Whitbourne writes, Sigmund Freud is to the field of psychology what Isaac Newton is to physics. His ideas about the unconscious became the foundation upon which later theories were built. Yet, although nobody can deny the degree to which his ideas have shaped our view of ourselves and despite him being the most famous psychologist in human history, our culture still seems to be—again using *his* term—ambivalent about Freud and his theories.

Freud's reputation remains as controversial as it was a century ago. While he has been called a genius, a founder, a master, and a giant among the makers of the modern mind, his detractors see him not just as a misguided psychologist, but also as a dictator, a liar, a fraud—in a word, a charlatan. Charles Darwin, that other great maker of the twentieth-century mind, immediately found an enthusiastic readership for his

Origin of Species and is not nowadays subjected to any fundamental questioning—despite the outrageous claims he made about human origins. For Freud, it has never been easy. His subversive, disturbing, and unconventional theories about human nature were met, from the very beginning, with horrified reactions. In 1910, Professor Wilhelm Weygandt exclaimed to the Hamburg Congress of Neurologists and Psychiatrists that Freud's theories were not a matter for discussion at a scientific gathering, but rather a matter for the police.

The parties quarrelling over Freud's legacy have such polarized opinions that the chances of their ever agreeing are extremely slim. Moreover, scientific research has provided us with confusing conclusions. Some research confirms a few of Freud's contributions. Fisher and Greenberg, for example, concluded in 1977, and later on in 1996, that certain concepts, including the infamous Oedipus complex, could be supported by empirical evidence and Kahneman showed that experiments have confirmed Freud's insights about the role of symbols and metaphors in unconscious associations. Others claim that Freud's ideas set back the study of psychology and psychiatry by 50 years or more. While neuroscientist and Nobel laureate Eric Kandel argues that psychoanalysis still represents the most coherent and intellectually satisfying view of the mind, many others criticize it for being a form of art at best and a fraud at worst.

Why does this battle seem to be colored by intense emotion? Could it be that beneath the vigorous accusations, there are deeper, more secret resistances? Freud was far from flawless, both in his theories and his personality, but this can be said of nearly every other genius in history. Is there some unconscious—or, dare we say, psychoanalytic—reason that he has become the eternally famous, yet controversial discoverer of the human mind?

Few know that this most unconventional explorer of the forbidden realms of sexuality underwent a personal struggle every step of the way. His propositions on libido were hardly less scandalous to him, conventionally bourgeois as he was, than they were to most of his readers. Yet he considered it his fate to "agitate the sleep of mankind."[68] Concealment, hypocrisy, and the polite evasions of bourgeois society were the nemeses of his psychoanalysis. Its unsparing inquiry rudely intruded upon the most heavily guarded aspects in the human psyche. Is it any wonder, then, that humanity has defended itself with angry denial as psychoanalysis has reached into the deepest and darkest regions of the psyche, aggressively pulling out repressed emotions and wishes? After all, as Freud's biographer Peter Gay observes, "the mind is more resistant to analysis, and even description, than the history of species."[69]

Perhaps it's the terrifying reflection of our psyche, which we see as we gaze into Freud's merciless mirror, that has caused psychoanalysis both to be so influential and to have been met with such reservation and resistance. The latter response is almost like the culture's revenge on behalf of its broken image of itself as healthy, rational, self-controlled, and morally refined. Freud considered all of us "sick"—different from the truly neurotic only in the degree of intensity, but not in essence. By demolishing the high walls that had separated the "normal" person from the "mentally disturbed," he finally exposed the psychic disturbances that a normal person could hide quite easily. We all became psychological beings, possessors of realms so secret that we kept them hidden even from ourselves. We became pretenders and concealers—in every dream, in every slip of the tongue, in every fleeting thought that we efficiently brushed away.

Moreover, we were exposed as irrational, driven by forces unknown to ourselves, while on the surface our choices and decisions might seem cool and thoughtful. Suddenly, we were deprived of our self-control and faced with unconquerable dark and strange worlds that influenced our every action, unbeknownst to us. Freud explicitly identified his task as being to "struggle with the demon"—the demon of irrationality—in

68 Peter Gay, *Freud: A Life for our Time* (New York: Norton, 1998).
69 Ibid., vi.

a "sober way."[70] This "sober way" was merciless in its exploration of hidden forces. It's easy to understand why we would be shocked by the shattering of the myth that small children are sexually innocent or horrified to hear that a healthy child would wish for his father's death. It's just as easy to understand why women would be repulsed by the idea that they were possessed by "penis envy" and why the idea of us having erotic feelings toward our mothers or fathers would be intolerable.

Freud stoically claimed that all of us, children and adults, normal and mentally disturbed, are innately perverse and unconscious murderers. He presented a whole underworld that exists beneath our socially acceptable masks. In this underworld are innumerable unspeakable wishes and fantasies, both erotic and violent. Freud messed with us, on a personal level: Our psyches were his guinea pigs, scrutinized by his suspicious "soul-microscope." For breaching the heavy defenses of our psyches, we shall never forgive him.

According to Freud, all normal people have to endure an inner split. It is the heavy price we must pay for entering civilization. Civilization divided our psychic world into different compartments the moment it started labeling some of our wishes as wrong and forbidden. It was human culture that invented the subconscious. All of a sudden, a large portion of our urges had to be pushed into the dark cellars, unacknowledged even by ourselves, since we wanted to think that we were exactly what our culture wished us to be. This was the birthplace of repression, when our wishes went underground. Since then, we have been doomed to be split forever: unable to live without cultural limitations and, at the same time, unable to be truly free.

The denial of passionate needs—for the sake of family concord, social harmony, or respectability—was inevitable. Fearful of unchecked passions, civilization deemed it necessary to brand the most insistent human impulses as ill-mannered and immoral. No man should feel sexually attracted to his mother or daughter and no girl should wish for

70 Gay, *Freud*, xvii.

her mother's death. Yet, deep down, the wishes persist. Denying them distorts us mentally, emotionally, and physically: Erotic excitement is turned into anxiety and unacceptable wishes become "symptoms." Repression had taken a heavy toll, but unearthing repressed secrets was no less painful and so it was that Freud, the invader of our secret thoughts, established himself as an unwanted cultural hero.

Digging out a buried city

The Freudian revolution did not start with great certainties, but with intent listening. At first, it was Freud's mentor and colleague, physician Josef Breuer, who, through the young Bertha Pappenheim, gained extraordinary insight into the therapeutic advantage of listening to one's patient. The treatment of this "hysteric," whom Breuer would later immortalize under the pseudonym "Anna O.," marked the starting point of psychoanalysis and, more generally, a total revolution in the treatment of mental illness. Following her father's fatal illness and eventual death, the young woman had developed peculiar symptoms that culminated in the development of two distinct, highly contrasting personalities, one of which was extremely unruly.

Breuer and his highly intelligent patient unintentionally established a spontaneous procedure that Pappenheim would eventually entitle her "talking cure."[71] Talking proved cathartic as it awakened important memories and allowed for the release of powerful emotions she had been unable to recall or express when she was her normal self. Her symptoms turned out to be residues of feelings and impulses she had felt obliged to suppress. The discussion of bizarre symptoms, like the inability to drink water, led to the liberating revelation of unconscious associations. Together, they could see, for the first time, the intricate ways in which the psyche made irrational and elusive associations, like a confused spider that weaves a complex web and then gets caught

71 Louis Breger, *Freud: Darkness in the Midst of Vision* (New York: Wiley, 2000), 73.

in it. It became apparent that full consciousness of these unwelcome associations led to their disentanglement.

The depth of this revelation can be more fully appreciated when one considers the context in which it occurred: The medical world had thus far ignored the psychological element of mental illnesses. The mind had been thought of as totally dependent on the body, the nervous system, and the brain. The very term "neurosis" derives from "nerve." Listening to what a hysteric woman had to say was, in itself, a revolution.

However, a peculiar incident gave Breuer such a fright that it made him drop Bertha's case and pass it on to a colleague. On the evening of the day on which all of her symptoms had been brought under control, he was called to her once more. Breuer found her confused and writhing with abdominal cramps. When asked what the matter was, she replied, "Now comes Dr. B's child." Freud commented many years later that at that moment Breuer had held the key in his hand, but, unable or unwilling to use it, he had dropped it. It was one thing to recognize hysterical symptoms as meaningful responses to particular traumas. It was quite another thing to touch on the sexual origins of Bertha's hysteria. It must have shocked him to encounter, for the first time, the phenomenon of "transference": the patient's tendency to project onto the therapist feelings they harbor for beloved persons, such as ambivalence toward his or her father or mother or erotic infatuation.

What made Freud more willing to fully penetrate the psyche? For Freud, any reservation regarding taking the final step into the dark regions of the human mind was no less than a craven desertion of the field of battle. Moreover, he saw Breuer's rejection of the elemental and shocking truths that were being revealed by the process as a plain instance of psychic "resistance"—the attempt of the conscious mind to push away the all-seeing eye of the true analyst. Breuer's rational objection to sexuality was, in Freud's view, irrational. First, the conscious mind experiences deep psychic turmoil, then it covers it up with reasonable justifications. Yet, according to Freud, the conscious mind was akin to a display window that presents only what the shopkeeper wants shoppers to buy.

Freud remained unshaken. In fact, he made it a rule that his patients should report everything, however frivolous or senseless, that came into their minds. A neurosis, he once wrote, never says anything foolish. When the patient spoke about seemingly unrelated subjects, even technical and boring subjects, Freud would listen. When a patient became silent, he would ask what was going on in his or her head and would refuse to accept "nothing" as an answer. Nothing was innocent and any irrational association that others might dismiss as coincidental was of great significance to Freud.

Around the year 1892, this approach slowly gave rise to the technique of free association. Freud disposed of the more acceptable hypnosis upon realizing that uncensored talking was a far superior investigative device. He took it upon himself to keenly listen to what his patients had to teach him. The analysands were not reduced to mentally broken people. They were his "instructors" and he turned listening to them into more than an art—he turned it into a method, a road to knowledge that was slowly mapped out for him by the analysands. Yet, he was far from the classical image of the silent, poker-faced psychoanalyst common in movies. He was an active, almost aggressive listener, interpreting his patients' confessions rapidly and skeptically, probing to gain access to deeper levels of distress and keenly searching for cracks and breaches in patients' conscious presentation. One of his first patients, Baroness Fanny Moser, grew so annoyed with this that she demanded that he stop "asking her where this or that came from, but let her tell [him] what she had to say."[72]

Listening to his first patients, Freud learned how to use the thinnest, most elusive threads of thought to access the underworld of hidden motives. When "Miss Lucy R." entered treatment, he could recognize the value of his purposeful attentiveness. Her most obtrusive symptom,

72 Gay, *Freud*, 70.

which he managed to cure after nine weeks, was the perception of the offensive smell of burnt pudding, which was associated with feelings of depression. Instead of minimizing this peculiar hallucination, he let it guide him to the origins of her malaise. It was clear to him that there had to be a reason why a particular smell should be linked to a particular mood.

This woman, an English governess employed by a wealthy widower to take care of his children, was secretly in love with her employer. When her love for him was met with indifference, she decided to leave him, but that necessarily meant losing contact with his beloved children. While contemplating the prospect of losing her connection to the children, she burned her pudding.

Such early experiences convinced Freud that his profession failed to probe the hidden nature of mental illnesses. He began to assign primacy to the psychological dimension in mental work. For the first time, the psyche was given an independent status and considered a world unto itself. Carefully listening to patients was paying off and so, as Freud's official biographer Ernest Jones put it, he gave rise to the first true depth psychology. This breakthrough into the enigmatic and strange world of the psyche was enabled by what we call "excavating thinking."

The more conventional type of thinking, "superficial thinking," could never tap into such psychic depths. The reason is simple: It can recognize as real only that which appears on the surface of one's mind, only that which is consciously available and presentable. In a way, it is akin to a strictly materialistic approach, whereby only objects that are immediately perceivable exist. It never questions or inspects that which is beneath the surface; it interacts only with the surface. To Freud, who had, in his twenties, analyzed his fiancée's letters to him with an attention to minutiae worthy of a detective, the display of thought and emotion was only ever a cover-up. The very purpose of this display was to hide away one's innermost reality. Therefore, one could never come to understand human behavior unless one used excavating thinking. This type of thinking even manifested in Freud's way of looking at people. In the words of musicologist Max Graf, Freud's eyes "seemed to look at man from the depths."[73]

For the excavating thinker, there is always something deeper and so one should constantly search for that which is hidden underneath the surface. Indeed, Freud associated his process of inquiry with the archaeological excavation of a buried city. The enlightened archaeologist walks on the earth with the constant suspicion that underneath his or her feet there lies a whole world of antiquity. Similarly, Freud declared that the student of hysteria is like an explorer discovering the remains of an abandoned city, with walls and columns and tablets covered with half-effaced inscriptions. He or she may dig up these artifacts and clean them and then, with luck, the stones will speak. These worlds are gradually buried through the process of repression. To the analyst, the patient presents the new and visible city he has built atop the buried ruins of those forgotten cities of the past. The analyst becomes the archaeologist of the psyche. He "must uncover layer after layer of the patient's psyche, before coming to the deepest, most valuable treasures."[74]

It should not surprise us, therefore, that Freud avidly read about archaeology in his free time, much more than he read about psychology, and followed the progress of excavations with the excitement of an amateur. His analysis room was packed with Greek, Roman, and Egyptian antiquities, so much so that one of the patients who came to be treated at Berggasse 19 was reminded not of a doctor's office, but rather of an archaeologist's study. In a letter to a friend, Freud compared an analytic success of his to the discovery of Troy by the celebrated digger Heinrich Schliemann. With Freud's help, a patient had found, buried deep underneath fantasies, "a scene from his primal period ... into which all left-over riddles flow ... It is as if Schliemann had dug up Troy,

73 Gay, *Freud*, 156.

74 Jean-Michel Rabate, *The Cambridge Introduction to Literature and Psychoanalysis* (New York: Cambridge University Press, 2014), 201.

considered legendary, once again."[75] When he found, in another case, that his analytic results were incomplete, he compared the situation to the problems faced by "explorers fortunate enough to bring to the light of day after long burial the priceless though mutilated remnants of antiquity."[76]

Excavating thinking revolves around one central principle: Whatever appears on the surface of consciousness is always but a representation, a replacement for or an attempt to cover up something else. Since anything that is on the surface—any thought, emotion, or behavior—is only intended to replace something deeper, excavating thinking interprets that which is apparent on the surface as a series of symbols that must be deciphered. This is evident in the countless discoveries, controversial to this day, made by Freud: Anxiety replaces sexual excitement and is a twisted form of repressed erotic desires; addiction to cigars (like any other addiction) replaces masturbation; dreams of flying replace the excitement of the child when lifted up in the air by his parents; and a dream of a broken pencil symbolizes impotence, or the fear of impotence. For excavating thinking, there are no accidents in the universe of the mind. Every event, no matter how accidental it may seem, constitutes a knot of causal threads that are too remote in origin, too large in number, and too intricately intertwined to be readily sorted out. By adopting this approach, Freud could more easily follow the strange threads of the mind, even when they seemed to lead to the most improbable of places, in complete defiance of coherence and rationality.

Only excavating thinking can detect the most elusive signs of an underground city. It clings to clues, like the smell of burnt pudding, that superficial thinking would usually dismiss or prefer not to see.

75 Gay, *Freud*, 172.
76 Frank F. Scherer, *Freud's Orient: Early Psychoanalysis, "Anti-Semitic Challenge", and the Vicissitudes of Orientalist Discourse*. A dissertation. York University Toronto, Ontario, 2010. https://central.bac-lac.gc.ca/.item?id=NR80539&op=pdf&app=Library&oclc_number=890511509, 109.

It even admires the subtleties and intricacies of these "great art works of psychic nature," as Freud put it.[77] Superficial thinking is incapable of reaching into the complex worlds of the subconscious and even if it could, it would get lost in the endless connections that make up the irrational rationale of psychic patterns.

Without getting into self-analysis, we can begin to see this endless net of associative connections through the following thought-experiment: Consider a random object, such as the name of a city, a body part, or a natural phenomenon, and start generating feelings, emotions, images, and memories, even absurd ones, that arise in relation to it. By constantly asking, "What does this remind me of?"—a typical excavating-thinking question—we can come to appreciate the extent of our associative connections. In the brain, one thing always leads to another in an endless web of connections that may be sensible or absurd—or both. Our brain creates these webs of associations automatically and these associations affect our thinking without us realizing it. Now think about how, whenever you look at the body part or city you called to mind, the object instantly leads you along this unconscious chain of connotations. It is for this reason that our thoughts often become so entangled that we cannot remember exactly what led us to a certain thought.

Superficial thinking never really interests itself in these intense associative activities, instead focusing only on the final result—whatever the mind ultimately chooses to present to the world. Such thinking leads us to believe our own rational and tidy thoughts and accept the pretenses of others. It does not take the trouble to consider the depths of irrationality, unconscious motivations, self-deceptions, and mental manipulations. It is not difficult to understand the appeal of superficial thinking. Excavating thinking comes at the heavy price of losing one's naïveté. The ability to see everything that lies beneath the surface, including of yourself, leads to a true appreciation of the

77 Gay, *Freud*, 264.

saying, "Ignorance is bliss." As one of Freud's most famous patients, Dora, discussed her sexual matters with him, his excavating thinking noted that she kept playing with her little purse, opening and closing it and pushing her finger into it over and over. This, he realized, was a pantomime of masturbation. He once said that such is the lot of the skilled observer who can glean information from the faintest movement, the slightest flicker, for "he who has eyes to see and ears to hear becomes convinced that mortals can keep no secret. If their lips are silent, they gossip with their fingertips; betrayal forces itself through every pore."[78]

There are no weird dreams

Before any other patient sat on the famous couch, Freud subjected one patient of crucial importance to his intense excavating thinking: Freud himself. Though he seriously questioned the possibility of true self-analysis, he subjected himself to a most thoroughgoing self-scrutiny: an elaborate, penetrating, and unceasing survey of his fragmentary memories and his concealed wishes and emotions. His own person was, to him, simply another source of material. In this sense, his emerging psychology was also a desperate attempt to comprehend symptoms he shared with his patients.

When his father died in 1896, Freud could not help but analyze his process of grief. He translated his feelings into theory, drawing universal implications from his personal experience. While his father's death was, to him, "the most significant event, the most decisive loss, of a man's life,"[79] he put it to scientific use, distancing himself from his loss to gather material for his theories. For example, his excavating thinking allowed him to observe, beneath the grief, the phenomenon of survival guilt—the self-reproach that is regularly felt by survivors.

78 Forrest Robinson, "Twain and Freud," in *The Jester and the Sages*, eds. Forrest G. Robinson, Gabriel Noah Brahm, Jr., and Catherine Carlstroem (Columbia: University of Missouri Press, 2011), 44.
79 Gay, *Freud*, 89.

Freud ardently collected his dreams, memories, slips of tongue or pen, and instances of forgetting lines of poetry or patients' first names and allowed these clues to lead him from idea to idea through free association. When he dreamed that his old mentor had set him the strange assignment of dissecting his own lower body, he interpreted this dream as a reference to his self-analysis. In 1897, he sensed that great things were about to emerge from this self-analysis: "I believe I am in a cocoon, and God knows what kind of beast will crawl out."[80] A few days later, he had a breakthrough: Previously repressed childhood memories and forbidden wishes flooded his mind. He felt as if he were being pulled forcibly through his past as his thoughts made rapid connections. When he failed to understand the meaning of a dream or a fantasy, he felt despondent. He found the process exceedingly unpleasant, as almost every day his self-analysis revealed wicked wishes and discreditable acts, but then there were the days when "a flash of lightning illuminated the connections."[81]

Freud excavated his own buried city, on the basis of which he would formulate many of his fundamental ideas. His memories of his childhood infatuation with his mother and his jealousy of his father led him to claim that the Oedipal relationship was a general event in early childhood. His now wide-open subconscious also enabled him to unveil other universal principles, such as the unconscious feeling of guilt, the power of repressed aggressive feelings, the stages of sexual development, and the intricate mechanism of dream production.

Dreams, for him, represented the "royal road to the unconscious."[82] They seemed to spring from the deepest levels of the underworld and, for this reason, were exceedingly difficult to comprehend. The language

80 Moshe Gresser, *Dual Allegiance* (New York: State University of New York Press, 1994), 114.
81 Gay, Freud, 100.
82 Tracey Cleantis, "Freudian-Express: Dreams, The Royal Road to the Unconscious," *Psychology Today*, January 14, 2011. https://www.psychologytoday.com/us/blog/freudian-sip/201101/freudian-express-dreams-the-royal-road-the-unconscious.

of dreams was foreign to superficial thinking as dreams preceded rational dominion, like primitive cultures of prehistoric times. While most people, guided by superficial thinking, would simply wake up and say, "What a strange dream I had last night!", Freud believed that there was nothing "strange" about dreams. Even the most absurd or fragmented dream would reveal itself as a meaningful psychical structure under the scrutinizing inspection of excavating thinking. What we might consider a meaningless flow of random and distorted details was, in Freud's eyes, a sophisticated and meaningful web that invited us to enter the world of our true psyche. Whatever hints rose from this hidden world and reached the conscious mind were always carrying messages of one's deeper truth.

To decipher the meaning of a dream, Freud reasoned that it was necessary to understand the language of the dream. Despite seeming arbitrary, dreams do follow their own hidden rules and order. The dream-interpreter—who is now part paleographer, part translator, part codebreaker—needs to put hidden dream thoughts and explicit dream content side by side. These must be treated like two versions of the same content, only in two different languages. However, the only way of interpreting this apparently nonsensical picture puzzle is by ceasing to be astonished by the dream's absurdity and realizing that even if it seems crazy, it nonetheless has a logic of its own. Here again, Freud was guided by the basic principle of excavating thinking—that everything that appears on the surface is just a representation of or a replacement for something deeper. He realized that dreams represent thoughts as pictures and abstract ideas as concrete images. Slowly, by replacing each picture with a syllable or a word, the "stones speak" and the dream is revealed to be the bearer of a lucid message.

Freud's excavating thinking was remarkably penetrating when it came to dream interpretation. The first dream he undertook to interpret, as part of his painful self-analysis, is featured in his classic *The Interpretation of Dreams*. His interpretation is so meticulous that it stretches over no less than fifteen condensed pages. Even at that, after tracing each dream element to its origins in his recent and remote experience, Freud declared that his interpretation was fragmentary and that he could "dwell on it for a long time still … and discuss new riddles it throws up."[83] In his mind, no dream could ever be interpreted exhaustively; its associations were simply too numerous to permit the riddles to be wholly solved.

Freud believed that the manifest dream was only what our inner censorship would permit to float to the surface of awareness. The deepest truths of dreams were wishes that were rejected by our conscious mind; denied, they had to move to the underworld to be fulfilled in a different way, under the cover of a different language and form. Since humans harbor wishes that they do not wish to acknowledge in their uncensored form, they had to "dream them away." Even an anxiety dream, Freud controversially declared, holds within it a wish produced in the unconscious, but repudiated by the rest of the mind. Thus, a little boy dreaming of his father's death would wake up horrified; yet, this horror would be his conscious attempt to condemn the deeply buried part of himself that could actually wish for his father's demise.

While dreams were, for Freud, the ultimate guide, even the most ordinary slips and the most unsophisticated jokes afforded him access to the remotest regions of the mind. Misspelling a familiar name, forgetting a favorite poem, mysteriously mislaying an object, or even failing to send one's wife the usual bouquet of flowers on her birthday—these were all messages begging to be decoded, clues regarding desires or anxieties that the person was not free to acknowledge, even to him- or herself. By scientifically interpreting apparently causeless and inexplicable events, Freud again exhibited a profound law of excavating thinking: Any apparent randomness is but a gateway to a deeper and hidden order that governs the human mind.

---

83 Freud, *The Interpretation of Dreams*, 33.

Freud became interested in the theoretical relevance of slips in 1897, when he could not find an address he needed during a visit to Berlin. He was accustomed to paying attention to his own experience, but, as biographer Peter Gay writes, "[i]n these years of self-analysis he was exceptionally sensitive to the slightest hint of the mind's shifty and circuitous ways."[84] Upon analysis, Freud uncovered a complex web of associations and repressions. When correcting the manuscript of *The Interpretation of Dreams*, he wrote to a friend that no matter how hard he tried, the book would still contain "2,467 mistakes." He felt that this could not be a randomly selected number and hurried to analyze it. Here again, we can see that any error in thought, speech, or behavior was like a crack or a breach through which Freud could reach into the ocean of the subconscious.

Our irrational rationality

How rational do we think we are? In order to function as we do, we must think that we are perfectly rational. Continuously questioning our rationality would leave us in such a hesitant state that we might end up doing nothing. However, recent research seems to confirm the devastating news of our irrationality, first proclaimed by Freud more than 100 years ago.

Professor of Psychology Alex Todorov demonstrated a striking pattern in his research of "person perception"—our initial impressions of people. He briefly showed his students pictures of men's faces and asked them to rate the faces on the basis of various attributes, including likability and competence. The faces were not random: All were the campaign portraits of politicians competing for office. His students lacked this political context. Todorov compared the results of the elections to the students' ratings of the competence of the faces. In about 70 percent of cases, the election winner was the candidate whose

84 Gay, *Freud*, 125.

face had earned the highest competence rating. The implication is that however thoughtful voters might think they are, they often rely on an irrational assessment that takes place quickly and automatically[85]. As researcher Daniel Kahneman states, you might feel optimistic about a project because something about its leader reminds you of your beloved sister and you might dislike a person who looks vaguely like your dentist. Judgments are often determined by the unconscious feelings that precede them. When asked for an "explanation," we search our mind for presentable reasons. We then strongly believe the story we make up.

What drives us to adopt a certain position is too often unrelated to the reasons we later give. Before our slow intellect enters the picture, many things can happen: A deeper emotion in us, even a haunting memory of which we are not aware, may lead us to believe that a certain impression is "true" and "right." The "opinions" and "convictions" we sincerely regard as our own may be the product of unconscious and uncontrolled wishes and anxieties. Naturally, our reason doesn't like to think that it can be manipulated by deep feelings and emotions. We want to think that we are perfectly capable of separating our irrational feelings and emotions from our judgment. Yet, studies repeatedly undermine our self-image as conscious and autonomous authors of our judgments and choices.

Brief emotional responses may be the basis of "judgments of coherence" right now, as you evaluate the consistency and truthfulness of this text. Kahneman shows that it is our emotional attitude toward such things as irradiated food, red meat, nuclear power, tattoos, or motorcycles that actually drives our beliefs about their benefits or risks. Our reasoning mind, he claims, is more of an apologist for the emotions of our subconscious than their critic. When we search for information and arguments, we unknowingly limit ourselves to information that is consistent with our existing beliefs. When emotions are involved, first we make conclusions and only then do we look for arguments to support them.

85 Kahneman, *Thinking, Fast and Slow, 90–91.*

Freud clearly discounted rational or intellectual explanations for discord. He once observed that when differences of opinion make friendly relations impossible, "it is not the scientific differences that are so important; it is usually some other kind of animosity, jealousy or revenge, that gives the impulse to enmity. The scientific differences come later."[86] When we are guided by superficial thinking, which considers only that which appears on the surface as real, we relate directly to the statements that are made, never questioning their motives. If a person claims that he or she is angry for certain reasons, we believe what is said, just as we would expect the other to believe us when we vehemently present our own reasoning. It is for this reason that rational explanations and even striking evidence often fail to bring an argument to a close. Rationality was not the generating force behind the argument and rationality cannot be used against irrationality, which is driven by altogether different motives and passions. The greater the emotional intensity surrounding the argument, the more likely it is that it is born of subconscious motivations.

We hate to admit it, but we really are emotionalists more than we are thinkers. First, we have feelings about something, then we think about it. Think of yourself as consisting of three layers: Your lowest and most primordial is feelings and instincts; your middle layer is emotions; and on the top you have your thinking. All that you perceive is reacted to according to this order: instinct, emotion, thought. Your most primal feelings and instincts often assume the guise of a reasonable thought. This is because your thinking sometimes serves only to justify your irrational feelings and emotions. When we are taken aback by someone upon first meeting them, our reaction is obviously not caused by something he or she did; however, we tend to come up with some sound explanation. More often than not, we will look for further evidence that confirms our initial judgment, which makes it very difficult for us to change our minds; we will simply "dislike" this person. In the same

86 Gay, *Freud*, 220.

way, a research study found that parole judges were far less merciful when they were hungry and tired; their feelings overpowered their judgment—however, you can be sure that, if asked, they would have given a perfect explanation for rejecting each prisoner.[87]

Our irrational thoughts are simply disguised feelings and emotions. They hover over our heads all day long, nonsensical, unreasonable, reminders of an underground world beneath our feet. If we paid attention to them, they would disturb our functional behavior. That's why we censor them, pushing away the unwelcome mental activity—which is unwelcome because we don't understand it or don't want to face its annoying messages. This daily repression is our primary defense mechanism. An attempt to list all the unwelcome or strange associations that cross our minds over the course of even one day would make this abundantly clear.

But does this censorship really prevent the unwanted mental activity? No, it does not. In fact, it only makes the situation worse: By pushing away certain thoughts or feelings, we relegate them to the underground realm, where they control us without our knowledge. If we were to take the time to make a list of all of the associations we made in a day, we would realize that although we do our best, through superficial thinking, not to afford these forces and feelings any significance, they are responsible for shaping our so-called "rational thinking." These forces and feelings are not just outdated archaeological layers; they actively propel us toward choice and action. Freud's message to us is that, in order to truly understand ourselves, we must consider the irrational worlds within us. We must abandon the superficial thinking that restricts us to identifying only with the conscious mind and let our irrational thinking lead us to its origins in the ocean of the subconscious—where it was forged by feelings and emotions that we could not control. Only in this way can we minimize the danger of feelings and emotions disguised as rational thinking.

87 Kahneman, *Thinking, Fast and Slow*, 43–44.

With the help of excavating thinking, we can more easily identify the irrational thoughts that secretly shape our judgment, for example, when we try to logically justify our opinion while recognizing that there is some hidden tension we are trying to cover up or when we try to hide culturally unacceptable wishes, like violent impulses or erotic images, in a cultured discussion. Such primitive urges, which we try to repress, may eventually surface in the form of manipulative behavior, intense tension, or sudden outbursts of irrational expression. This is cause for great embarrassment: It seems that rational thinking can do nothing to change our emotional response—all it can do is repress it. Everyone knows, rationally, that we shouldn't feel insulted or jealous. However, intense emotional reactions do not seem to be affected by this knowledge.

Excavating thinking seems to be the only kind of thinking that can actually understand the language of feelings and emotions. It's like a bridge between the rational and the irrational. It is able to penetrate that which is incomprehensible and primitive in us and explore its "crazy logic." For that to happen, though, we must accept our irrationality and stop clinging so desperately to our conception of ourselves as completely logical beings. This can open up a whole new world for us and allow us to question any immediate reactions we have. Perhaps this is an emotional reaction rather than a mental one? Perhaps the rigid opinion—the political argument or film critique—that we are voicing is motivated by distorted childhood associations? An awareness of the deeper motivations that might drive us allows us to call into question the stories our rational thinking weaves so elegantly, including the way we might rearrange particular memories. It is more comfortable to overlook these underworlds, but disregarding them only broadens their scope of influence.

Mind over psyche

Although Freud never directly admitted this, his letters to friends prove that throughout his life he was also in contact with another type of subconscious—a positive subconscious. This other subconscious seemed to be the source of his greatest insights and creative leaps. On a few occasions, he wrote that "things are working in the lowest floor" or that "things ... are going forward soundly on a subterranean level."[88] When preparing for a writing project, he would wait for material to emerge from his unconscious and then he would experience what he compared to frightful labor pains. Whereas in his work he emphasized the subconscious only as the source of neuroses, it seemed that his deeper experience of the conscious and the unconscious was very different to that of ordinary people. It seemed like Freud experienced his conscious mind as a passing wave, while the larger portion of himself was akin to the unfathomable depths of the ocean, in which tremendous unconscious activities took place, finally giving rise to the conscious mind.

One might expect that this experience of himself would lead Freud to conclude that we are helplessly controlled by our own unconscious, but Freud was convinced that the unconscious could be a key to self-mastery.

The conviction underlying all of Freud's discoveries was that the human psyche obeyed its own hidden law and order. Freud believed that this hidden order of the mind had escaped the attention of psychologists because so many mental operations are unconscious. His rare excavating thinking seemed capable of penetrating the apparent chaos of subconscious activity and comprehending a significant amount of its order. Although Freud did not discover the unconscious, it had been a shadowy and poetic notion before he came along. He lent the notion of the unconscious precision and established it as the foundation

88 Gay, *Freud*, 142.

of a complete psychology. He was the first to attempt to outline the structure and dynamics of man's subconscious, making distinctions between the conscious, preconscious, and subconscious layers or describing the eternal conflict between libido, ego, and superego. Even if it was not accurate, his mapping of these "undiscovered provinces of mental life"[89] was clearly a bold attempt to show how the mind, our very own "wild" inner world, was a system, like solar systems and biological systems, that operated on the basis of observable laws.

This had far-reaching implications: If we could turn the psyche into a scientifically understandable system, we could also establish new order in the psyche. Understanding our chaotic mind could lead to us fully owning it for the first time. To Freud, this seemed possible, since the irrational world was that part of us that was ruled by inner logic that we could not yet understand. If we possessed a clear vision of this irrational world and saw our "inner house" as clearly as we see our outer houses, with their living rooms, attics, and cellars, we would be able to put it in perfect order. This new inner order would not be the result of repression, which is like sweeping dirt under the carpet; rather, it would be the natural outcome of a penetrating understanding. We repress only that which we fear and we fear things only because we do not know how to handle them. When we are capable of understanding our inner chaos, we no longer need to turn our gaze away from it. As Freud showed in his successful case studies, sometimes just admitting such feelings represented a leap toward a cure.

In his private life, Freud demonstrated time and again how his persistent self-analysis led him to conquer his mind. One of his heroes was the Carthaginian military commander Hannibal; however, Freud wished to triumph internally by heroically harnessing his "libido"—his volcanic emotions and restless energies—in pursuit of his life's mission and self-mastery. He called this "mastery through sublimation,"[90] that

89 Gay, *Freud*, 134.
90 Gay, *Freud*, 164.

is, refining one's instincts in a way that transforms libido into creativity, passion for knowledge, and love of mankind. The final result of his excavating thinking, which probed into the darkest regions of his psyche, was control gained through the order he imposed on the depths of the psyche. It was perhaps this inner power that enabled him to depart from the world so nobly. When dying of cancer, he asked his doctor, Schur, to put him to sleep. Schur was moved by Freud's extraordinary stoicism and dignity as he lay on his deathbed. He had never seen anyone die like that.[91]

Could we, too, strive toward such inner order? Most people take it for granted that their houses should be tidy and clean, but while we rearrange and renovate our homes regularly, our minds are permitted to contain many unnecessary thoughts. Unnecessary or useless thoughts are mental activities that don't serve constructive and creative aims. Examine how many of your daily thoughts fall into this category and then try to imagine how a mind that was free of such meaningless mental activity would function. It is clear that mental order results in improved clarity and better judgment. Taking note of all the unnecessary thoughts that contribute to a general sense of mental overload should not be the preserve of psychologists. After all, there is a reason for this inner hyperactivity: We still know far less about ourselves than we think we do.

---

91 Gay, *Freud*, 651.

CHAPTER 5

LEONARDO DA VINCI

Thinking from all perspectives, *or* Life as an unfinished work of art[92]

It's almost a cliché to begin a chapter on Leonardo with the *Mona Lisa*, his most famous painting, the riddle that he left for posterity. It is a seemingly innocent portrait of a woman without eyebrows, which Andy Warhol proclaimed an icon and John F. Kennedy treated like a state guest. If you travel to Paris and stand in the Louvre with 50 other visitors in front of this oil painting—which is surprisingly small and inconspicuous for such a tourist magnet—you may wonder what all the fuss is about. If you're lucky, however, you'll find yourself alone with the image for a few moments. Then, if you look at it a little longer—at the lady in the black dress whose exact identity is known to no one—you'll probably notice that it has a strange effect on you. But perhaps you think you have to see something in the painting because it is so famous? Or maybe *La Gioconda*'s gaze and enigmatic smile pose questions that cannot be answered? It is presumably for this reason that this painting has become so renowned and that the subject's gentle smile has been analyzed hundreds of times.

A small but subtle clue is provided by author and surgeon Leonard Shlain in his book *Leonardo's Brain*. Shlain subjects da Vinci to a kind

92 Unless otherwise stated, all translations in this chapter are by David A. Brenner.

of posthumous brain scan. One of his many claims is that Leonardo had a special understanding of the intricacies of human facial expressions. Leonardo knew, Shlain argues, that a person's face is made up of two halves that are only superficially symmetrical. Each half is controlled by the opposite hemisphere of the brain. For most people, the right side of the face is determined by the more rational left hemisphere. This is why people are better able to control consciously the right side of the face. In contrast, the left, less controllable side of the face more readily betrays what a person is feeling internally. However, the signs are so subtle that we barely notice in an ordinary conversation. Leonardo, Shlain contends, understood these subtleties intuitively. Shlain believes that's why the smile of the *Mona Lisa* seems so ambiguous: The artist has highlighted the right side of her face and shaded the left side. Other researchers have concluded that her mysterious smile seems more striking when looking at her eyes rather than her mouth. By painting using a certain technique, Leonardo achieved a remarkable effect: The viewer only sees the smile when looking at the whole picture. When the viewer looks closely at her mouth to see if she's really smiling, her expression appears neutral. The artist has given the image a bewildering depth that goes beyond mere portraiture. The viewer sees something in her face without realizing it consciously.

The shaded left half of the face, the illuminated right half, the odd facial expressions—these are only details, minor aspects of Leonardo's life work. But they do give an initial indication of what was so special about his perspective on objects, people, and the world. To begin with, it is generally agreed that Leonardo was an extremely keen observer. The same nuanced perception that led him to shade the left side of the *Mona Lisa*'s face is also evident in the copious notes he left behind. In them, Leonardo noted, for instance, how water moves below the surface and how the wings of dragonflies work: "The dragonfly flies with four wings, and when the anterior are raised, the posterior are dropped. However, each pair of wings must be capable individually of supporting the entire weight of the animal."[93] The British art historian Kenneth Clark contended that "the extraordinary quickness of his eye" is really only something that it has been possible to understand since the invention of slow motion.[94] Where others might only see flickering movements, Leonardo could distinguish individual movements.

He was literally able to *see more* than others. However, that alone doesn't adequately explain the oeuvre created by the Italian in his 67 years. Much of his work was lost or remained incomplete. (It may come as a surprise that he did not excel at finishing things.) But that which has survived—around fifteen paintings and his notebooks, with their thousands of drawings in his precise but peculiar mirror script—should be enough to astound anybody. It's simply impossible to understand how a person could possess such talent. Not only was Leonardo an extremely talented painter and sculptor who created some of the world's most celebrated works of art; he was also an extremely inquisitive and multi-talented scientist. Both the range and the depth of his gifts were enormous. He was a mathematician, a geologist, a cartographer, a botanist, a musician, an architect, an anatomist, a mechanic, an engineer, and a natural philosopher. Among other things, he designed a car, a functioning parachute, a submarine, and a forerunner of the helicopter based on his observations on the flight of the dragonfly. Thus, he occupies a unique position in history.

When approaching the work of this man, you will inevitably brush up against the realm of the mystical—simply because it isn't clear how he was able to create some of the things he did. A good example of this are Leonardo's maps. During the period when he was working for Cesare Borgia, the Duke of Valentino, he drew his employer a map of the town of Imola. The map itself is a work of art that sells well nowadays in poster and postcard form. It is also extremely detailed

93 Leonard Shlain, *Leonardo's Brain: Understanding Leonardo's Creative Genius* (Guilford, CT: Rowman & Littlefield, 2014), 43.
94 Kenneth Clark and Martin Kemp, *Leonardo da Vinci*, revised edn. (London: Penguin, 2015), 216.

and technically precise: Every house and street in Imola is represented on it. Moreover, the town can be seen from above, from a height of more than half a mile. In later maps, Leonardo adopted a perspective from an even higher elevation. But how was he able to do this? He was probably the first cartographer ever to draw bird's-eye views consistent with present-day depictions—and he did so without having important data or surveying equipment at his disposal. In his day, distances were basically measured by counting steps and maps were still decorated with dragons and castles. In contrast, Leonardo's realistic bird's-eye views seem to come from another time and place—it is like finding an espresso machine in a medieval kitchen.

As ordinary human beings, we tend to feel helpless when faced with such immense talent. Perhaps that's why people have responded to da Vinci so intensely. His activities have become the object of all sorts of rumors and every image he created has been searched for hidden messages and symbols. Some even claim that he was an extraterrestrial. Whatever about these fanciful attempts at an explanation, it seems that what was going on inside Leonardo's head is beyond the ken of mere mortals. But is this not a bit of an exaggeration? Certainly, it takes the talent of a Leonardo to paint a *Mona Lisa*, but if we refuse to be intimidated by him, we can identify how we might access his way of thinking. For the special thing about this *uomo senza lettere* [uneducated man], as Leonardo referred to himself, was his remarkable powers of perception.

Seamless transitions

Many people have talent and intelligence, but most display their gifts in fairly conventional ways. This applies to normal mortals as well as geniuses. Although there have been numerous brilliant artists and scientists in human history, none of them has been equally strong in both the arts *and* the sciences. There's a reason why Johann Wolfgang von Goethe's *Faust* is better known than his color theory and why Einstein didn't go down in history for his violin playing. A person's talent usually takes either an artistic or scientific direction. This was not the case with Leonardo. "No other individual in the known history of the human species attained such distinction in both science and art as the hyper-curious, undereducated, illegitimate country boy from Vinci," Shlain insists.[95]

As an illegitimate child, Leonardo did not receive proper schooling, nor was he permitted to attend university. However, these circumstances, which might nowadays be considered unjust and the cause of difficulties, may have given him a decisive advantage. School learning can lead to certain views and assumptions being taken for granted, which limits one's perspective. Leonardo, however, had an unadulterated view of things. His educational deficiencies meant that he was able to extend his curiosity to the entire world with little inhibition. He did not have to distinguish between that which was considered "important" and that which was considered "unimportant" or set meaningless priorities. He was free to contemplate the various facets of the world like a child who finds an oddly shaped rock on the road. In this lies the key to his way of thinking. Not only was he smart; he applied his intelligence to everything he encountered and never grew tired of learning. Let us now closely consider a few examples of Leonardo's work that are less renowned than the *Mona Lisa*: his anatomical drawings.

In 1489, the 36-year-old Leonardo succeeded in acquiring some human skulls. He must have been delighted, for he had long felt an urgent desire to examine and illustrate human anatomy. As a child, he had hauled dead lizards and wild animals into his room and taken them apart; later, he dissected larger animals. However, getting hold of human corpses was difficult. Moreover, dissecting human bodies was illegal unless you were a doctor. Leonardo's desire to examine corpses sprang from artistic motivations. He wanted to write a book containing

95 Shlain, *Leonardo's Brain*, 5.

everything that a painter needed to know and, according to his logic, it was not possible to draw a body without knowing exactly how it worked. Besides, he knew that the interior of a body defined its exterior forms. It was therefore necessary that a painter be familiar with anatomy.[96]

It should be remembered that human anatomy was poorly understood in the Renaissance era and the assumptions that were made about anatomical functions seem obscure from today's perspective. Leonardo accepted the consequences of this lack of knowledge—he'd have to look for himself and was clearly prepared to break the law to do so. He is even said to have sometimes paid grave robbers to get hold of corpses.

Leonardo's anatomical studies spanned decades and developed their own momentum. Over the years, he dissected over 30 dead bodies, removing the skin, sawing the bones apart, and opening up the skulls. The engineer in him began to appreciate the human body as a sophisticated "machine." Even though it invents multiple things with diverse instruments, "[h]uman subtlety ... will never devise an invention more beautiful, more simple or more direct than does nature," he remarked.[97] Having grown up in the countryside, Leonardo admired nature and valued direct observation more than anything else and considered "wisdom ... the daughter of experience."

Dissection could only take place at night by candlelight. As it was impossible to refrigerate a corpse in that era, the stench of the bodies must have been unbearable. Writing with the detachment of the scientist, Leonardo noted that the corpses decayed too quickly to be studied extensively. The gruesomeness of such work, however, cannot be detected in his sketches. These sketches demonstrate the gaze of a person looking for harmony who succeeds in finding it. Leonardo drew

96 Pedretti, Carlo (ed.), *Leonardo da Vinci on Painting: A Lost Book* (Libro A) (Berkeley: University of California Press, 1964), 134.
97 da Vinci, Leonardo, *The Notebooks of Leonard Da Vinci, Vol. 2* (New York: Dover Publications, 2012), 126.

his anatomical studies with delicate strokes, darkening them so they rose up from the page, almost as if they were three-dimensional. The result was precise anatomical images and refined drawings of extraordinary beauty. These scientific-artistic masterpieces were, for centuries, the most accurate anatomical drawings that had ever been made.

Multi-perspectival thinking

For these works, Leonardo developed a special drawing technique that elucidates a central principle of his mind. He appears to have had a mental predisposition that precluded the adoption of rigid positions in relation to his observation of the world. His thinking was *multi-perspectival*. It was during the Renaissance that artists discovered perspective, but no artist spent as much time exploring perspective as Leonardo. In his notes, he described precisely how a painter should relate the individual elements of an image to each another and how a painter had to work with shadows in order to obey the laws of perspective. This was not merely motivated by perfectionism. Rather, he was compelled by something much deeper. He was playing with perspectives in order to convey various aspects of an object. He deemed it inadequate to show a muscle, a bone, or an organ from only one angle. It was clear to him that the view from a particular perspective could never capture the essence of that thing. An artist had to think about and depict the other possible perspectives. Only thus could the artist get closer to the truth of a thing. Leonardo solved this problem by perfecting the "exploded-view" drawing, a multi-perspectival image that separates the object into its component parts. He would draw one part of a body several times on the same page, each time from a different perspective; he sketched a skull, for example, in profile, in cross section, and diagonally from above. This enabled the viewer to observe an object from several different perspectives at the same time. Just as a film about a person can portray that person better than a photograph, so Leonardo's simultaneous multiple views of the truth of a thing were more impartial than viewing it from a single perspective.

Multi-perspectivism is not a common way of thinking. Most people, including brilliant intellectuals, think rather *one-dimensionally*. Hence, we have an automatic, often unconscious preference for adopting a single specific perspective. Doing so is economical and efficient—or so it seems. Who has the energy to apply themselves to everything with the same élan? One-dimensional thinking corresponds to the efficiency-oriented spirit of our times—and perhaps to our natural predisposition as well. If you were to address a random person on the street, he or she would probably be able to tell you whether he or she approached life more as a rational, analytical person or as a feeling, emotive person, that is, more as a "scientist" or an "artist." Leonardo, by contrast, does not seem to have been so one-dimensional. It is for this reason that his experiments and observations, which today would be called "scientific," blend seamlessly into his art, such as when he painted the muscles and tendons of a figure with anatomical precision. He thought of his art as science, as can be seen in his treatises on the subject of painting, for example. Art historian Michael Ladwein writes that "Leonardo's method of combining science and art in his way of working reveals an entirely new kind of consciousness."[98] Leonardo's inexhaustible thirst for knowledge probably derived from his feeling that his understanding was never complete; there were always other levels and views to consider. For him, art and science weren't in opposition; they were, rather, distinct means of describing the same reality.

A puzzling polyvalence

An additional example of Leonardo's multi-perspectival thinking is so famous that millions of people today carry it around, possibly without

98 Michael Ladwein, *Leonardo da Vinci: The Last Supper. A Cosmic Drama and an Act of Redemption* (Forest Row: Temple Lodge, 2006), 31.

even realizing it. The *Vitruvian Man*, Leonardo's drawing of a naked, upright man, which looks like a double-exposed photo as the man is simultaneously adopting different body positions, is on the back of the Italian €1 coin. Leonardo drew the *Vitruvian Man* about a year after having started to examine human skulls. It is a study of proportions, drawn in pen and ink, that illustrates the ideal mathematical relationship of human body parts. Although the *Vitruvian Man* has come to symbolize Leonardo, it was not actually his invention. The idea is based on descriptions by the Roman architect and engineer Vitruvius, who, in addition to his work in urban planning and materials science in the first century BCE, expounded the doctrine of the "well-formed body." His idea was that the body of an adult man with outstretched arms should fit into both a square and a circle. The center of the body, according to Vitruvius, was the navel. If one were to place a compass on the naval of a person who was lying on the ground and draw a circle around him or her, the tips of his or her fingers and toes would touch the circle that was created. The square would be based on the distance between the person's head and the soles of his or her feet, which was supposed to match the total length of the outstretched arms. Vitruvius himself did not illustrate this ideal description. This was undertaken later by draftsmen. Compared with Leonardo's elegant version, however, those drawings seem almost inept. Only Leonardo managed to create in a single drawing a harmoniously proportioned figure that fit into both a circle and a square. He succeeded in this by using a different center point for the square than the circle—locating it in the figure's groin. The result is a perfectly proportioned geometric figure into which the human body fits as if it were an abstract form. The effect of the image is enhanced by the way in which Leonardo put the two views, circular and square, on top of each other, instead of on two separate pages. Thus, he added a further dimension to the image: that of *time*. The *Vitruvian Man* can thus be seen from two different temporal perspectives, as if shifting back and forth between two body positions (like a lenticular or "wiggle" picture). Only a person who was accustomed to thinking about a single object from different perspectives could have conceived of such an image.

Ironically, one of Leonardo's most admired artworks immediately began to fall apart upon its completion. He had painted the 40-square meter fresco *The Last Supper* over the course of three years—in what would, fittingly, become the refectory of the Dominican monastery of Santa Maria delle Grazie in Milan. As he was painting it, the inventor in him went wild. He renounced the traditional fresco technique, whereby colors were applied to damp plaster, as this necessitated working rapidly. He experimented with a method that suited his slower manner of working. He drew directly onto the dry wall and, in contrast to the customary procedure, used a color mixture that had egg yolk and linseed oil as its base. Thus, he could repeatedly revise the image. The painting, likely his most famous after the *Mona Lisa*, was finally completed in 1498. Even during Leonardo's lifetime, the work created a considerable stir. Art connoisseurs traveled long distances to see it. The French king, Francis I, wanted to remove the entire wall and have it brought to France. But it quickly became apparent that Leonardo's choice of technique had been a major error of judgment. The damp wall absorbed the paint, which then faded, crumbled, or broke off. As early as 1550, Leonardo's first biographer Giorgio Vasari could only make out "a muddle of blots"[99] on the wall of the refectory. Over the centuries, the image was repeatedly restored, not always particularly sensitively. It is really only because of the many copies made by previous admirers that it can still be admired today.

The Last Supper is a fascinating image for several reasons. Firstly, Leonardo demonstrated in the painting that he had not only mastered the laws of perspective, but could also deftly manipulate these laws. What he thereby achieved for art is considered groundbreaking. *The Last Supper* is full of precisely calculated perspectival "errors." Leonardo,

99 Peter D'Epiro and Mary Desmond Pinkowish, *Sprezzatura: 50 Ways Italian Genius Shaped the World* (New York: Anchor Books, 2001), 170.

for instance, knew that whoever entered the monastery's refectory would be looking at the image from below. Yet he wanted viewers to have the impression that they were seeing it at eye level. He therefore intentionally distorted the perspective. As a result, the figure of Jesus is one-and-a-half times larger than his dining companions and the table they are sitting at seems too short: In total, thirteen people are crowding around a table that should only accommodate eleven. In addition, there is a trick of perspective in the background of the painting: The space there, which at first glance looks like a rectangle, actually tapers off to the rear. Consequently, the picture looks like an extension of natural space.

The Last Supper is not only remarkable because of the way in which Leonardo played with geometric perspective. The work itself is so polyvalent that it allows for a seemingly infinite number of interpretations—including conspiracy theories. Probably the most famous of these is brought to life in Dan Brown's international bestseller *The Da Vinci Code*. On closer inspection of the painting, we realize that it is not possible to say exactly what is happening in what should be an unambiguous scene. Are we observing the moment when Jesus declares to his disciples, "One of you will betray me"? Or is it the moment of the Eucharist? There is evidence to support both hypotheses and we have to conclude that *both* are valid, that is, there are two simultaneous temporal levels, past *and* future. Some interpretations even claim that there is foreshadowing at work in the painting: Jesus is crossing his feet under the table in an unnatural-looking manner—they are in the position they will later assume on the cross. The art historian Leo Steinberg characterized the painting as "a marvel of compressed meanings." He discerned in *The Last Supper* "an intellectual style that constantly weds incompatibilities, visualizes durations in one seeming flash, and opposites in marvelous unison."[100] Steinberg is certain that Leonardo

100 Leo Steinberg, *Leonardo's Incessant Last Supper* (New York: Zone Books, 2001), 72.

deliberately painted it in such a way that no unambiguous—one might say one-dimensional—interpretation would be possible.

One could spend a great deal of time scrutinizing *The Last Supper*. What seems at first glance to be the artful representation of a famous biblical scene gradually becomes, not unlike the *Mona Lisa*, a mystery.

New glasses needed

"The source of Leonardo's extraordinary creativity was his ability to access different ways of thinking," avows Bulgarian journalist Maria Popova.[101] So what might we learn from Leonardo that might benefit our own thinking? To answer that question, we should take a look inside Leonardo's head and, quite literally, his brain.

Whether we look at the world from more of a rational-linear perspective (e.g. biology) or more of an emotional-non-linear perspective (e.g. expressive dance) is reflected in the way our brain is structured and how it organizes the world. In popular-scientific terms, these tendencies are often equated with the dominance of the right- or left-brain hemispheres. This hemispheric model is a simplified understanding of how the brain operates. It assigns each half of the brain a distinct, clearly defined role. Accordingly, the left brain is specialized in rational, analytical, and linguistic processes while the right brain is specialized in creative and emotional processes. The model is considered outdated because the brain's functioning cannot be explained schematically. Both sides of the brain are involved in reason, emotion, and language. However, it is true that humans have certain preferences about which area of the brain they use for particular activities. Hence, the model continues to be useful because it clarifies existing tendencies, as well as specific personality attitudes. "There are

101 Maria Popova, "Leonardo's Brain: What a Posthumous Brain Scan Six Centuries Later Reveals about the Source of Da Vinci's Creativity," Brainpickings. http://www.brainpickings.org/2014/11/17/leonardos-brain-leonard-shlain/.

different emphases of personality in the hemispheres with their different components and capabilities,"[102] observes Dr. Onur Güntürkün, who is researching the interaction of the brain hemispheres at the Ruhr University of Bochum. On the basis of these emphases of personality, a person assembles a self-image that determines how he or she encounters everything in life. It's like having a pair of glasses screwed tightly to your head. Rarely does one encounter a person who is able to switch perspectives with ease. Leonardo, however, seems to have been able to do just that.

Shlain observes interesting peculiarities in Leonardo's notes and works, as well as in descriptions of his personality. The structure of a brain and the extent to which both hemispheres are functionally specialized, as indicated by various neuroscientific studies, depends on factors such as gender, right- or left-handedness, and sexual orientation. The most specialized brain of all is that of a heterosexual man who is right-handed. In the case of most right-handed heterosexual men, the left brain is dominant. Interestingly, the brain of a left-handed person is not simply the mirror image of that of a right-handed person, but rather tends to be more symmetrical. The same is true of women and homosexuals. In addition, the *corpus callosum*, that band between the two hemispheres that allows for the exchange of information, can also act as an impediment to the use of one of the hemispheres. It tends to be more pronounced in left-handed and homosexual men than in right-handed men, neuroscientist Sandra F. Witelson concludes. These findings are generalizations, not facts that apply to every individual. The statistical values arrived at through various studies are distributed along a bell curve: They therefore apply to a large proportion of people, but not everyone. It is remarkably revealing to consider Leonardo in light of these findings, despite the caveats: He was left-handed (but able to work ambidextrously) and wrote from right to left in his notebooks, making use of a highly peculiar "mirror script." It is presumed that he was gay:

102 Tobias Hürter, "Ich bin Zwei," trans. D. Brenner. Die Zeit, no. 25, 2013.

He never married, had no children, and hardly mentioned women in his notes, regarding them solely as visually interesting material for his artworks. He was once arrested and jailed as a young man on the charge of committing homosexual acts (which were regarded as a crime in that time and place). His presumed homosexuality, his left-handedness, and his use of mirror script are all indications that Leonardo's brain was more symmetrical and his brain halves more interconnected than those of the average person. Shlain sees Leonardo's love of metaphors and puzzles as another indication of this. The right hemisphere can understand things like metaphors, body language, humor, and tone of voice. In other words, cooperation between the right and left hemispheres is necessary to appreciate metaphors and puzzles—and Leonardo communicated effortlessly and extensively in metaphors and images.

A brain such as Leonardo's could be considered *symmetrical* or *balanced*—or even *androgynous* as the traits generally associated with the left half of the brain—analytical rationality—traditionally connote masculinity, while those associated with the right hemisphere—creativity, emotion—connote femininity. It is essential to understand this in order to access multi-perspectival thinking. As psychologist Mihály Csíkszentmihályi writes in *Creativity: Flow and The Psychology of Discovery and Invention*, a book for which he and his team interviewed 91 particularly creative people, "In all cultures, men are brought up to be 'masculine' and to disregard and repress those aspects of their temperament that the culture regards as 'feminine' whereas women are expected to do the opposite. Creative individuals to a certain extent escape this rigid gender stereotype."[103] In tests, Csíkszentmihályi explains, it has been repeatedly observed that creative girls behave more dominantly and forcefully than other girls and creative boys are more sensitive and less aggressive than other boys. "A psychologically androgynous person in effect doubles his or her repertoire of responses

103 Mihály Csíkszentmihályi, *Creativity: Flow and the Psychology of Discovery and Invention* (New York: HarperCollins, 1996), 45.

and can interact with the world in terms of a much richer and varied spectrum of opportunities. It's not surprising that creative individuals are more likely to have not only the strengths of their own gender but those of the other one, too."[104]

The recurrence of androgyny in Leonardo's paintings and sketches is striking. It is difficult to assign a gender to the face of *Mona Lisa*, the portrait of John the Baptist, and the image of the disciple John in the *The Last Supper*. However, it would be reductive to attribute Leonardo's way of thinking solely to psychological androgyny.

There are experts who believe that each brain hemisphere has its own consciousness, as well as its own capabilities. One such expert is British psychiatrist Iain McGilchrist, who argues in his book *The Master and his Emissary* that perhaps the most important function of the *corpus callosum* is not to exchange information between the two halves of the brain, but rather to act as an impediment to one of the halves.[105] This is significant because the consciousnesses—or perspectives—of the hemispheres are both complementary and contradictory. McGilchrist's thesis is that we live in an epoch dominated by left-brain consciousness, according to which we engage with the world using abstract, rational, or generalizing thinking. However, the right brain creates a worldview in which things repeatedly change and can never be understood in all their detail. Leonardo's multiple talents might have arisen from an elegant fusion of these perspectives. He was a pacifist who designed war machines and he was a compassionate vegetarian who bought and then released birds at the market and yet dissected animals without inhibition. Such behavior may seem arbitrary, but it can also be considered evidence of Leonardo's ability to adopt diverse perspectives. He knew that a specific standpoint could never be a universal one. There is much to suggest that this is precisely why he was so creative.

---

104 Ibid., 71.
105 Ian McGilchrist, *The Master and his Emissary: The Divided Brain and the Making of the Western World* (New Haven, CT: Yale University Press, 2012).

Left- or right-handed, homo- or heterosexual, anatomically female or male—it is rare that we can change these aspects of ourselves, even if we want to. But can we, as McGilchrist would put it, challenge the dominance of the left brain and become more symmetrical (as it were) in our thinking and the perspective we adopt? A definitive answer to this question is still pending, but there are already multiple indications that it may be possible. Contrary to what was once believed, the brain doesn't stop developing as soon as it's fully grown; rather, it changes throughout one's lifetime. Everything we experience and learn—whether we're doing physics or belly dancing, creating oil paintings or reading this book—has an influence on the brain's structure. However, our point of view can only be changed by the awareness that our brain is capable of producing two ostensibly opposing views of life and the world, two divergent ways of thinking, each of which is perfectly valid. There are two independent units endowed with consciousness that exist in a single individual. As a result, we can become more aware of aspects of our perception that we normally disregard or dismiss as insignificant. A person who prefers to adopt a more emotional perspective would do well to engage with rational thinking too. A person guided by logic, on the other hand, would benefit from allowing him- or herself to see things irrationally or emotionally. Doing so may feel unusual or even unpleasant at first. After all, we are going against the grain of our self-image. Ultimately, though, it leads to thinking that is more flexible and more creative. The aim is not to avoid taking a position, but rather to improve the possibilities of our perception. Every inflexible perspective is a form of (self-)deprivation.

Leonardo's blurred boundaries

Art historian Kenneth Clark has characterized Leonardo as "the most relentlessly curious man in history."[106] If one assumes that Leonardo was a multi-perspectival thinker, it becomes clear why he never ceased his searching: As long as there was another aspect to illuminate, he couldn't be satisfied—and there was always more to know.

However, there seems to be a broader context for this way of thinking. Leonardo seems to have had a kind of "unity consciousness"—not in the esoteric sense, but as a genuinely experienced intellectual and emotional perception that things were interconnected. In one of his notebooks, he proposed the following principles for the development of a perfect spirit:

1. Study the science of art.
2. Study the art of science.
3. Develop your senses—learn, above all, to see.
4. Realize that everything is interconnected.

These four points indicate the mental attitude behind Leonardo's multi-perspectival thinking. Art and science were inseparably interconnected for him—which is why they flowed effortlessly into one another in his work. He distinguished the interconnectedness of things in recurring parallels, links, and patterns. For instance, he described how waves and ripples on the surface of water resemble the structure of human hair. In addition, he realized that a stone thrown into the water produced circles resembling soundwaves. Such multi-perspectivism involves repeatedly looking at aspects of reality without drawing clear lines of demarcation between them.

106 BBC Culture, "Leonardo da Vinci's groundbreaking anatomical sketches," October 11, 2014. https://www.bbc.com/culture/article/20130828-leonardo-da-vinci-the-anatomist.

Perhaps it is because of this multi-perspectivism that Leonardo never organized the notes he took. He might write an entry in one of his notebooks and years later scribble another idea on the same page. This has infuriated many later scholars, but, for Leonardo, it was logical to do this. Categories didn't matter to him. Every idea and observation he wrote down was connected with all the other thoughts he had recorded. A visual expression of this blurring of boundaries is his famous *sfumato* technique (which is another artistic innovative contribution that he made to the depiction of perspective). Previously, artists had sketched out the silhouettes of their figures in black and then painted them. Leonardo explained that the perimeter of a body is neither part of the body itself nor part of the surrounding space and would blur the boundaries between his figures and their surroundings when painting them.

If you want to experiment yourself with multi-perspectival thinking, you could try questioning your "male" or "female" perspective. This may not particularly groundbreaking as gender boundaries are much less rigid nowadays than they used to be (a development that Leonardo would probably have approved of). However, one's actual gender identity—as any psychiatrist will attest—is a matter that one usually regards as settled. What if you were to play around with it to become aware of the extent to which you view the world through the eyes of "man" or "woman" and then look at it differently? How does your perception change? Do you see more or different aspects of reality than you did before? You can try this with any perspective that comes to mind—if you're a dedicated meat-eater, for example, you can adopt the perspective of a vegan. Or you can adopt some other perspective that's wholly unfamiliar to you. You can even attempt to do more than explore another perspective intellectually. We usually only adopt beliefs that we like. But how would it be to become a vegan temporarily, if you're a meat-eater (or vice versa)? How does it feel to live differently? In a certain sense, your mind is no different to your body. If you move it too little or always make the same movements, it will become stiff and inflexible. When you adopt perspectives that are unfamiliar or untried, it's like gymnastics for the brain: Your thinking becomes more elastic—and more creative.

CHAPTER 6

SOCRATES

The philosophical lover, *or* Do not fear the nothingness[107]

The Greek philosopher Socrates always generated enthusiasm, confusion, and antagonism. Today, almost 2,500 years after his death, little has changed. However, while the Athenians once confronted a Socrates of flesh and blood, whom they both honored and felt antagonized by, researchers today are divided over a more fundamental question—specifically, who exactly was the historical Socrates and what did he really teach? This question arises because Socrates, who was so exceptional that all thinkers that came before him have been labeled "pre-Socratic," did not write down what he taught. For Socrates, words were living things that had to be repeatedly questioned and filled with meaning. Writing, Socrates claims in the dialogue *Phaedrus*, is similar to painting: "For the offsprings of painting stand there as if they're alive, but if anyone asks them anything, they remain most solemnly silent."[108] Once words are written down, they lose their force and become frozen on the page. This attitude is an early indication of Socrates' way of thinking.

But before we address his thinking, we must first deal with the "Socratic problem," that is, how to distinguish Socrates' ideas from those

107 Unless otherwise stated, all translations in this chapter are by David A. Brenner.
108 Plato, *Phaedrus*. Translation quoted from Plato, *Complete Works*, ed. John Cooper (Indianapolis, IN: Hackett, 1997), 552.

of Plato, his most famous student, who documented the teachings of his master. Although two other contemporaries, the comic playwright Aristophanes and the politician/historian Xenophon wrote about Socrates, neither of them produced as much material as Plato. At the same time, the Socratic dialogues and speeches chronicled by Plato are philosophically much richer than those of Aristophanes and Xenophon. Plato's writings contain some of the most brilliant elements of Socrates' written legacy, which begs the question: Was Plato documenting the ideas of his teacher or was he using the figure of Socrates to communicate his own ideas? Many people assume that Plato was appropriating his teacher to convey his own ideas. This would provide a plausible explanation for contradictions between the sources and inconsistencies in Plato's statements about Socrates. This question is highly relevant to this chapter because we want to get to the bottom of Socrates' way of thinking, not the thinking of some "hybrid creature I call Platsoc,"[109] as biographer Paul Johnson once wrote disparagingly.

Although researchers have been discussing this question for hundreds of years, no consensus has ever really been reached. Each person must therefore answer the question for him- or herself. You might side with the camp that thinks the "real" Socrates can principally be seen in the early Platonic dialogues. Paul Johnson remarks that at the outset Plato was "still innocent enough, that is, still sufficiently enraptured by Socrates' thinking and method, to reproduce both accurately."[110] Yet later, Plato is thought to have used the figure of his teacher as an instrument for sharing his own concepts, especially his "Theory of Ideas." Thus, in order to distill the real Socrates from the texts, we ought to read only Plato's earlier works. This approach is controversial because it isn't sufficiently clear how Plato's texts should be ordered chronologically. Others have tried to find the "real" Socrates by comparing Plato's works with the other sources. Accordingly, whatever is not present in Aristophanes or Xenophon must be regarded as dubious

109 Paul Johnson, *Socrates: A Man for Our Times* (New York: Viking, 2011), 97.
110 Ibid., 10.

in Plato. This approach is understandable, but it has its drawbacks, the most notable of which is that there is hardly any overlap between the texts of Plato, Xenophon, and Aristophanes. Still others maintain that the doctrine of archetypal forms, the "Theory of Ideas," is purely Plato's and that the "real" Socrates would never have advocated such a doctrine. However, the Ideas are implicit even in the early dialogues that everyone considers "genuinely" Socratic.

On the other hand, if you take every sentence that is attributed to Socrates in Plato's writings to be something that Socrates actually said, then you will be left with a complex portrait of the philosopher. This Socrates is a radical thinker who would laugh at how his teachings are treated as dogma by many philosophy students today.

Socrates claims in the third book of Xenophon's *Memorabilia* that a person's traits "are reflected in the face and in the attitudes of the body, whether still or in motion."[111] If he's right, then Socrates' face and body allow us to observe how unknowable he was. His contemporaries described him as ugly. He always walked barefoot, he bathed irregularly, and he wore only a thin cloak, even in the winter. At the same time, he was a man whose appearance made an impression: He built up his body in the *gymnasion* and his voice was melodic—he never raised it gratuitously. On the rare occasion when he was angry, he would speak softly. Moreover, he could drink plenty of wine without losing his self-control. And he permanently had a serene expression on his face, as the Roman philosopher and orator Cicero noted admiringly.

Socrates must have confused his countrymen. His teachings were provocatively contradictory. He might convincingly defend a certain position in one dialogue only to argue the opposite in the next. At times, it seems as if he were denying humanity any possibility of true wisdom; at others, he advances lucid philosophical ideas. In accordance with the spirit of his age, he pays tribute to the eroticism of beautiful boys;

111 Xenophon, *Memorabilia*, ed. E.C. Marchant. http://www.perseus.tufts.edu/hopper/text?doc=Xen.%20Mem.%203&lang=original.

however, he doesn't touch them. And he has distinctly mystical features: He communicates with an inner voice, his *daimonion*, and consequently sometimes just stands still and stares into space for long periods.

Reduced versions of Socrates pale in comparison to this image of a philosopher. They hold him up as the skeptical rationalist and moralist, a logical thinker and religious man devoid of mystical qualities and erotic interests. This view of the philosopher is attractive as it is less complex and fits the Western notion of a philosopher. But Socrates wasn't a philosopher in the way we imagine philosophers to be today. Rather, he lived in a Renaissance-like ambiance, in which philosophy, science, poetry, and mysticism intermingled, each enriching one another, forming a complete image only when combined. We must imagine him in this context. The narrow categories we use today would have seemed artificial and oddly incomplete to him.

How Socrates behaved depended on whom he was dealing with. According to Sanderson Beck in his *Confucius and Socrates*, "Socrates ... apparently taught and discussed many issues for several hours almost every day for a period of at least twenty-five years and perhaps for forty or more. Because he claimed little or no doctrine of his own but rather attempted to elicit the truth from others by his questioning, it's likely that he discussed many different subjects with different people; these people in searching their own minds and value systems may indeed have taken away widely different philosophies from their encounter with him."[112]

Our position on the "Socratic problem" is as follows: We take Plato literally and assume that the Socrates depicted in his works is authentic. How well the seeming inconsistency of Socrates' character and statements fit with his way of thinking will be revealed in the next few pages.

---

112 Sanderson Beck, "The Socratic Problem," in *Confucius and Socrates: Teaching Wisdom*. http://www.san.beck.org/SocraticProblem.html.

A midwife of truth

Socrates chose an unusual site for his philosophical investigations. He did not philosophize in airy, venerable halls but in the *agora*, that intemperate heart of Athens. This central square, where the gods had their temples and the government its institutions and where statues commemorated heroes, was abuzz with life. You had to raise your voice to have a discussion. The Greek sun beat down, crowds thronged, and the smell was unpleasant. For the *agora* was also a market and a meeting place. Day after day, the Athenians congregated there, exchanging gossip and shopping for fish, figs, and bread. It was here that Socrates walked in his bare feet amid the noise and heat, tearing the Athenians away from their daily routines. As historian Bettany Hughes puts it, he was "frighteningly unpredictable."[113] He would unexpectedly stop an unsuspecting passerby to ask him a fundamental philosophical question: "Most excellent man, are you who are a citizen of Athens, the greatest of cities and the most famous for wisdom and power, not ashamed to care for the acquisition of wealth [...], when you neither care nor take thought for wisdom and truth and the perfection of your soul?"[114]

It is thus that Xenophon came to know Socrates. Socrates' preferred audience consisted of adolescents and other youths. The young Xenophon must have caught the philosopher's eye for Socrates came up to him and asked innocently where one could buy certain household items. Then, out of the blue, he asked Xenophon, "And where might one obtain a brave and virtuous man?" Xenophon responded with confusion, whereupon Socrates suggested that the lad join him to pursue the matter further.

---

113 Bettany Hughes, *The Hemlock Cup: Socrates, Athens and the Search for the Good Life* (New York: Vintage Books, 2012), 23.

114 Plato, *Apology, in Plato in Twelve Volumes, Vol. 1*, trans. Harold North Fowler, introduction by W.R.M. Lamb (Cambridge, MA: Harvard University Press, 1966). http://www.perseus.tufts.edu/hopper/text?doc=Perseus%3Atext%3A1999.01.0170%3Atext%3DApol.%3Apage%3D29.

This procedure was typical for Socrates. He compared himself to a gadfly bothering a noble but sluggish horse. He wished to remove people from their routines and open their eyes to the fact that they were taking their lives for granted instead of calling them into question. Some were offended, which is hardly surprising. It is safe to assume that he was at times a real nuisance at the *agora*. Nonetheless, many felt drawn to this barefoot philosopher, who was so unlike the other thinkers of his time because Socrates showed them how philosophy was relevant to their lives. Cicero would later write that Socrates had been the first to "call philosophy down from heaven and set her in cities and even to bring her into households and compel her to inquire about human life and customs as well as matters good and evil."[115]

In that epoch, there were two groups of philosophers in Athens: One taught *what* people should think, the other *how*. Socrates clearly belonged to the latter group. He was not inclined to explain the world to others. He was not interested in ready-made concepts, but rather questioned everything, including his own opinions. He saw himself as a "midwife" who helped others "give birth" to their own wisdom. This method, called *maieutics*, was practiced in dialogues with his fellow citizens. Socrates rarely gave simple lectures on specific topics; instead, he would pose questions like, "What is justice?", "What is truth?", or "What is courage?" He did not present himself as a teacher, but as a student, claiming that others were teaching *him*. This flattered his interlocutors, encouraging them to explain the world to him. Little did they know what they were getting into. As Socrates continued to ask them questions—in a friendly manner, sometimes apologizing for his "naïveté"—the supposed knowledge of these "explainers" was revealed to be a pretense.

The confusing philosopher never let himself be put off by an obvious or automatic answer. He kept posing questions until it was clear that his

115 Marcus Tullius Cicero, *Cicero and the Natural Law*, trans. Walter Nicgorski. http://www.nlnrac.org/classical/cicero.

interlocutors' definitions or opinions were ill-considered because they had contradicted themselves or because their answers applied only in limited circumstances. Thus, Socrates broke through the self-assurance with which his discussants made their claims, repeatedly demonstrating that their answers were actually empty, no matter how good they might sound. Those who spoke to Socrates were ultimately left feeling that they essentially knew nothing at all.

Socrates was not doing this to show off or to make people feel foolish. If these had been his motivations, he probably would not have gained such an enthusiastic following.

If we study Socrates' dialogues, we can observe what kind of thinking Socrates wanted to present to his auditors. He was leading them away from *overconfident thinking* and toward *direct thinking*. Overconfident thinking, as evidenced by the matter-of-factness we exhibit when we act like we know what love is, or justice, truth, or courage, was a kind of arrogance that Socrates sought to expose. "But how do we know that something is just?" Socrates would ask. "Who taught us *that*?" In reality, we make use of these terms without ever having truly defined what they mean. The meaning of these terms seems so obvious to us that we don't deem it necessary to question them. Whenever we think we know more than we actually do—which is almost always the case—overconfident thinking is at work. By contrast, direct thinking doesn't take anything for granted. It is based on the assumption that everything we think about the world can—and *must*—be questioned. Those who don't challenge themselves live according to a unexamined hodgepodge of ideas that they have adopted from others. Direct thinking could also be termed "adventurous thinking" because it always involves a journey into the unknown.

It is no coincidence that Socrates' most famous words were "I know that I know nothing." For centuries, people have been fascinated by this statement. This is somewhat ironic considering he probably never voiced exactly these words. The alleged quotation comes from Plato's

Apology, in which the philosopher tells of the Athenian Chaerephon, to whom the oracle in Delphi proclaimed that no one was wiser than Socrates. "Whatever does the god mean? What is his riddle? I am very conscious that I am not wise at all," Socrates marvels. He proceeds to describe how he investigated the matter in his own way by conversing with a statesman in Athens who had been deemed wise. "When I examined this man [...] I thought that he appeared wise to many people and especially himself, but was not. I then tried to show him that he thought himself wise, but that he was not. As a result, he came to dislike me [...]; so, I am likely to be wiser than he to this small extent, that I do not think I know what I do not know."[116]

Thus, Socrates never maintains that he doesn't know anything at all. His "not-knowing" (Plato prefers this term to "ignorance") is an awareness that human beings have their limits and that there are things no one can know. A cobbler may know much about sandals and an orator a great deal about rhetoric, but their knowledge is that of the specialist. For Socrates, acquired knowledge was always fixed and inflexible. It wasn't *wisdom*. Wisdom could never be captured, written down, or learned by rote. It was achieved when the mind suddenly expanded to make room for a realization. Such moments of wisdom were always fleeting. That which you understood about "love" today would have to be understood anew tomorrow.

It is for this reason that Socrates did not write down his teachings. If he had, people would have passed down his explanations as well-thought-out wisdom. However, that was not his aim. He did not want to communicate specific content, but rather sought to teach a strategy of thinking. He displayed a readiness to question his insights over and over, to examine them anew, or even to argue the opposite. Socrates taught that those who think they have understood everything are denser than those who recognize that their knowledge has limits. Paradoxically, "not-knowing" is a superior form of wisdom.

116 Plato, *Apology*, 21.

In the dialogue *First Alcibiades* (attributed to Plato), Socrates attempts to teach this mode of thinking to his favorite student. Alcibiades is a wealthy, distinguished Athenian. He is barely 20 years old and as handsome as he is arrogant and vain. He considers himself a natural political talent and therefore believes that he should be involved in decision-making about war and peace. To launch his political career, he intends to speak before the Athenian public assembly. However, Socrates takes the young man to task, giving him a proper intellectual thrashing. In the process, he makes use of three typical Socratic devices: irony, logic, and naïve questions. By means of irony, Socrates demonstrates the arrogance and superficiality of what Alcibiades says. Through logic, he exposes the contradictions in the young man's responses. And he deliberately poses naïve questions to reveal the obvious flaws in Alcibiades' opinion of himself. For instance, he asks Alcibiades what he would like to advise the assembly about. Medical questions? The art of shipbuilding perhaps? A doctor or a shipbuilder would be more suited to advising on these issues as each is clearly an expert in such matters. So in what field is Alcibiades an expert? Alcibiades must confess that he hasn't studied anything that qualifies him to advise on affairs of state. Next, Socrates asks Alcibiades to define what right and wrong are—since knowing the difference is undoubtedly essential for a future politician. The young man admits that he has never really thought about this. He uses the words "right" and "wrong" without having reflected on them. Moreover, he can't have learned their true meanings from anyone because no one knows exactly what they mean. The Athenians, for instance, were able to justify a war that their enemies deemed outrageously unfair. Through Socrates' insistent questioning, Alcibiades becomes tangled up in inconsistent definitions. After having been overconfident at the start of the dialogue, he is now completely confused. He laments, "[B]y the gods, O Socrates, I myself do not know what I mean but I really seem to be in a strange condition, for when you question me, it seems one way at one time, and another at another."[117]

117 Ariel Helfer, *Socrates and Alcibiades: Plato's Drama of Political Ambition and Philosophy* (Philadelphia: University of Pennsylvania Press, 2017), 53.

The experience Alcibiades describes is called *aporia* (Greek: "puzzlement," "hopelessness"). Aporia is an important component of *direct thinking*. It is the moment when your own beliefs break down. It's a highly significant moment, according to Socrates, because it is only when people experience aporia that they really start thinking. Overconfident thinking may present a shiny façade, but it conceals a shaky edifice that is built upon untested ideas and contradictory data. Once such thinking has collapsed, the way is cleared for thinking that is independent, creative, and inquisitive.

Nothing remains of Alcibiades' overconfidence at the close of this dialogue. He stands before Socrates like a child who is learning about everything for the first time, which is exactly what the philosopher wanted. He explains to Alcibiades that whoever wants to govern others must first be able to govern him- or herself. But in order to do this, it is necessary to practice direct thinking. For only when you are able to question the foundations of life are you truly able to make your life your own. It is because of your own knowledge, Socrates states, that you are really able to act freely. Those who do not know themselves are nothing more than slaves. This does not apply solely to Alcibiades, he explains, but also to Socrates himself, as well as every other person. Knowledge that has been acquired or that has never been questioned gives rise to overconfident thinking, whereas not-knowing generates a different kind of wisdom that cannot be conceptualized. Direct thinking is therefore not a purely deconstructive process that causes all beliefs to collapse in on themselves, leading people to drift through life. Deconstruction is, rather, the precondition for direct insight. At its core is a willingness to question one's own knowledge and recognize the limits of appropriated knowledge. Ultimately, this is the only process that allows one to "give birth to" authentic knowledge of one's own. It is for this reason that Socrates labeled himself a "midwife."

Self-knowledge as caring for the soul

Socrates was a direct thinker who refused to merely recycle the thoughts of others. For him, "an unexamined life was not worth living,"[118] as he was in the habit of saying. Consequently, his method of choice was dialogue and words were the medium that he and his interlocutors used to draw ever nearer to the truth. Socrates appreciated the importance of the quality of his medium and thus became a master of words.

At first glance, Socrates seems to have been in line with his contemporaries in this regard as the Athenians of the fifth century BCE valued rhetoric highly. However, most Athenians were interested in rhetoric chiefly for political reasons: The city-state was a direct democracy in which every free male citizen could appear in the public assembly and avail of his right to speak. The audience was comprised not of politicians, but rather of laymen. If your speech was well composed and compelling, you would be more likely to win over your audience; the power of persuasion went hand in hand with the very real power of politics. If you wanted to be influential, you could call on a sophist, an educated professional who could teach you the art of public speaking. The sophists argued that the content of a speech was less important than its external form. A good rhetorician could talk more convincingly than experts on subjects about which he knew nothing. The sophists thus perfected the art of speech as manipulation and obfuscation—which still plays such a decisive role in politics today.

Socrates' attitude to language was the opposite to that of the sophists. He worked against teachings that had more surface than substance. Socrates' own mastery of rhetoric is evident in the *Phaedrus*. In this dialogue, Socrates is strolling through the countryside with an interlocutor to whom he delivers an impromptu yet persuasive lecture on the sense of falling in love—after which he gives an even more captivating speech arguing against falling in love. It is clear that he

118 Plato, *Apology*, 33.

knows exactly how to manipulate listeners using words and how little doing so has to do with truth.

On the other hand, in the dialogue *Gorgias*, he sets out to redefine rhetoric or, more accurately, to determine its true significance. Ironically, he does this in conversation with Gorgias, one of the greatest rhetoricians of the time. Although Gorgias may be a great orator, he turns out to be much like everyone else once Socrates interrogates him: He starts to contradict himself and ends up feeling uncertain of what he really thinks. Socrates uses the exchange to present his own view of things: Words should not conceal the truth; rather, they should lead one to it. Rhetoric has no meaning in and of itself; it is purely appearance as long as it does not serve the pursuit of wisdom. It is probable that Socrates would have heartily agreed with Nietzsche's dictum that "[e]very word is a prejudice."[119]

As Socrates emphasized the importance of not using words in an unreflective manner, defining one's terms is at the heart of his philosophy. He is credited with having stated that "[t]he beginning of wisdom is the definition of concepts." Whether or not he spoke these words, the remark illustrates his attitude perfectly. The effort to define a concept *is* the philosophical process of inquiry; it *is* the process of direct thinking. Accordingly, many of Socrates' dialogues begin with the question "What is this?" Those who engage in overconfident thinking think they already know the answer to the question of what a term means. Direct thinking occurs when one draws nearer to the meaning of the concept itself. Aristotle, Plato's student and one of the most famous philosophers of antiquity, took up this idea when distinguishing between the nominal definition of a thing, which only reflects opinion, and its real definition. The latter represents what a thing *is* and not what people think about it. A genuine definition therefore measures the essence or nature of a thing—that is, it measures a thing *directly*.

119 Friedrich Nietzsche, *Werke in drei Bänden*. http://www.zeno.org/nid/20009241035.

Liberating a thing from preconceived notions facilitates a direct encounter with the thing itself—with its soul or, to use a more modern word, with its *nature*. This process also leads to self-knowledge. When we expose all of our appropriated knowledge through dialogue, the ensuing insight is a product of our "naked" self. It is for this reason that Socrates repeatedly refers to the inscription at the temple of the Delphic oracle: "Know yourself." Searching for truth, to Socrates, meant caring for the soul. "For I go around doing nothing but persuading both young and old among you not to care for your body or your wealth in preference to or as strongly as for the best possible state of your soul."[120]

Here, Socrates' way of thinking acquires a direct practical significance. For him, the pursuit of (self-)knowledge was the sole basis for conducting oneself properly. He believed that we act wrongly because we think we know about something when in reality we know nothing about it. Trying to make bread without an understanding of baking is not likely to prove truly catastrophic. However, using moral concepts when we lack direct knowledge of them can lead us to make disastrous choices. Socrates alerts Alcibiades to these consequences when they are discussing the possibility of him having a career as a politician: "Don't you realize that the errors in our conduct are caused by this kind of ignorance, of thinking that we know when we don't know?"[121] It is this kind of thinking that leads a completely inexperienced man like Alcibiades to believe he is capable of taking part in deliberations over war and peace. The problem, Socrates contends, is not that the young man lacks knowledge; it is, rather, that he is ignoring his ignorance (i.e. his "not-knowing"). In turn, Socrates derives a higher—or *direct*—morality from having pursued knowledge, since a person who questions him- or herself should realize that he or she does not possess any moral concepts of his own. All he or she has is the morality that has been learned or appropriated from others. However, that morality can never be considered one's own. Consequently, one is liable to violate this

120 Plato, *Apology*, 28.
121 Ibid., 575.

morality because one has no independent insight into its value. Direct morality is the result of having conducted independent inquiry. Those who examine notions like "justice" and "the good" derive their actions from such examination. Socrates believed in humanity and maintained that a person could only do the wrong thing if he or she didn't know better.

One could say that Socrates had too much faith in humanity. Doesn't every individual who asks about "the good" arrive at a different conclusion? However, Socrates' faith in humanity illustrates a remarkable aspect of direct thinking. As already outlined, direct thinking is the opposite of overconfident thinking. The latter is based on information that has been acquired externally. This information is always contradictory as opinions inevitably vary. Hence, one could rightly claim that it is impossible to find a "justice" that is universally applicable. Socrates, however, saw things differently. He claimed that we could use his thinking strategy to recognize the universal principle of something like "the good."

This approach is the basis of the Theory of Ideas that Socrates explains to his young Athenian companion in the *Phaedrus*. In this dialogue, Socrates is taking a stroll in the countryside with Phaedrus—a highly unusual act for a philosopher who disliked leaving the city. "Landscapes and trees have nothing to teach me—only the people in the city can do that,"[122] he asserts. Perhaps it was the prospect of Phaedrus' company that induced him to leave the city. Sitting under a sycamore tree by a babbling brook, Socrates tells his young student a legend, a poetic story, about the soul: It enters a body after having lost its wings and descended from the heavenly realm. On Earth, the soul-filled person retains an unconscious memory of that divine kingdom and its qualities: the good, the true, and the beautiful—those things that "truly exist." Thus, when a human in the material world observes objects or other humans and sees in them something good, true, or beautiful, he

122 Plato, *Phaedrus*, 510.

or she is recalling the original forms of these things, that is, the Ideas. A good person does not "possess" the good. Rather, the good is reflected at the beholder *through* the person. "That process is the recollection of the things our soul saw when it was traveling with god."[123]

Thus, Socrates believes that there is a different way of understanding a thing than merely possessing information about it. If you really want to know that thing, you must experience its essence directly. Direct thinking leads one to recognize the "Idea" of a thing. The next time you see something beautiful—a sunset, for example—you can make yourself aware of this principle. To Socrates, beautiful things (like sunsets), true things (like philosophy), and loving deeds (as in relationships) were forms on Earth that recalled the essence of beauty, truth, and love in the realm of Ideas. Accordingly, when we look at a sunset or feel love for someone, we are associating ourselves with the essential Idea of "ultimate" beauty or love. Direct knowledge in this context implies that we know the inmost nature of a thing, not just its superficial or situation-bound appearance.

Thus, it is clear that direct thinking consists of three stages: 1) recognizing one's own pseudo-knowledge about a thing; 2) becoming aware of one's own ignorance (or "not-knowing"); and 3) directly encountering the Idea of the thing in itself. As a result of this process, a human being can tap into a kind of autonomous intelligence that is awakened when that human being liberates him- or herself from preconceptions and prejudices and observes a thing without any ready-made assumptions.

True and false stability

Through his questions, Socrates challenged a mental mechanism that does not like to admit defeat. Researchers have known for years that

123 Plato, *Phaedrus*, 527.

people have a tendency to overestimate themselves. This common cognitive distortion is known as the *overconfidence effect.* This effect has frequently been studied by asking test subjects how confident they feel about the correctness of particular ideas or answers. Surprisingly, they are often most incorrect when they are especially certain of something. But the effect extends even further. It transpires that we constantly make serious mistakes when assessing our knowledge and abilities. In a study conducted on college students, Marsha T. Gabriel and Joseph W. Critelli found that all of the participants rated their own intelligence too highly. In addition, male participants frequently overestimated their attractiveness. A survey at the University of Nebraska, in turn, found that 94 percent of the professors observed ranked their teaching competence as above average.

At first, this behavior appears senseless, even dangerous. Researchers have long puzzled over how self-overestimation took root as a fundamental tendency of human behavior. Then, in 2011, Dominic Johnson and James Fowler presented the interesting results of their research on the "overconfidence effect" in the journal *Nature.* Using model calculations, they found that overestimating one's own abilities could give one a competitive advantage under certain conditions. A person who has an inflated sense of his or her own skills and abilities exhibits greater confidence—and sometimes actually experiences greater success. Just think of an arrogant businessman or those people whose self-confidence compensates for their rather average appearance. But it is not only individuals that overestimate themselves; nations do so too—which can have catastrophic consequences. By way of example, Johnson and Fowler cite the global financial crisis of 2008 and the Iraq War that commenced in 2003. Overconfidence also causes politicians and entrepreneurs to misjudge situations, have unrealistic expectations, and make wrong decisions. It is no wonder that Scott Plous, Professor of Psychology at Stanford University, has identified the overconfidence effect as potentially the most dangerous of all cognitive distortions.

Yet there's an even deeper level to overconfidence. Behind supposedly certain knowledge, there lies a fundamental desire for security. This derives from our interest in survival—we want to *know* where we stand. We prefer having mistaken beliefs to not knowing at all. Who among us has never passionately insisted on a certain point, even though we were not completely sure that we were right? Our beliefs about the world produce a mental system of coordinates that we use to orient ourselves. We have almost no doubts about this system, especially when it comes to life's fundamental questions. There are some things that we simply regard as certainties. But why should that be so? Overconfident thinking cannot answer this question. Nor does it seek to answer it as doubts come with confusion and uncertainty, which can transform a self-assured person into a confused child.

That is the problem with this way of thinking: It pretends to give us security when it is actually unstable. It cannot tolerate challenges or too many uncertainties because these could cause its confident thought structure to collapse. At the same time, this mode of thinking senses, whether consciously or not, that its beliefs are pieced together from information and experiences that barely stand up under scrutiny. After all, our knowledge always contradicts itself. What we learn at school does not necessarily match the information provided by our families. And this information, in turn, is likely to contradict what our neighbors or people in other countries think. This raises a fundamental question: What do we actually know? Is there any assumption that cannot be taken away from us? Ultimately this question leads us to conclude that everything we know is uncertain. That is an uncomfortable thing to discover—which is why most of us are extremely careful about protecting ourselves from such a realization. We prefer insisting on particular beliefs and principles to having the rug pulled out from under us. This is reflected in our absolute confidence in science. Most of us are not scientists ourselves and cannot adequately understand the research conducted by scientists, yet we are inclined to believe everything their studies claim to demonstrate. People are more likely to believe, for instance, in the existence of an overconfidence effect if we cite a few studies, as we have. The reason for this is simple: We're deeply invested in a form of thinking that overestimates itself, as well as being invested in believing unconditionally that information means "truth."

Certainly, scientific inquiry and information play an important part in our lives. But it is also clear that information cannot provide the answers to all of life's questions. If we want to know what a good life looks like, we will not present scientific studies as evidence. We can try to do so, but the results will not be particularly satisfying, for we can explore the subject from all possible angles—sociological, psychological, anthropological, etc.—without arriving at a definitive answer. An independent understanding is thus indispensable if you want answers to fundamental questions. But this does not arise on its own; you must cultivate such understanding in yourself.

An absolute requirement for direct thinking is the ability to tolerate confusion and not-knowing. Consequently, this way of thinking calls for courage. Socrates had such courage. He was an intrepid thinker. Confusion did not trouble him in the least. Some of his conversations, especially the early dialogues, seem to go on endlessly without ever achieving a result. At some point, the dialogues simply end in aporia. For Socrates, this was not a problem because he knew that confusion is only frightening if you don't understand it. It should be viewed not as a monster that invades your mind and forces confusion upon you, but rather as a necessary middle stage on the path to insight. It is not possible to instantly leap into knowledge; rather, you must cross through the "valley of aporia" to arrive at knowledge. Upon realizing this, the state of confusion becomes less frightening.

Direct thinking creates a form of stability that self-overestimating thinking can only dream of. The latter mode of thinking is constantly at work maintaining its beliefs, which requires energy and a certain rigidity that can be *mistaken* for stability. However, this is a big misconception. Beliefs do not produce any certainty because they can always be unsettled.

The only true stability lies in the ability to question everything in life. Those who are not afraid of confusion or not-knowing will still be standing on both feet when all of their beliefs have crumbled. Whenever the ground beneath their feet disappears, they discover anew that they are able to fly. It is necessary to learn to love this state of affairs in order to produce new insights that are not based on old information.

It is direct thinking such as this that allowed Socrates to face his death so calmly. After his fellow Athenians had condemned him to die by poison for having "seduced the youth" and for "blaspheming against the [local] gods," he spent his final days doing what he liked most: engaging in philosophical conversations with his visitors. Indeed, he even composed poetry for the first time. He rejected the possibility of escaping—which would not have been difficult—because he didn't want to leave Athens. Instead, he calmly drank the cup of hemlock on his last day. Death is the ultimate confusion, the ultimate not-knowing—and, by then, Socrates was already on good terms with both.

The philosopher as a Greek lover

If you view Socrates as he is depicted in painting and sculpture—dignified and stern—you might think he was a totally spiritualized person who was utterly disinterested in human affairs. This could not be further from the truth. Granted, Socrates was a calm and collected person, but there was a powerful fire burning inside him. His dialogues are full of lyricism and sensuality. He likewise ignited in his listeners a passion that they found difficult to explain. In the words of one contemporary: "For when I hear him, [...] my heart leaps [...] and tears fall from my eyes [...]. And I see the same thing happening to others."[124]

124 J.B. Engelmann (ed.), *Sokrates und seine Zeit. Eine historische Schilderung für Jünglinge und Jungfrauen*, trans. D. Brenner (Frankfurt am Main: Andreä, 1812), 117.

What kind of man was capable of eliciting such reactions? What kind of philosopher felt the need to leave his house every day, always seeking contact with others instead of ruminating in a quiet room? Who, in his conversations, repeatedly ensnared the truth, courting and rewording it in poetic terms? It is no coincidence that the Greek word *philosophy* literally means "love of wisdom." But that phrase isn't quite appropriate since the kind of affection implied by the Greek *philia* is a friendly form of love. Socrates and wisdom were far more than just friends.

If we wish to understand his relationship with wisdom, we must read Plato's *Symposium*, regarded by many as his masterpiece. The honorable men present at this banquet decide not to get drunk, but rather to take turns making speeches about Eros, the god of sexual love. Eros sees to it that people are gripped by desire and passion and find themselves attracted to the object of their desires. Socrates' speech is the philosophical high point of the evening. He surprises those present by telling a story about his teacher Diotima, who taught him "the nature of love." Diotima once presented Socrates with a curious interpretation of Eros: She explained that the god represents the desire of mortals to become immortal. An ordinary man is driven by this desire to the bodily act of love and renders himself "immortal" by producing children. But Diotima stated that there is also a higher form of procreation and erotic love. "[T]here surely *are* those who are even more pregnant in their souls than in their bodies, and these are pregnant with what is fitting for a soul to bear and bring to birth. And what is fitting? Wisdom and the rest of virtue."[125] Thus, the erotic urges of the philosopher draw him or her toward wisdom. He or she gets closer to wisdom by extending his or her desire from a single object to a common principle. Diotima describes the gradual recognition of beauty in this way: The philosopher grasps that a body he desires does not possess beauty, but rather participates in the principle (or Idea) of beauty. He or

125 Plato, *Symposium, in Complete Works*, ed. John Cooper (Indianapolis, IN: Hackett, 1997), 491.

she gradually develops an increasingly comprehensive view of objects of beauty: beautiful bodies, beautiful virtues and actions, and the spiritual beauty of philosophical knowledge. Lastly, he or she encounters the beautiful *in and of itself.* Diotima considers this spiritual experience, this becoming one with the originary Idea, to be the supreme goal of erotic fulfillment: "[F]rom one body to two, and from two to all beautiful bodies, then from the beautiful bodies to beautiful customs, and from customs to learning beautiful things, and from these lessons he arrives in the end at this lesson, which is learning of this very Beauty, so that in the end he comes to know just what it is to be beautiful."[126] This desire, or *eros*, becomes the mediator between the human and the divine—that is, the realm of Ideas.

Diotima trained Socrates well. He followed her teachings his entire life. Thus, we can understand why Socrates seemed to feel a fiery desire for beautiful young men, but never acted on his desire—not even with the magnificent Alcibiades, who complains bitterly in the *Symposium* that Socrates is too cool toward him. Socrates did not use *eros* to achieve physical satisfaction, instead using it as a path to transcendence—precisely as he had been taught by Diotima. Above all else, Socrates loved and adored the truth; he was literally seized by a yearning for *it.* He was not some dry philosopher; rather, he was an erotic lover in his entire approach to thinking.

You could even say that Socrates and his interlocutors in the *Symposium* were engaged in some sort of subtle love play. The conversation resembles an act of procreation that gives birth to knowledge. In his dialogues, the philosopher drew increasingly close to his object, literally penetrating it more and more deeply. Ideally, he would finally come so close to it that he would experience a direct encounter, a direct insight, that had nothing to do with knowledge in the ordinary sense. This direct encounter—this becoming one—lends direct thinking its erotic quality.

126 Ibid., 493.

We can conceive of erotic thinking in relation to a long-term romantic relationship. At the beginning of such a relationship, the partners are full of desire for each other—seized by *eros*, as the ancient Greeks would say. After a while, though, that feeling fades or disappears altogether. Each partner seems to know the other too well to feel the same excitement as in the beginning. Everything about the partner has become familiar. We anticipate what they will choose at a restaurant before they have ordered; we know how they look after waking up in the morning; we don't have to guess what kind of music they like. However, this kind of information does not represent our *partner*, but only our *knowledge* of them. If, for some reason, we succeed in forgetting everything we know about them—for example, because we suddenly experience them in an unknown situation or because we haven't seen them for a long time—then the encounter is once more a direct one. We are in love again, even if only for a short time.

In a sense, Socrates was in love his entire life. He spent his days continuously resetting his thinking to a state of not-knowing. In this way, he encountered the world as if for the first time. He repeatedly felt compelled to overcome the distance between himself and things, the nature of which he would deeply penetrate.

If you wish to apply this mode of thinking, think about a moral choice you have to make. Let us say you have to decide whether you should donate a certain amount to charity or whether you should use that money to treat yourself to something nice. If you ask five of your friends for their opinions, you will get five different answers since each will respond based on their existing assumptions. If you take this approach, you never get any real insight, even if you spend a lot of time in thought. Ultimately, you will simply choose the answer you find most convincing. But the conflict will persist: You will not have actually attained clarity; rather, you will only have rid yourself of other options. Instead, try practicing direct thinking. Put aside all the information and assumptions you have about the choice. Perhaps it would be easier for you to write all of this down to stop these thoughts from running through your head. Once you have fully emptied your mind, consider the matter anew. Observe it. Do not resist the fact that you do not know anything right now. Perhaps your brain feels completely blank. Perhaps it feels confused or unpleasant. If you manage to stay calm and avoid blindly grasping at solutions in this empty state, you will find that the mist will eventually disperse on its own. And suddenly a new direct insight will arrive, as if out of nowhere. This moment is an almost sensory experience, direct contact with the thing itself. And in this moment, you will have brought philosophy down from heaven to Earth, as Socrates once did.

CHAPTER 7

HANNAH ARENDT

Active thinking, *or* Eichmann as a metaphor

In 1964, German journalist Günter Gaus interviewed Hannah Arendt for his TV program *Zur Person*. Their conversation began with a peculiar debate. Gaus kept insisting on defining Arendt as a "philosopher," but Arendt gently resisted accepting the title. Gaus looked perplexed.[127] Arendt was clearly part of the rich tradition of German philosophy. She had been the student of such great thinkers as Martin Heidegger and Karl Jaspers; she was the acclaimed author of major philosophical classics, such as *The Origins of Totalitarianism* and *The Human Condition*; and everything she had written had been in dialogue with the ideas of Socrates and Kant, Hegel and Heidegger. So why would a thinker of such stature and depth deny being a part of the philosophical world?

It was of great significance to Arendt that she be considered a "political theorist" rather than a "philosopher." As we delve more and more deeply into her mind, this denial of the term "philosopher" will serve as a major key to unlocking her unique way of thinking. The reason for her refusal of the term was never as superficial as mere pedantism about her exact field of inquiry. It was her stance in the

127 Stack Altoids, "Hanna Arendt 'Zur Person' full Interview," April 8, 2013. https://www.youtube.com/watch?v=dsoImQfVsO4.

world, her fundamental life statement, around which her entire ... well, *philosophy* revolved.

One way of comprehending the distinction she made would be to observe her growing distance from her most influential direct teacher, Martin Heidegger. Arendt's early encounter with Heidegger at the University of Marburg was thrilling—so thrilling that it led to a four-year secret love affair between the 35-year-old married teacher and the 18-year-old Jewish student.

Arendt was not the only one who was enthused by Heidegger. Students flocked to his lectures as rumors spread that here, once again in history, "thinking has come to life." In Arendt's words, the spiritually hungry students shared the feeling that finally "there exists a teacher; one can perhaps learn to think." Forty-five years after her initial encounter with the great philosopher, Arendt wrote:

> People followed the rumor about Heidegger in order to learn thinking. What was experienced was that thinking as pure activity ... can become a passion which not so much rules and oppresses all other capacities and gifts, as it orders them and prevails through them. We are so accustomed to the old opposition of reason versus passion, spirit versus life, that the idea of a passionate thinking, in which thinking and aliveness become one, takes us somewhat aback.[128]

However, Arendt gradually discovered that her interest in the act of thinking did not accord with "thinking as pure activity"—which, in so many ways, is the definition of "philosophy." Over the years, she began to develop a critical distance from philosophical introspection, in particular Heidegger's. As she became aware of her own unique mode of thinking, she grew more and more disturbed by what seemed to her to be a profound lack of concern on Heidegger's part—a self-immersion

128 Hannah Arendt, "Martin Heidegger at Eighty," *New York Review of Books* 17/6 (October 21, 1971), 51.

that so distanced him from the actual world that its most essential characteristic was "its absolute egoism, its radical separation from all its fellows."[129] Arendt was troubled by this type of thinking, which kept contemplating itself in a closed circle and never considered its actual relationship with the world.

Though not directly linked, Heidegger's explicit involvement with the Nazis proves this point as it seems to confirm Arendt's sobering realization that the act of philosophy, however deep it may be, does not necessarily lead to moral engagement in the world. This illustration of the disconnect between philosophy and action must have shaped her thinking: She came to see the two as different domains without a bridge between them that would enable philosophy to lead to thoughtful action. Twenty years after their separation, Arendt forgave Heidegger for his Nazi involvement and the two resumed their friendship until Arendt's death in 1975; however, she would never again conceive of thinking as being directed toward the purity of philosophy, which was what she had learned from her master.

The Heidegger of her youth, back in 1924, had been "the hidden king [who] reigned in the realm of thinking."[130] Nevertheless, Arendt slowly but surely began to be influenced by other thinkers. She started to doubt the traditional identity of philosophy and became interested in Heidegger's own master, the philosopher Edmund Husserl, who called for a quiet revolution in philosophy that would lead it away from self-occupation: "Back to the things themselves!" When Arendt moved to the University of Heidelberg and met Heidegger's friend, Karl Jaspers, his concrete approach led her to experience a revelation: "Philosophizing is real as it pervades an individual life at a given moment."[131]

---

129 Hannah Arendt, "What is Existenz Philosophy?" *Partisan Review* 8/1 (Winter 1946), 50.

130 Elisabeth Young-Bruehl, *Hannah Arendt: For Love of the World* (New Haven, CT: Yale, 1982), 44.

131 Ken Booth, *Theory of World Security* (Cambridge: Cambridge, University Press, 2007), 198.

Arendt realized that she could not sympathize with the act of introspection, which she defined as thinking that "rebounds back upon itself and finds its solitary object within the soul."[132] Introspection, to her, implied isolation from the world: One ceases to be interested in the world and finds only the inner self to be of interest. In this isolation, "thinking becomes limitless because it is no longer molested by anything exterior; because there is no longer any demand for action."[133] Through introspection, one becomes indifferent to the world and learns to expect nothing from the "bad outside world." When the world and action have been rejected, introspection can fill up a life: "It annihilates the actually existing situation by dissolving it in mood, and at the same time it lends everything subjective an aura of objectivity, publicity, extreme interest."[134] This tendency toward introspection, Arendt felt, had been her youthful error.

Unprotected by shielding introspection, Arendt embarked upon a journey away from traditional philosophy. She owes her final transformation to a far greater movement in history, an intervention of the "bad outside world" that "molested" her thinking and propelled her to become engaged in ways unimaginable.

"I could no longer be a bystander"

"When I was young," Arendt recalled in 1963, "I was interested neither in history nor in politics. If I can be said 'to have come from anywhere,' it is from the tradition of German philosophy."[135] However, during the early 1930s, this naïve apolitical attitude steadily morphed into an anti-academic approach that led her to focus more and more on current affairs. When the Nazi party demonstrated its increasing power in the

132 Hannah Arendt, *Rahel Varnhagen* (Baltimore, MD: The Johns Hopkins University Press, 2000), 10.
133 Ibid.
134 Ibid., 21.
135 Hannah Arendt, *The Jew as Pariah* (New York: Grove Press, 1978), 245.

1930s election, she grew less tolerant of thinkers who seemed indifferent to the darkening political situation. Finally, in 1933, when the Reichstag was set ablaze, leading to a series of arrests, Arendt's philosophical thinking was completely overturned.

Arendt's experience during that year can be thought of as the beginning of a union between philosophy and action. This was demonstrated by her courageous choice to stay in Berlin. Though she had been considering emigration for months, she felt she could no longer be a bystander. She offered her apartment as a way station for those fleeing Hitler's regime. For the first time, she felt satisfaction that derived not from thinking, but from acting and resisting in the actual world. This participation in the escape effort was her introduction to the realm of action, which would later be the basis for one of her most original contributions to political theory.

In her interview with Günter Gaus, Arendt explained that the series of illegal arrests in 1933, which led to political prisoners finding themselves in the cellars of the Gestapo or concentration camps, was "such a shock to me that ever after I felt responsible."[136] This newfound sense of responsibility, she added, wiped away any trace of innocence. She became even more disengaged from academic thinking as a result of yet another, more personal shock. As the "general political realities transformed themselves into personal destiny as soon as you set foot out the house," Arendt discovered, to her horror, that friends she had known and trusted were voluntarily collaborating with the Nazis. "This wave of cooperation," she said, "made you feel surrounded by an empty space, isolated. I lived in an intellectual milieu ... and I came to the conclusion that cooperation was, so to speak, the rule among intellectuals ... And I have never forgotten that. I left Germany guided by the resolution that 'Never again!' I will never have anything to do with 'the history of

136 Marco Goldoni and Chris McCorkindale, *Hannah Arendt & the Law* (Oxford: Hart Publishing, 2012), 3.

ideas' again. I didn't, indeed, want to have anything to do with this sort of society again."[137]

Arendt had lost her naïve faith in the moral goodness of thinkers. She started to search elsewhere to formulate an understanding of evil and the conditions under which right judgment and action can emerge in the world. It was then that she entered into the political domain, shifting from being an intellectual and apolitical thinker to being fully engaged, with an unambiguous political and historical stance. She felt strongly that philosophy failed to offer substantial meaning to the world, as it vehemently ignored the core of human existence—man as an acting being. Its focus on speculative and metaphysical thinking meant that it was unable to offer anything of substance to the political realm, where people come together, judge, and act.

Arendt's shift from philosophy to politics kept her out of the realm of thinking for some time. She escaped to Paris, where she immersed herself in anti-war, pro-Jewish, and pro-Zionist action. She began to think not in individual terms, but in collective terms. She went from perceiving herself as a citizen of the world to recognizing that "when one is attacked as a Jew, one must defend oneself as a Jew." Since problems surrounding Jewishness were not her own problems, her personal problem was, in fact, a political problem. Rejecting the psychological thinking that put the subject at the center of existence, she started to tell her individual story from a historical perspective as a part of a "we" consciousness. The person was a part of general structures, fundamentally shaped by the conditions of his or her birth, neighborhood, and the group to which he or she belongs. The problems of the human condition, Arendt concluded, lay in those general structures—or, in other words, in the political sphere.

Thus, Arendt strongly believed that any real change, any revolutionary renewal, could only take place in the political realm. Any movement that did not enter into the political arena and did not

137 Young-Bruehl, *Hannah Arendt*, 108.

translate its ideology into concrete goals to change the actual situation would remain abstract and ineffective. To act in this world, one had to become politically involved. It is for this reason that Arendt was critical of movements such as the women's movement or the Zionist movement, which operated chiefly in what she called the "social realm" and dealt with social questions. In Paris, she observed the French socialists busying themselves with class struggles, but noted that they remained apathetic toward international affairs—as a result of which they were utterly unable to deal with the Jewish Question. She was also astounded by the Jews' failure to think politically beyond their small sphere of concern and their consequent lack of awareness of the general destiny of their people.

When Jewish hopes collapsed in 1937, many Jews began to propose a "return to the ghetto": withdrawing from the European cultural community into Jewishness. Arendt recognized this as a catastrophically wrong response at a time when the enemies of the Jews were growing in power. She believed that political insight had to emerge, that Jewish reconstitution could only come about in a political context, in a struggle against the forces that threatened it. Retreating implied a failure to realize that Europe as a whole was facing destruction. It was no longer acceptable to conceive of Zionism as an isolated movement. She argued for a new "Jewish politics" and a Jewish army to fight against Hitler and even legally help defend those who assassinated Nazi figures.

Arendt's thought process was not overturned by some inner revelation independent of external events and circumstances. Such a revelation would be highly characteristic of philosophers. The uniqueness of Arendt's thinking was partly attributable to the way she transformed in tandem with the historical and political shift that took place in Europe. Her kind of thinking was deeply intertwined with the flux of changes occurring in the world. It was *active thinking*.

Active thinking is a highly engaged form of thinking. It prepares one to act in the real world. Moreover, active thinking is, in itself, already a form of action. In the very act of thinking, one is aware that one is a responsible participant in the world. Although thinking is often conceived of as a way of retreating from the world—disengaging from the actual flow of events to engage in silent introspection—active thinking entails a commitment to think responsibly, to understand that it is only through full engagement that we can rightly judge and consciously act.

Thinking, for Arendt, was the tool with which humans could bring new awareness to their actions. There is no daydreaming in active thinking, nor does it allow for self-immersion that makes one forget all about the world. It is the complete opposite of aimless and involuntary thinking. Through Arendt, thinking became a powerful tool of engagement.

Arendt's political thinking was not limited to what one would usually consider politics: parliament and government members negotiating certain decisions on behalf of their voters. Politics, to her, was the public realm in which people come together, judge, and act, the realm of exchange, interaction, and dialogue. The ability to think politically implied an ability to think in a way that makes one capable of judging and acting in the real world.

Arendt claimed that philosophy and politics—which had, in Ancient Greece, been inseparable—had gradually separated, with philosophy eventually becoming pure thinking, completely detached from worldly affairs. However, this was more than just the problem of philosophy: The way in which individuals think tends to be uninvolved and irresponsible, unaware of the crucial role of thought on an individual level in the world of action. To put it bluntly, ordinary thinking is almost like non-thinking, like switching off voluntary activity that can investigate and make judgments. Arendt hoped to liberate thinking from "thinkers" and return it to individuals to allow them to develop their own capacity to truly and actively think. It was out of this critical awareness that Arendt's political theory emerged.

The man who stopped thinking

At the end of the war, while still in Paris and actively engaged in helping Jewish refugees and anti-Fascists, Arendt began to develop her unique union of thought and action. Her focus was gradually shifting from political activity toward an ambitious attempt to bring forth a new political science. This attempt first took shape in her seminal book, *The Origins of Totalitarianism*. This book, written by an unknown woman whose training was in philosophy and who had never before written a book about history or political theory, was met with overwhelming critical acclaim and set her on the path to international fame.

In *The Origins of Totalitarianism*, Arendt, grappling with the horrors of evil regimes such as Nazism and Stalinism, carefully delineates the characteristics of totalitarian control. She identifies four such characteristics: The first is an ideology that explains all of history, justifies the regime and its politics, and relates a myth of a superior people and an internal enemy; the second is total terror, as demonstrated in the Nazi concentration camps and the Soviet labor camps; the third is the destruction of natural human bonds; and the fourth is governing through bureaucracy, thereby creating a general sense of a faceless controlling power.

Perhaps most striking is Arendt's insight—or warning—that the very existence of such regimes signifies a highly dangerous possibility for mankind: that politics, as the public realm in which people can talk and act, can disappear altogether. Politics is made possible only under certain historical conditions; certain forms of government can emerge and eradicate politics, first by systematically dehumanizing one group of people and later another group—making humans superfluous. Even democracies are at risk of adopting totalitarian elements when, for example, a victory over non-democratic regimes leads to the justification of the use of any means necessary to force democracy on another country or when, as happened in the US during the 1950s, a patriotic morality initiates a crusade against free-thinking in the name of democratic values. The awareness of totalitarian elements should be deeply assimilated in order to prevent well-disguised totalitarian control from taking hold, even in the most democratic nations.

On a deeper level, Arendt recognized that totalitarianism was the anti-political process that led to the shutting down of all thinking. This could also happen when, without being forced to do so, people enter a state of thoughtlessness and avoid participating in the political realm. Arendt was very critical of democracy as we know it—people handing over all responsibility to a select few who represent them in the political realm. She believed that the only antidote to totalitarianism was "participatory democracy" or the "council system": spontaneous organs of the people that are not organized along party lines or with the involvement of their leaders. Here, Arendt's active thinking is in evidence. Engaged and responsible thinking on the part of the individual was the key to preventing evil from taking over the political realm.

In *The Human Condition*, Arendt continued to develop her "new political science," focusing on the failure of philosophy to offer humans genuine ways of acting and participating in the world. She described how thinkers move away from the world, considering disinterest in the world of action as a higher value. Since the days of Socrates, she claimed, philosophers had been more concerned with how philosophy could be practiced with the least amount of interference from the political realm. Her question was: How shall we take the political realm seriously? Or, in other words, how can people turn thinking into a tool of action? Arendt intuited that bringing thinking into the world of action would empower people to think in order to act. It could also shift the attention of philosophers to a world in which political events—world wars, totalitarianism, and atomic bombs—desperately demanded such an approach to thinking.

Driven by her wish to see a new form of action in the world, Arendt highlighted the crucial importance of maintaining the *vita activa*—the life of action or the political life. Arendt distinguished the term "action" from "labor" and "work," which signified far more limited human activities, like taking care of vital necessities and being productive. Action took place when one initiated something new and unpredictable in the world and was completely dependent on the constant presence of others. In other words, for action to happen, there needed to be a public space. The material needs of labor and work could be met in one's private space, but the condition of action was plurality, humans relating to one another.

Arendt was concerned that this public space and the *vita activa* were gradually diminishing in importance. She felt that ever since the Christian era, the public life had lost its deep political meaning. Action had been reduced to one of the necessities of earthly life and freedom had become associated with the unworldly domain of contemplation. Only in *vita contemplativa*—one's inner world—could one find truth and freedom. Additionally, the distinction between the public realm and the private realm had become blurred. Nations had become like vast households, bureaucratically taking care of all of the social and economic needs of the individual, as a result of which the public space—the space of freedom—had been replaced with the "social space."

This is another clear example of Arendt's *active thinking*. Arendt wished to revolutionize philosophy by redefining man as an acting being. Her hope was that thinking, when focused on action and human affairs rather than contemplation, could lead to a new form of action in the world. In her time, in which the devastating results of Stalinism and Nazism appeared to signal the "end of ideology," there seemed to be no role for intellectuals. Arendt seemed to be trying to give new meaning and significance to the act of human thinking.

Arendt hoped that free thinking could become man's last resort at times when moral structures had collapsed and one had to judge for oneself what kind of action is right in such a world. Her approach sought to protect the freedom of the political realm when all else failed. She believed that at such times, the only reliable moral compass was asking oneself, "Would I still be able to live with myself if I did such a thing? Would I be able to bear the memory of my deed?" She rejected moral ideology and encouraged people to think for themselves and to be guided by their own *active thinking*.

This was the crux of Arendt's political thinking. It centered on maintaining the individual's ability to think and to judge, since the absence of thought was the root of all evil. Evil could thrive only in humans who stopped thinking. On the other hand, thoughtfulness—our ability to enter into a dialogue with ourselves, to look into our experience and turn it into meaningful story to tell others and themselves—was the only hope for a genuine morality. Thinking can lead people to consider the past and so move in "the dimension of depth, striking roots and thus stabilizing themselves, so as not to be swept away by whatever may occur."[138]

Those who do not have this ability, Arendt warned, will do wrong. Her most controversial example was Adolf Eichmann, whose trial in Jerusalem she covered in a series of articles for *The New Yorker*. Until then, Arendt had investigated the ultimate evil of totalitarianism as a general phenomenon. Eichmann's case finally gave her the opportunity to look evil in the eye and try to identify the deeper forces and ideas that constituted the preconditions for the emergence of totalitarian forms. She, like everyone else, was expecting Eichmann to be an inhuman monster, however, she was shocked to realize that he was not, that there was nothing there. It was this absence, this vacant space, that had enabled Eichmann's evil. While the majority of humanity is bewildered in the face of extreme evil and seek an "explanation" for how anyone could do such things, Eichmann's evil lacked any depth.

Observing Eichmann with great intensity, Arendt eventually came to realize that her earlier notion of "radical evil"—a demonic

138 Young-Bruehl, *Hannah Arendt*, xxx.

evil inherent in the human being—needed to be revised. Though utterly incomprehensible, the crimes committed by the Nazis could not be explained away by painting them as monsters and demons who had engineered the murder of millions. There was something else, something that was perhaps no less fearsome, that had made this possible: the banality of evil—man's capacity to do wrong when he does not engage in the act of thinking.

When confronted with extreme evil, Arendt claimed, it is tempting to "indulge in sweeping statements about the evil nature of the human race";[139] however, one thing is certain: "that everyone could decide for himself to be either good or evil in Auschwitz." People like Eichmann simply turned off their thinking and judging faculties and therefore had no real motives. At his trial, Eichmann revealed himself as having no independent will or thinking faculty. He could mechanically recite moral maxims—which demonstrates how useless such maxims are when they have not been reflected upon. By testifying factually and remorselessly that he had only obeyed another's will, he was saying that he was not a person. He renounced responsibility and even this renunciation did not concern him.

Thus, Arendt felt that Eichmann's deeds were unpunishable and unforgivable—there was no person left whom one could ever forgive. Moreover, noting Eichmann's bureaucratic mentality, she judged him incapable of telling right from wrong, which made him, at least in a sense, not truly "guilty." To even deserve the right to be considered "guilty," Eichmann would have had to be conscious of the nature of his crimes. His deeper crime was that he had stopped thinking. He had been far more devoted to mindless extermination and the sense of belonging to a movement than he had been to the ideology behind them.

139 Eric Voegelin, *Hitler and the Germans* (Colombia: University of Missouri Press, 1999), 39.

While many who read Arendt's series of articles felt that she was "soulless," she felt that she had finally been cured of the kind of emotional involvement that precludes good judgment. For her, this was the beginning of a new political morality based on the human capacity to actively think in a way that would enable the act of judging. Since only thinking could condition one against evil-doing, people had the moral obligation to deeply engage in thinking in order to rightly judge. However, even good people fear making judgments. They feel that judging would make them seem arrogant and over-confident. Arendt's poignant response to that was: "if you say to yourself in such matters: who am I to judge?—you are already lost."[140]

Are we thinking or just daydreaming?

Many complain nowadays that their thinking is too "active." What they mean by "active" is that their brain is chattering too much, that there are too many thoughts of worry and distress, frustration and struggle, going on in their mind. Some express a wish to quiet their stormy, over-thinking brain and attempt to do so using different meditation and relaxation techniques. Indeed, mental quietude—especially when life's challenges are proving unbearably intense—seems quite appealing.

However, Arendt tells us that our thinking is not active enough and that humans tend to shut down the activity of right thinking and judging. Arendt's own way of thinking makes it clear that, most of the time, we are not really actively thinking. We are daydreaming. Daydreaming may be intense at times; however, when it comes to developing a brighter style of thinking that can lead us to consciously engage with the world, it leads us nowhere. Voluntary thinking, gathering one's mental forces to realize something for oneself, is quite a rare phenomenon in most people's lives. Interestingly, recent research confirms Arendt's criticism of human thinking.

---

140 James W. Bernauer, *Amor Mundi: Explorations in the Faith and Thought of Hannah Arendt* (Berlin: Springer, 2012), 6.

Research on cognitive bias demonstrates that the human brain does not really like to think. In fact, most of the time it operates in a mode of maximal energy preservation. It uses mental strain only when it doesn't have a choice, for example, when confronted with difficult tasks in the office or when facing other acute and demanding challenges. Most of the time, it does not activate itself voluntarily. It shifts to an "automatic pilot" mode, a state of associative and reactive thinking.

This is understandable. One can never know when an emergency will strike and demand a tremendous degree of strenuous concentration, so, in circumstances that do not demand such mental engagement, there is no point having an unnecessarily active mind. The "automatic pilot" mode seems perfectly suited to more automatic activities, such as talking with friends, watching TV, and cooking dinner. This "automatic pilot" mode is defined in the field of cognitive bias as the brain's bias toward *cognitive ease*.

If you suspect that cognitive ease relates to the brain's love of laziness, you are right. The brain naturally prefers to be in an effortless state, in the same way that the body does not like straining itself at the gym for more than a short while. Mental strain is akin to a muscle being pushed to its limit; before long, the brain seeks an escape path toward relaxation and aimless wandering. Moreover, for the brain, the privilege of being lazy implies that there is no threat and that everything is going well. It is for this reason that cognitive ease is associated with good mood and good feeling.

However, things become more complicated when we come to realize that cognitive ease is also associated with truthfulness. This means that an easy answer is also considered a true answer and a quick judgment is considered a right judgment. Distinguishing right from wrong is too often guided by a hidden wish of the brain not to think about things too much. According to research, most of our judgments derive from our lazy system of thinking rather than our brain's capacity to deeply engage in consideration and thoughtful observation.

This becomes even more uncomfortable when we take Eichmann into account. Though Eichmann's case is far more disturbing than any failure of judgment we are likely to make in our own lives, he represents a man who preferred to put his thinking to sleep—indeed, a man for whom not thinking and not judging became higher values. The consequences, in his case, were devastating. However, if we forget, just for a moment, about the extreme deeds in which he was involved, we may well come to recognize that we, too, prefer not to think too much.

Arendt's genius lies not in her drive to turn us all into philosophers, but rather in her drive to demonstrate how our tendency not to think might weaken our humanness and our ability to fully participate in the world. Seeing thinking as a burden—the preserve of intellectuals or an unnecessary activity when all is well—is dangerous. Everyone likes to think of themselves as "individuals" nowadays, but Arendt states that only through volitional thinking—going beyond the brain's tendency to minimally and intentionally think—can one claim genuine independence of thought. For Arendt, an individual is a person who initiates thought processes and passionate inquiries and not simply someone whose brain functions just enough for him or her to react when needed and to make hasty and superficial judgments.

The entire field of cognitive bias is dedicated to outlining the many ways in which the human brain judges without exerting itself. By "judging," we mean assessing the truthfulness of something. The fundamental failure of thinking, as demonstrated by this field of research, is automatic thinking or "fast thinking," which is at the root of all cognitive errors. Arendt's active thinking seems to tackle this fundamental bias. Perhaps active thinking, which is intentional and effortful and motivated by a wish to correctly judge, can minimize cognitive errors. But how exactly should one engage in such thinking?

One of the most persistent cognitive errors made by the human brain is believing that the repetition of something, be it a statement or an experience, is an indication of its truthfulness. This, almost humorously, starts with what is called the "attentional bias." If one's thinking keeps producing a certain thought, one's perception will be deeply affected by this recurring thought. For this reason, patients suffering from anxiety disorders and chronic pain pay increased attention to information relevant to their conditions, such as angry or painful facial expressions. We are not only easily persuaded by the repetition of our own false thoughts. The "illusory truth effect," for example, relates to the human brain's tendency to believe that certain information is correct merely because it has been frequently exposed to it. As one research study has shown, if you repeatedly hear that "Basketball became an Olympic discipline in 1925," you are more likely to accept this statement.

Perhaps the bias about which Arendt is most deeply worried is the "bandwagon effect," whereby people do certain things simply because other people have already done them. The more people do something, such as adopting a belief or a trend, the greater the likelihood that you will follow. You would act the same as those other people, regardless of your own beliefs, which you may ignore or override. For instance, as soon as a particular product becomes popular, more people "get on the bandwagon" and buy it. Another example is the way in which many choose to vote in elections: They vote for the candidates or parties that are more likely to succeed—at least according to the media.

Why? One major reason is our automatic thinking, which absentmindedly accepts that which we repeatedly experience. It is essential to understand that the judgments we make are shaped by repetition, whether that which is repeated is true or false. Thus, it is clear how dangerous it can be to fully give in to the automatic system. This is true not only in relation to what Arendt terms "banality of evil," but also in relation to what we might call the "banality of goodness."

Even one's morality—the set of values and actions one considers "good"—can easily become little more than a lazy habit. People who "do good" are often people who do not think too much as noble maxims, such as "Love thy neighbor," can turn into yet another enemy of thoughtfulness, which Arendt advocates as the only true freedom. Good ideologies, in this respect, are not essentially different from bad ideologies. All ideologies put the brain to sleep, relieving it of the responsibility to think for itself.

When we adopt a certain ideology, a certain fixed moral principle, we thereby take a "position" in the world. For example, we may become "leftists" or "rightists" in our political worldview. This may endow us with a sense of confidence. We always know what we stand for—the "good"—and what we reject, the "bad." The downside of taking such a position is that we tend to stop examining new political situations or political complexities. In other words, we stop thinking in the belief that we have already done as much thinking as is necessary in relation to these matters. We become blind followers of our own ideology or morality. Interestingly, Arendt rejected ideology and, to the great disappointment of many of her activist students and colleagues, refused to support either conservative or liberal views. Moreover, she rejected the impulse to influence others as a teacher and to tell others what to think and how to act. She felt that commitment to a certain worldview "can easily carry you to a point where you no longer think."

It is not sufficient to merely shake off all ideology as this alone does not lead to active thinking. Shaking off ideology or external morality, Arendt tells us, results in a great sense of responsibility, since it is now completely up to us to consider and judge right action in the world at every given moment. This calls for the cultivation of great awareness as we are no longer adopting a fixed position. We must scrutinize the assumptions of our automatic thinking and question our moral habits, reassessing past actions and asking ourselves important, challenging questions.

The following thought experiment is a good starting point for awakening our active thinking. Think of every individual life as a small country that is run by the individual him- or herself. Whatever choices and decisions this individual makes represent his or her vision of how the whole world should choose and decide. Thus, one becomes a paragon of behavior and action for all to follow and life becomes a matter of great responsibility. What actions would you take if you were completely aware that you were setting an example for 8 billion people? Imagine this immense responsibility attaching to every aspect of your life. Such an experiment can help instill in you the sense of global responsibility that Arendt was hoping could become second nature to humans.

Love of the world

"I've begun so late, really only in recent years, to truly love the world," Arendt wrote in a letter to her mentor, Karl Jaspers. "Out of gratitude, I want to call my book on political theories *Amor Mundi*."[141] Although this book was eventually entitled *The Human Condition*, Arendt's wish to replace the philosophical tradition of *contemptus mundi*—"contempt of the world"—with "love of the world" reveals a deeper motivation for her *active thinking*. In contrast to the thinking of the reclusive and self-immersed philosopher, her thinking could never turn its back on the world. Rather, it faced the world, observing "men in their infinite plurality" (in Lessing's words), seeking a sense of community, and finding purpose only as a part of the great human web. Arendt's thinking was never a monologue. It was dialogic and relational by nature, since Arendt's deepest experience of the world was that the world can form only in the interspaces between humans in all their variety.

Arendt was fully aware that the "interaction" with one's fellow human beings was not considered characteristic of great thinkers, nor was it a condition desired by them. Yet her unique type of thinking was driven by the conviction that truth can exist only where it is humanized by discourse, hence her enthusiasm about the "council system," which she believed to be the only political structure that could fully prevent

141 Young-Bruehl, *Hannah Arendt*, xxiv.

totalitarianism: people coming together to act together. Her hope did not rest on theories and concepts, isolated from human activity, but on the "uncertain, flickering and often weak light that some men and women, in their lives and works, will kindle."[142]

Arendt's "loving" thinking expressed itself as *active thinking* also in the sense that it was founded on the commitment to embrace the world instead of escaping it. Whereas many view thinking as an inner "haven," away from the cruelties or disappointments of the outside world, Arendt viewed her "thinking space" as an opportunity to love the world through the active life of the mind. Philosophically, she struggled to frame thinking in a way that would allow one to withdraw from the world into a "thinking space" without ignoring or demeaning the world. This turned into her last literary project, which she never managed to complete: her three-volume *Life of the Mind.*

Arendt's sudden retreat from the political realm into the world of philosophy in *Life of the Mind* surprised many. Her life seemed to have come full circle: She had moved away from philosophy toward political thinking, then returned to philosophical immersion. However, this was a sudden shift only on the surface; Arendt had simply turned toward *inner* politics. She divided the inner world into three mental systems: thinking, judging, and willing. She hoped to establish a vision of good mental governance whereby these three mental faculties would check and balance each other like three branches of government. She held that no one faculty should dominate the other two. Each should live and have its freedom. The precondition for such mental harmony is the internal freedom of each. There should be no silencing or refusing to hear the other, even in one's inner republic. For example, she suggested a peace treaty between thinking and willing, a treaty that would end a long historical and philosophical struggle during which it seemed that one had to be sacrificed in order for the other to prevail. Being together

142 Hannah Arendt, *Men in Dark Times* (New York: Harcourt Brace Jovanovich, 1968), ix.

with oneself was a second mode of human plurality and achieving harmony in this inner plurality was another form of her "love of the world."

In her last book, Arendt finally exposed her own way of thinking: thinking that stands back from the world of human affairs not in order to avoid conflict or to "contemplate," but to search for meaning and to tell a meaningful story. In searching for the meaning of deeds, even evil ones, humans could win the privilege of judging. The role of thinking is to lay the groundwork for us to make good judgments about the world. It prepares us to meet whatever we must meet in our daily lives. Thinking can allow one to nullify one's opinions and prejudices until one no longer depends on preconceived systems and can encounter phenomena objectively. Judging, the outcome of right thinking, is the true political activity of the mind. It is through such thinking that we become fully engaged in the world. To make good judgments, we cannot remain at a remove from reality. There is a moral obligation to enter the real, concrete, and factual world. More than that, doing so is an act of love.

It is worth considering how our lives might change if we turned our thinking into a tool of engagement. For the most part, human thinking is like a precious resource that is wasted arguing with the world instead of creatively collaborating with it. Thinking is too often used as a way of disengaging from the world. At other times, it can be intensely focused on resistance and struggle, internally pushing away that with which it is presented. What would happen if, when facing a challenge, we determined not to waste the precious resource that is our thinking and instead chose to use it as a tool for constructive and creative action that would fully respond to the challenge? What would happen, for example, if instead of sourly thinking, "I can't bear this workplace," you thought, "How could I creatively contribute to changing this workplace?" Simply imagine your thinking as an active collaborator that is fully responsive and committed to confronting the challenge with which it is presented. Perhaps this reorientation could lead to *real action*, rather than automatic re-action.

CHAPTER 8

CHARLES DARWIN

Dynamic thinking, *or* A force like a hundred thousand wedges[143]

As we were conducting the research for this chapter, we arrived at a point at which we had to stop and reflect for a moment. We tried to think back to a time when evolution and natural selection were not yet self-evident facts. We found it impossible to do so. This illustrated how Darwin's ideas have become a fundamental part of our reality. His explanation of how species emerge—indeed, how *we* came into existence—has become so firmly established in our heads that it is no longer possible to look at nature differently. Go ahead and try. Try not to think about evolution as you wonder why kangaroos have pouches on their bellies or why humans and chimpanzees resemble each other so closely. You'll likely find this very difficult (unless you're a creationist, in which case you will probably not want to read this chapter).

This is exactly what makes Darwin's ideas so special: They have become general knowledge. The same cannot be said of Einstein's general theory of relativity, for example. One reason for this is surely that Darwin made an effort to present his theory in language that would be comprehensible to the general public. Darwin's most important

143 Unless otherwise stated, all translations in this chapter are by David A. Brenner.

work, *On the Origin of Species*,[144] is one of the few specialist texts that is widely read by laypeople—another likely reason for this is that Darwin is explaining life itself, how we ourselves came to be.

It is even more surprising that this explanation, without which we can barely imagine our world, is not even 160 years old. Darwin didn't publish *On the Origin of Species* until November 1859. Until then, scientists had largely accepted the dogma that species didn't change because God had arranged it that way. Darwin's magnum opus pulled the rug out from beneath everyone's feet.

You would think the man who had managed this feat would have to have been a rebel who did not care much about what others thought and enjoyed controversy. Nothing could be further from the truth. It is an irony of history—and of Darwin's own life—that these highly revolutionary ideas originated in a man who sought to avoid social disturbances of any kind. Darwin was a well-respected man from a distinguished family. He lived conservatively, loved consistency, and loathed excitement and big social events. He was very close to his deeply religious wife and knew that she would not respond well if he illustrated a mechanism of nature that operated without God. Biologists of his time likewise assumed the existence of a creator god—or at least pretended to do so. And, after all, it was already an era of discontent in Europe. Darwin did not want to make matters worse. In the face of radical political currents, Darwin and many of his contemporaries felt a need for stability and thus clung to conservative values. The Industrial Revolution had made many jobs obsolete and there was a mood of social unrest in the air. The elites of European society were skeptical of new ideas that might fuel this subversive atmosphere.

144 The complete title of the first edition is *On the Origin of Species by Means of Natural Selection, or the Preservation of Favoured Races in the Struggle for Life*. For the most part, this chapter makes reference to the 1859 edition, which can be accessed at http://www.gutenberg.org/files/1228/1228-h/1228-h.htm and as a variorum edition at http://darwin-online.org.uk/Variorum/index.html.

Darwin's theory of evolution was a real powder keg. Not only did it challenge traditional notions, but it overturned what people regarded as the natural order of things and humanity's role in the cosmos. This was all perfectly clear to Darwin. It quite literally gave him a severe case of indigestion. Around the time he was making his first notes on the mutability of species, he developed inexplicable bodily symptoms that would accompany him throughout his life. He felt unwell so often that he set up a special corner in his study where he could throw up. The thoughts that agitated him were inconsistent with his character and the way in which he wanted to present himself to the world. Darwin was a reluctant revolutionary. Those visiting the Darwins' home encountered a polite British gentleman who cultivated roses and bred pigeons. No one suspected that these hobbies had a deeper motivation: Darwin wasn't merely amusing himself; rather, he was seriously observing his flora and fauna, insistently pursuing the innermost mechanisms of nature.

Darwin had already outlined his theory in its basic form shortly after returning from his legendary journey on the surveying vessel HMS *Beagle*. He knew that species were mutable, that the Lord God had neither personally shaped every bird's beak, nor placed the animal it belonged to on a specific little spot of ground. Yet it was a long time before he finally came out with his ideas. The 20-year period that elapsed between him taking his first notes on evolution and the appearance of *On the Origin of Species* so bewildered many later researchers that it has gone down in history as "Darwin's Delay." If circumstances hadn't compelled Darwin to publish his theses, they might not have been published until after his death—perhaps hastily assembled from his notes. But the naturalist's hand was forced and his ideas moved from his study in rural Downe onto the world stage. As unpleasant as he found it at the time, this development ultimately suited him perfectly. You might just say that the struggles Darwin discerned in nature, that constant but creative grappling of opposing forces, were likewise taking place inside him.

A look behind the veil

In the fall of 1836, Darwin returned from his trip on the HMS *Beagle*. He immediately made his way to his family home, where everyone was still asleep. Without waking a soul, he went to bed. The next morning, after the others had sat down to breakfast, Darwin appeared, surprising his assembled relatives, who hadn't seen him for five years. After his father had recovered from the initial shock, he looked at his son and remarked: "Why, the shape of his head is quite altered."[145] That could scarcely have been the case, considering Darwin was already a fully grown 22-year-old man at the time of his departure. However, the words of his father were apt: Even if the shape of his son's head hadn't changed, something had most certainly transpired inside it. To Darwin, who had displayed a lack of interest in his classes at school—"Nothing could have been worse for the development of my mind,"[146] he later noted in his autobiography—the journey on the *Beagle* had been his first real intellectual challenge.

The research vessel had been sent by the British Navy to survey the South American coasts. Darwin went along as a companion to the young captain, Robert FitzRoy, but his presence also gave the trip a bit more prestige: A naturalist on board made for good optics. Although he suffered seasickness throughout the voyage, Darwin was ecstatic. The exotic, colorful flora and fauna that he saw cast him into a "delirium of delight."[147] Yet this "delirium" did not prevent him from observing what he saw attentively, nor did it stop his mind from working at full

145 David Quammen, *The Reluctant Mr. Darwin: An Intimate Portrait of Charles Darwin and the Making of His Theory of Evolution*, Great Discoveries Series (New York: W. W. Norton, 2007), 22.
146 Charles Darwin, *The Autobiography of Charles Darwin, From the Life and Letters of Charles Darwin*, ed. his son Francis Darwin. http://www.gutenberg.org/files/2010/2010-h/2010-h.htm.
147 Heike Le Ker, "Darwins Selektionstheorie: Der zaudernde Evoluzzer," *Der Spiegel*. http://www.spiegel.de/wissenschaft/mensch/darwins-selektionstheorie-der-zaudernde-evoluzzer-a-601504.html.

speed. He made observations, collected samples, and dissected captured animals. He wondered why there were marsupials only in Australia and nowhere else. What about the useless stub wings of certain bird species that could not fly? And why did he find a layer of hard white rock formed from crushed coral and seashells in a horizontal band on the face of a cliff on the island of Santiago, 13 meters above sea level? This rock face must have been underwater at some point in time. Could this be evidence that the Earth was not static, but in motion?

In 1835, Darwin landed on the Galapagos Islands in the Pacific Ocean after more than three and a half years of travel. This isolated group of volcanic islands is situated about 600 miles from the mainland. At first glance, the place did not seem particularly inviting. "The dry and parched surface, being heated by the noon-day sun, gave to the air a close and sultry feeling, like that from a stove: we fancied even that the bushes smelt unpleasant,"[148] he asserted. Although he suffered greatly from the heat, Darwin enthusiastically gathered what he had discovered over five weeks, from birds and insects to iguanas, and packed them all into his collection on the *Beagle*. As he hiked across the Galapagos, he had fun with the giant tortoises, trying to ride on their backs, although he usually quickly fell off. The islanders made him aware that the shape of a turtle's carapace revealed which island it had come from. However, it was not only the turtles that were special. There was also something odd about the birds hopping and flying around him. Why, he mused, did the mockingbirds he had found on San Cristóbal Island look different to those on the neighboring island of Floreana? The former had dark feathers on their breasts, white bands on their wings, and longer beaks. Darwin started playing with the idea that the different species could have evolved from common ancestors. Perhaps this happened without the Creator's guidance and was ultimately unplanned. "If there is the slightest foundation for these remarks, the zoology of archipelagoes will

148 Charles Darwin, *A Naturalist's Voyage Round the World: The Voyage of the Beagle*, 399. http://www.gutenberg.org/files/3704/3704-h/3704-h.htm.

be well worth examining; for such facts would undermine the stability of species,"[149] Darwin noted.

Nowadays, it is hard to appreciate just how outrageous this statement was. In Darwin's time, biology was not a secular discipline. Many serious observers of nature were clerics who were searching for and finding traces of the Creator in the natural world. British researchers and philosophers of that period argued that God had singlehandedly created the world, down to its last detail, and located each species on a particular patch of the Earth. Why precisely in that location was something only God knew, for "[s]cience *was* in a certain sense religion."[150] The general term for this view was "natural theology" and William Paley was the author of the standard work on natural theology. In *Natural Theology*, Paley presents an idea that is still well known today—the idea of a god as a "watchmaker." There was a simple logic behind this. Paley asserted that every "design must have had a designer. That designer must have been a person. That person is GOD."[151] A designer created works that were complete; they did not have to evolve. The progeny of cats, chickens, or flowers might have differed somewhat from their parents, but there would never been any fundamental changes. "Species have a real existence in nature, and a transition from one to the other does not exist," British philosopher and historian of science William Whewell had insisted in the 1830s.[152] By doubting the immutability of the species, Darwin was challenging not only God, but also the foundations of contemporary science.

---

149 Darwin Correspondence Project, *The Correspondence of Charles Darwin, Volume 1: 1821–1836.* http://www.darwinproject.ac.uk/correspondence-volume-1.

150 Eve-Marie Engels, *Charles Darwin* (Munich: C.H. Beck, 2007), 54.

151 Ibid., 54. Incidentally, this notion has many supporters even today; the principle is also called "intelligent design."

152 William Whewell, *History of the Inductive Sciences: From the Earliest Times to the Present*, vol. 3, 1837, quoted in David L. Hull, *Darwin and His Critics: The Reception of Darwin's Theory of Evolution by the Scientific Community* (Cambridge, MA: Harvard University Press, 1973), 68.

When he arrived back in England, Darwin had in his possession 1,529 animals conserved in alcohol, 3,907 skins, bones, and dried specimens, as well as notebooks filled with 2,000 pages of geological and zoological observations. Now he would have to see what he could learn from all of those bones, beaks, and claws. He was only able to work his way through this collection slowly and with the help of other scientists. He discussed birds that he had brought from the Galapagos with the ornithologist John Gould. The distribution of various kinds of mockingbirds across the islands wasn't the only notable discovery; the distribution of the finches was equally interesting. Without realizing it, Darwin had returned with fourteen distinct but closely related species of finch. Like the mockingbirds, the finches differed externally, particularly their beaks. It must have occurred to Darwin how absurd it would have been to explain this using natural theology. Why would God have distributed closely related species of birds on neighboring islands? Why bother changing a bird's beak dozens of times? For Darwin, this seemed to fly in the face of all common sense. He began to suspect that there was a connection between the animals' habitats and the physical forms of their species. Could the birds have adapted to the feeding conditions of their respective islands? If so, certain birds would have short beaks for cracking open fruits and others would have longer beaks for finding larvae in the bark of dead branches.

As Darwin examined his *Beagle* souvenirs, or had them identified by researchers, he became increasingly convinced that the distribution of species across the planet was not arbitrary. There was a logic to it, deriving from the interaction between geography and living things (or "organic beings," as Darwin preferred to call them). Closely related creatures had spread out across habitats that varied widely in the living conditions they afforded, but were quite close geographically. These included the mockingbirds and finches of the Galapagos, the zebra species in Africa, and the (extinct) giant sloths that Darwin had excavated in South America, where he had also observed smaller (non-extinct) species of sloth. However, it was also possible to find very different species in similar habitats, if these habitats were located far apart from one another. In the European wetlands, for example, there were muskrats and beavers, whereas, in the wetlands of South America, there were capybaras and nutrias. In Australia, and nowhere else, there were marsupials. "It was evident," Darwin noted decades later, "that such facts as these, as well as many others, could only be explained on the supposition that species gradually become modified; and the subject haunted me."[153]

Although Darwin was an extremely precise, even pedantic observer, this alone does not explain his discovery. Others had been confronted with the same exact facts and had not drawn the same conclusions. There was one crucial difference in the way Darwin observed things: His thinking was dynamic; he saw movement everywhere. To him, it was obvious that nature was highly variable. This diversity simply did not accord with the rigid tenets of natural theology—and it wouldn't accord with them unless it were forced to do so.

Rather than trying to reconcile his ideas with natural theology, Darwin allowed his thinking to be dynamic, like the nature he was observing. Thus, he could explore that which was behind the movements he witnessed in nature. Most of his contemporaries, however, were dependent on static thinking. Nature was a fixed matter for them and there was not much leeway for any kind of movement. This is not surprising considering their thinking derived from a rigid belief system. The God who had created their world was eternal and unchangeable. Accordingly, His creation had always been the same. This way of thinking did not allow for the dynamic connections that Darwin saw between species and their environment. Everything had its place, in which it remained. There were no interconnections or interactions, just facts that could, at best, be observed and described. If the skeletons of giant sloths were discovered, then these had indeed existed at one time, but they no longer existed now. The smaller sloths

153 Darwin, *Autobiography*.

alive today were not a sign that the species had evolved. If you bred pigeons and each generation looked a little different, this was not a sign of development; rather, it merely indicated a slight deviation from their actual, unchanging form.

The difference between Darwin's point of view and that of his contemporaries is akin to the difference between a visually stunning nature documentary and a shaky two-dimensional still. Darwin's colleagues were confronted with nature that was vibrant, colorful, and pulsating, yet they only perceived a tiny fraction of the movement that was actually occurring in it. The reason was simple: Ordinary thinking does not like changes, so it ignores them. Its range of movement is therefore highly constrained. It can generate minor theories and ideas, but never thoughts that question everything that went before. When inquiring into the causes of phenomena, it always stops at the point beyond which an established precept might get subverted.

Darwin, by contrast, could not ignore the fact that plants and animals varied greatly within the same species. Rather, he was able to see that these changes had to be of *central* significance in nature. The more material he collected, the more evident it was to him that nothing in nature was fixed for all eternity. Once one had accepted that species could evolve, then "the veil had been lifted," as Darwin wrote in his "Notebook C." The "veil" was the traditional notion that life on earth was unchanging, which derived from the biblical story of Genesis, in which all species were constructed in their final form in a singular act of creation.

The formula of nature

At the beginning of October 1846, a single container remained unpacked among the thousands of treasures that Darwin had brought back from his journey on the *Beagle.* Preserved inside this container were barnacles. These peculiar animals live in water and attach themselves to rocks, whales, and ships. Darwin had gathered these particular barnacles off the coast of Chile. When he finally unpacked them, he merely intended on writing an essay about them. Instead, he spent the next eight years at his desk, studying the alcohol-conserved barnacles. He observed them under the microscope; some specimens weren't much larger than a pinhead. He was struck by how difficult it was to categorize these creatures, which sometimes resembled mussels and sometimes resembled snails. These little animals were extremely diverse, both within their genus and their species. As for their sexual features, some barnacles were androgynes, others had a clear gender, and the rest were somewhere in between. Darwin repeatedly wondered where one subspecies ended and another one began. Astonished by what he had found, he grasped that nature was infinitely more variable than he had supposed. Until then, Darwin had believed that variations in wild species would be much rarer than variations in domestic animals. The barnacles showed him that the opposite was true.

It was this variability that caused him such difficulty in his attempts to systematically classify these animals. Until then, no one had been able to classify them satisfactorily; however, Darwin wanted to change that. At the same time, he was critical of the existing systems that biologists used to group living organisms. It troubled him that, even though their systems were understandable, no one questioned what their classifications of nature were actually trying to accomplish. Some were categorizing animals according to their external characteristics, others according to their internal structure. In Darwin's view, this was inadequate. Dynamic thinking seeks out not simple facts, but rather processes—and the foundations of those processes. Darwin wanted to know not only *what* it was that linked animals within a species, but also *why* they were linked in that way. However, the question of *why* was not being posed by the other taxonomists, for they were thinking statically under the assumption that the ultimate answer was already clear—as always, that answer was: God's will. Thus, they were not trying to find the causes of links between species, but merely, as Darwin lamented, "to discover the laws according to which the Creator has willed to produce organized beings."[154] To him, these were nothing but "empty, high-sounding sentences."[155]

Darwin clearly had his own ideas about how to classify species. His journey on the *Beagle* had taught him that connections between species could be observed almost everywhere. Other researchers had also found clues. For instance, the naturalist Richard Owen had highlighted the similarities between the skeletons of reptiles and birds. However, he had not realized what Darwin began to see with mounting delight: that nature makes use of certain blueprints over and over and that there had to be a deeper reason why it did so. Unlike most of his colleagues, Darwin had already accepted that evolution was a fact. Where there was development, there had to be an origin as well. It was precisely this origin that Darwin anticipated whenever he discerned the similarities between the blueprints. "We see in these facts some deep organic bond, prevailing throughout space and time,"[156] he claimed.

Almost a decade before he began studying the barnacles, he had scrawled a picture in his "Notebook B" under the heading "I think": a structure that looked like a leafless tree. At the end of each branch, he wrote a letter that stood for a particular species. The result was a picture according to which every animal and every plant, every frog, bee, and shrub, stemmed *from a single, originary root.* From this common source, the endless variety of forms found in nature developed. Classifying species was not just about describing their external or internal features, but also about uncovering their shared origins. Embryology proved quite helpful in this regard. Darwin believed that "the embryo comes to be left as a sort of picture, preserved by nature, of the ancient and less modified condition of each species."[157] In their early stages of development, the

154 Quammen, *The Reluctant Mr. Darwin*, 103.

155 Ibid.

156 Ibid., 193.

157 Charles Darwin, *The Origin of Species by means of natural selection or the preservation of favored races in the struggle for life*, vol. 2 [1859]. https://oll.libertyfund.org/titles/darwin-the-origin-of-species-vol-2.

feet of lizards and mammals, birds and humans all correspond to the same basic form. Adult moths and flies look very different, but as larvae they are remarkably similar. Barnacle larvae, in turn, are very similar to the larvae of brine shrimp. Consequently, Darwin classified the barnacle as a subclass of crustaceans. His systematization of the animal world went much deeper than that of his colleagues. The reason for this was simple: The others had constructed systems for reproducing static facts whereas Darwin had pursued a principle of movement.

After working on barnacles, Darwin began to breed pigeons. Some people may have been surprised as this activity was not deemed appropriate for a man of his social class. Undeterred, Darwin joined two pigeon clubs and interbred the birds until his home turned into a veritable dovecote. He had a plan. The causal link that he saw in nature was simple and elegant: Organic beings that reproduced almost always varied in their characteristics. These variations could be inherited, as a result of which species gradually changed. Darwin therefore knew *what* was taking place in evolution, but he lacked evidence of *how* it occurred. But his idea of the *how* had already emerged in his feverish younger years, as had the rest of his theory. Back then, Darwin had been wondering about why species changed. He was vaguely aware that there had to be some sort of selection for certain traits (and not others) to be inherited. However, he did not yet understand how this selection worked. As he was mulling it over, he chanced upon *An Essay on the Principle of Population* by British economist and social philosopher Thomas Robert Malthus. In this essay, Malthus describes how population is always growing faster than the food available for it, which inevitably leads to hunger, illness, and competition. The essay got Darwin thinking. Until then, he had believed that a population would only expand insofar as it could provide for itself from existing resources. Now he came to believe that Malthus had unwittingly described a deeper principle of nature that affected not just humans, but *everything.* Based on his own observations, Darwin knew that animals produce more offspring than the environment can continuously feed, a circumstance that limits their ability to reproduce themselves. Hence, there had to be a regulatory mechanism for preventing a single species from inundating the world, a natural selection for deciding which offspring would survive. After having read Malthus, he connected the dots: Nature, through its limited food supplies, its predators, and its changing ecology, could exercise relentless pressure on living beings—pressure to adapt to the environment. Evolution occurred because those living things that could best adapt to the natural conditions survived and reproduced. This natural selection was the engine of evolution. And the evidence for this? Domesticated plants and animals such as pigeons. The breeder selects the animals most suited to breeding and makes sure that they reproduce. Through this artificial selection, he or she can deliberately reinforce specific characteristics. In the wild, nature takes on the role of breeder and selects the best specimens—for instance, animals that have the least trouble finding food or that predators have the most trouble spotting. Thus, it is evident that Darwin did not breed carrier pigeons, runt pigeons, and turbits merely as an unusual form of recreation. Rather, he set out to understand the law he had discovered and to support his thesis. His goal was to establish that nature had its own inherent developmental logic that would make a divine designer superfluous.

Here, too, Darwin's dynamic mode of thinking is evident. While others still had a romantic-religious idea of nature, in which birds sang and flowers bloomed in praise of their Creator, Darwin regarded the most beautiful flower as a form with a purpose. Species were developing in a coevolutionary dynamic: If a flower had a certain shape, there had to be an animal in nature whose body was built to match that exact shape. The entire range of nature resulted from a natural process that had generated variety out of a few forms by means of pressure and friction. "The face of Nature may be compared to a yielding surface, with ten thousand sharp wedges packed close together and driven inwards by incessant blows," Darwin commented.[158] Nature wasn't "peaceful." It was a bubbling cauldron, endlessly cooking up variations.

Nothing ever stays the same

Now we have a question for you. Please respond as honestly as you can. (Don't worry—we won't tell anyone how you respond.) *Do you love change*?

If you answered "no," you aren't alone. If truth be told, most people can't stand change. Unless their lives are utterly unbearable, the status quo is always more attractive than having things change in unpredictable ways.

In case you answered "yes," either you are one of those rare people who are remarkably flexible, courageous, and adaptable or you aren't being completely honest with yourself, which would be understandable. After all, we live in a time when we are expected to show the greatest possible flexibility—be it in our relationships ("Honey, I'd like to try out an alternative to monogamy"), in our communications ("I'm just about to operate, but I can answer a few e-mails quickly"), or in our jobs ("Could you relocate to Cape Town next week?"). We hardly dare to admit that we like our everyday lives to be stable.

But this desire is utterly human. In fact, it's so deep-seated that many would prefer to stay in an unpleasant job or relationship rather than changing something in their lives. Even in life-threatening situations, people resist change, even though they realize that doing so will have negative consequences. Studies have revealed that most patients who have survived complicated heart surgery do not change their lifestyles, despite being told that they will die if they do not. In business, too, this

158 R.C. Stauffer (ed.), *Charles Darwin's Natural Selection: Being the Second Part of His Big Species Book Written from 1856 to 1858*. http://darwin-online.org.uk/content/frameset?itemID=F1583&viewtype=text&pageseq=1.

problem is familiar. One of the greatest difficulties executives face is that employees resist new initiatives and methods—even if these would improve their day-to-day experience of their jobs.

One reason for this is our biological programming. Our system always strives to remain in or return to a state of equilibrium. This principle, called *homeostasis*, applies to our body chemistry, but also to our psyches. Just as the human body works to keep calcium and blood sugar levels stable, the brain strives to maintain a "normal" mental state. The brain likes structures and regular processes and sticks to them with great persistence. When there are changes, particularly sudden changes, it responds by resisting them. Although the brain can adapt to new conditions (it is actually very good at it), it prefers the status quo.

This points to a fundamental misunderstanding. Homeostasis is utterly vital for the body. Within a very limited range, the body can tolerate fluctuations, but beyond this range, alarms go off. For instance, if you have a fever, your temperature only needs to rise a few degrees to become dangerous. Thus, it makes sense that the body resists change. Psychologically, however, things are quite different: Clinging to the status quo often results in resistance to change and development. We would benefit from being a lot more flexible; if we focus too much on homeostasis, we're likely to stagnate mentally.

The mistake of static thinking is that it assumes that movement in life is the exception and calm is the normal state. It always follows the urge to remain in equilibrium or to return to that state. As a result, we're both slow and reluctant to change and most people are constantly searching for something that will never change. That "something" could be God, but it could also be an exclusive relationship or a certain ideology. Thus, you don't have to be a theologian or a believer to have this pattern of thinking—it's a typically human mental tendency. Static thinking tends to see developments as exceptions and fixed structures as a desired state. Changes are threatening because the outcome is always open. It is no coincidence that one of the most serious accusations people can make in a relationship is: "You've changed."

On closer inspection, this accusation is absurd because it is clear that nothing in life stays the same. On the contrary, life *is* movement and development, as Darwin recognized. Life *is* constant change. As the American writer Alison Bonds Shapiro recalls in her blog on *Psychology Today*: "Like many people, in an effort to maintain homeostasis, I wanted to think of my life as more or less unchanging or changing very slowly, as something that was permanent. Having a stroke taught me the truth about the illusion of permanence in a hurry. Ignoring the presence of change may give us a temporary sense of stability, but it is an illusion." According to Shapiro, even our physical bodies are regularly undergoing change: "Our bodies are constantly shifting, growing, shrinking, developing new set points for homeostasis, accommodating new information. Whether we look or not, this process is happening in every moment."[159]

So at this moment, as you read this book, countless dynamic processes are happening in and around you that you are not even noticing. We might not change as fast as barnacles, but we are clearly not static beings. For living organisms, there is no such thing as a motionless state. Just think about a typical hospital scene in a TV series: A patient is dying and the EKG tracking the patient's heartbeat suddenly becomes a flat line. It is not a coincidence that EKG monitors are such a ubiquitous dramatic symbol in film and television; we all know that moving and being alive are really one and the same.

The pursuit of mental and psychological balance is important. However, a basic misunderstanding holds that a balanced state of mind is possible only in peaceful circumstances. The fast-paced world in which we live and the unsettling news with which we are inundated daily strengthen this belief. A typical response to this is to minimize

159 Alison Bonds Shapiro, "Getting out of the way. The Balance between Homeostasis and Growth," *Psychology Today*. https://www.psychologytoday.com/intl/blog/healing-possibility/201103/getting-out-the-way-the-balance-between-homeostasis-and-growth.

changes in our lives by organizing everything to exclude any and all fluctuations. Yet, doing so has two major drawbacks. First, it means you also minimize the possibility of your own development, because new circumstances lead to growth. Second, you lose the ability to respond adequately to changes that cannot be avoided, which can be fatal in a crisis.

If you wish to switch from a static to a dynamic way of thinking, you first need to abandon the notion that anything in life is permanent. You must realize that even the most peaceful moment in your life was full of movement. You were breathing. Your body was working silently, but intensively, in countless places all at the same time. And the world around you was like a whirlwind—even if you were sitting in a peaceful meadow in the mountains. You would have been better able to appreciate this if you had been looking at the meadow from the vantage point of an ant. The peace in that moment was not the result of you and the entire world standing still; rather, nothing was happening in that moment that excited or upset you.

In other words, we feel peaceful when we think of our surroundings as being in well-balanced harmony. The trick is to stop associating harmony with immobility. From a psychological perspective, harmony is simply the absence of resistance. Once you realize that life was never meant to stand still, that you yourself are not a static being but an organism that is designed to change, you no longer have to waste your time resisting such change. Evolution never stops moving. By accepting that fact, you're giving yourself the opportunity to experience a different peace—one that is much more stable than a peace that depends on nothing happening.

What humans and bananas have in common

Nowadays, everyone knows Darwin's name. Many think that he more or less invented evolution. That's not correct: Ideas about the development of species go all the way back to the ancient Greeks. The most famous evolutionary theorist before Darwin was Jean-Baptiste de Lamarck, whose work influenced Darwin; however, Lamarck's theories weren't widely accepted. Darwin was different to his predecessors in that he provided a compelling rational explanation of how evolution *had to* occur and included extremely plausible evidence. He could both describe evolution and explain its impetus—or at least a very important impetus for it. He himself recognized how important the principle of natural selection was for ideas. It became the pulsating heart of his theory, the principle that would lead to the overturning of all previous teachings about evolution.

When, in 1859, Darwin finally published *On the Origin of Species*—which, at 500 pages, he still deemed too short—he characterized the entire treatise as "a long argument" for the theory of natural selection. However, this was not something the world wished to hear. Decades later (and even now, to an extent), the world pushed back against this part of Darwin's work, despite having (for better or worse) already accepted evolution as a fact. People had their limits. It was bad enough that human beings, like all other creatures, should have evolved from other forms, that *homo sapiens* wasn't specially fashioned at the wheel of a divine potter, but instead had monkeys for grandparents (in a manner of speaking). As a young man, when sketching out ideas in his private notebooks, Darwin had initially tried to keep human beings separate, but he quickly jettisoned his concerns about including them. Humanity, he proclaimed courageously, was no exception to the process of evolution. His contemporaries were able to accept this part of his theory of evolution, even though many were offended. The wife of an English bishop, after hearing about it, is alleged to have cried in horror: "Let us hope that it isn't true. But if it is true, let us pray that this will not become widely known."

However, the idea of natural selection seemed to many, as Darwin's biographer David Quammen puts it, "profoundly materialistic and gloomy … both literally and figuratively dispiriting."[160] The theory of evolution itself was gracious enough to leave a certain amount of leeway for God. It remained possible for people to imagine that a divine creator had set the entire process in motion. In that event, human beings still had a special role to play, because at some point God might have personally arranged for them to emerge, with the mental faculties that set them apart from the rest of the animal kingdom. But if one were to accept Darwinian natural selection, then even this last bastion of human superiority would be lost. The implication was that humans and animals were, in principle, the same—evolutionary material that, owing to random circumstances, had been formed at times into spiders and at other times into bananas, wolves, or humans. Despite the limited appeal of his thesis for his contemporaries, Darwin was unreservedly committed to it. Ironically, although his book was titled *On the Origin of Species*, it did not provide any explanation for the earliest origins of life—for its "emergence." Instead, it described "only" the evolutionary logic of its variety of forms. Still, with respect to this evolution, Darwin was certain that it was not guided by any god-like figure. He even went one step further, suggesting that the idea of a god could itself be a product of evolution—an idea that had developed among humans as an instinct that served as a reference point for moral decisions.

Darwin's materialism was uncompromising. It even went too far for the person with whom he had developed a theory of natural selection. The biologist Alfred Russel Wallace had recognized the connection between geological changes of the Earth, the geographical diffusion of animals, the transformation of species, and, like Darwin, the principle of selection. It was because of him that Darwin had to go public with his theories in the first place: The elder scientist was worried that the younger scientist was about to preempt him. However, 10 years after *On the Origin of Species* was first published, Wallace backed down, publishing an essay in which he claimed that natural selection could not be the reason why the human brain had developed. He wrote of a

160 Quammen, *The Reluctant Mr. Darwin*, 206.

"higher intelligence" that must have shaped this particular apparatus. Darwin was disappointed, though not necessarily because he objected to the idea of divinity in and of itself, for Darwin's theory of evolution does not oppose the *existence* of a god, "any god, personal or abstract, immanent or distant. … What it challenges is the supposed godliness of Man—the conviction that *we*, above all other life forms, are spiritually elevated, divinely favored, possessed of an immaterial and immortal essence, such that we have special prospects for eternity, special status in the expectations of God, special rights and responsibilities on Earth. That's where Darwin runs afoul of Christianity, Judaism, Islam, and probably most other religions on the planet."[161]

This is the ultimate consequence of Darwin's dynamic thinking. Not only did he include humanity in the process; he also acknowledged that it was anything but complete. He grasped something we still struggle with today: We are neither the "pinnacle of creation," nor in any other sense a finished product. Most likely, none of us will experience evolution in real time in our own lives. Yet it continues to occur, including for humans, and nobody knows what its outcome will be—or whether it will ever end. If you could ask Darwin today, he would presumably say that it will never come to an end. His view of the world did not require starting or end points—the most important aspect was the process—nor did it require an outside being to guide the process, because there wasn't anything outside the process. Everything was part of nature: life, death, evolution, curiosity, intelligence, and good and evil. While others regarded his theses as cold, inhuman, even cruel, Darwin regarded a godless nature as profoundly awe-inspiring. In the conclusion to *On the Origin of Species*, he wrote: "There is grandeur in this view of life, with its several powers, having been originally breathed by the Creator into a few forms or into one; and that, whilst this planet has gone cycling on according to the fixed law of gravity, from so simple a beginning endless forms most beautiful and most wonderful have

161 Ibid., 210.

been, and are being, evolved."[162]

Darwin knew that anyone who thought that 3 billion years of evolution—a process that had produced all living forms—was less impressive than seven days of biblical creation had failed to understand the magnitude of his theory.

If you want to test dynamic thinking, go ahead and try a new way of working. Static thinking is always based on fixed points. Thus, when it comes to tasks, it is always goal-oriented. It works toward the point at which a project is completed and you can finally relax—the supposed "state of normalcy." This approach doesn't work, because there are always more tasks to be completed. This way of thinking also has another weakness: Many people are overwhelmed by their tasks, particularly in larger projects. The goal appears enormous—and therefore unattainable.

Dynamic thinkers, on the other hand, work in a process-oriented manner. They know that movement, not peace, is the normal state of things and can therefore relax much better during the process. Instead of setting the final goal, they simply focus on the next step. In this way, dynamic thinkers are almost certainly more efficient because they can better respond to each stage of their task, instead of getting irritated by how far they are from the goal. So go ahead and tackle a task in a process-oriented way, instead of a goal-oriented way. It will change your experience of work significantly.

162 Darwin, *The Origin of Species*.

CHAPTER 9

JIDDU KRISHNAMURTI

Negating thinking, *or* A vessel with many holes

In 1908, Jiddu Narianiah, a South Indian minor civil servant, was due to retire from his lifelong government service. However, he came to realize that with his meagre pension, it would be impossible to maintain his large family. He had been a member of the Theosophical Society for over 26 years, so he turned now to its bright, charismatic president, Annie Besant, and requested a job. After some convincing, Besant consented and offered him the role of assistant secretary in the esoteric section of the society's headquarters in Adyar. Narianiah bought a tiny house outside the Adyar compound and transferred his family from their home in the village of Mandanapalle. It was in the unusual atmosphere of the Theosophical Society—an organization dedicated to the exploration of the hidden mysteries of nature and the latent powers of man—that an extraordinary drama would unfold.

Based on the prophecy of the nineteenth-century founder of the Theosophical Society, Helena Blavatsky, Annie Besant was convinced that the coming of the "World Teacher," the next Messiah, was imminent. She sought psychic help and became close to clairvoyant Charles Webster Leadbeater, whom she helped advance through hierarchy of the Theosophical Society. Determined to locate the great teacher, Leadbeater one day stumbled upon Narianiah's two sons, who were bathing in the sea at the Adyar beach. Surprisingly, his clairvoyant gaze was drawn not to the brilliant and awake Nityananda, but rather to the peculiar older brother, the 14-year-old Krishnamurti. Krishnamurti, he noticed, seemed vacant and had a unique selfless "aura." Intrigued, Leadbeater spent days observing the boy, who was vague, said little, lacked interest in worldly affairs, and had eyes that gazed out at the world, seeing beyond horizons. It was these same traits that had worried his schoolteacher, who had suspected that he might be intellectually disabled.

The eccentric British mystic recognized the thin and ill-nourished boy as a great being and later as the "vehicle" for the advent of the bodhisattva Maitreya. Leadbeater was told by invisible Masters that if the boy's body was correctly prepared, Maitreya would "enter" his mind and take over. Leadbeater took the two boys under his wing, gradually weaning them off from their father's influence. Krishnamurti and Nityananda were taken from the confines of their tiny house and moved into the grand Theosophical Society headquarters. They were introduced to a world of luminous Masters and initiates, past lives and splendid incarnations. Thought forms and visual images circulating in the atmosphere of Adyar were made manifest to the young neophyte Krishnamurti. At the same time, the boys were thoroughly stripped of all Indianness and turned into perfect British gentlemen. They were only allowed to speak in English, they learned how to eat with a spoon and fork, and they wore Western clothes.

The boy Krishnamurti was given everything he wanted, from orange juice to a Rolls Royce. Nobody was allowed to sit on his seat or touch his tennis racket. He was not allowed to drink alcohol or eat meat or meet people who were coarse or unrefined. A special group of boys was selected to play with him. Many years later, the adult Krishnamurti wondered how, under these special conditions, indoctrinated with the esoteric teachings of the Theosophical Society, he had, as a boy, remained unaffected and vague. It was as if he had been born without a formal character or personality. Though visibly obedient and unresisting, he didn't seem to care what was happening around him. He was like a vessel with a large hole in it; whatever was put into it spilt out, leaving nothing behind. This capacity played an important role in his later ability to effectively shake off the Theosophical conditioning to which he had been subjected.

Eventually, the boys were torn away from their family and homeland and moved to Europe. There, they felt lonely and deserted. They seemed to have lost interest in the Theosophical teachings and when asked about the heavy burden of being considered an incarnation of a deity, the adolescent Krishnamurti ridiculed the whole thing. The first significant crack in his impeccable obedience appeared in 1922, when he was 27. After an intense spiritual awakening that was both mystically illuminating and physically agonizing, Krishnamurti was left with the awareness that he was no longer a seeker of truth, but at one with the truth. He joyously developed his own language of inner freedom that clearly departed from Theosophical terminology. A second crack soon appeared. News reached Krishnamurti that Besant and other members of the society had declared themselves the twelve apostles of the "World Teacher." A new world religion must be established, they announced, with Besant as its head. Mystical initiations, real or imaginary, led members to make self-aggrandizing proclamations. Krishnamurti responded to all this with bewilderment and distress.

The deepest rift was caused by Krishnamurti's young brother's severe illness and death. Still faithful to the invisible Masters of the society, Krishnamurti had been assured by "them" that no harm could come to Nityananda. His brother's untimely death brought an end to the future the two brothers had excitedly been envisaging together and shattered Krishnamurti's entire philosophy of life. His explosive sorrow brought him face to face with the actual. He abandoned all references to the Masters and freed himself of the visual imagery of the Theosophists, declaring that all images were projections of the mind. He felt that a new vision had been revealed to him: a vast, wordless perception triggered by the intensity of sorrow.

This inner transformation manifested in his speeches. Facing a gathering of thousands, instead of communicating the orthodox Theosophical teaching, he expressed a feeling of oneness with the universe. He shocked and bewildered Besant and other members when he rejected the role of teacher and promoted a state of constant inner revolution in his listeners. It was clear that neither his formative years spent in the Theosophical Society nor the time he spent among British aristocracy had molded his thinking. His mind had been watching and listening and now, after a long gestation, there had been a volcanic eruption of energy. He demanded that others question as he had questioned and break away from knowledge to perceive anew. He was in revolt and no authority satisfied him. "For all this life," he declared, "I have struggled to be free—free from my friends, my books, my associations. You must struggle for the same freedom. There must be constant turmoil within you."[163] He saw the truth not in symbols or images that condition the believer to see exactly what he or she expects to see. Truth was the open sky, the flower, life as a whole.

Yet these early speeches only prepared the ground for an unforeseeable finale, a dramatic twist in a plot that had been carefully designed over the course of 18 years, using significant resources and kindling great hopes. One can only imagine the religious thrill and intense faith that throbbed in the audience of 3,000 people that gathered to hear him at the 1928 summer camp in the eastern Netherlands. Despite the immense devotion of his audience, Krishnamurti emphasized the need to abandon all sources of authority, especially the "World Teacher." The news spread rapidly. On hearing what he had said, Annie Besant, who was, in many ways, not only his spiritual

163 Mary Lutyens, *Krishnamurti: The Years of Awakening* (New York: Farrar, Straus and Giroux, 1975), 248.

mentor but also his adoptive mother, fell seriously ill. A year later, standing in front of the Ommen camp, this time in Besant's presence, he finally announced his determination to dissolve the order of which he was the president. The talk he gave was a seminal expression of his position, which remained unchanged throughout his life. "A belief," he lucidly proclaimed, "is purely an individual matter, and you cannot and must not organize it. If you do, it becomes dead, crystallized … If an organization be created for this purpose, it becomes a crutch, a weakness, a bondage, and must cripple the individual and prevent him from growing."[164] He went on to say that he did not want followers, as his sole concern was to set man absolutely, unconditionally free.

Krishnamurti's total rejection of authority in relation to thinking became legendary, distinguishing him from all other gurus and religious figures. After the dissolution of his order, he came to be regarded as a secular philosopher, hostile to any religious belief. "My teaching," he wrote immediately after resigning from the society, "is neither occult nor mystic for I hold both as limitations placed on man in his search for truth."[165] The group of young people who had always gathered around him dispersed and the international media lost interest in the "World Teacher." For a long time, he led a life of anonymity, traveling his individual and determined journey alone. When he resumed his public teachings, there were no teachers or disciples. Instead, he spoke of "learning," a state of shared intense curiosity and freedom to explore. He wished to serve only as a mirror in which the listener could see him- or herself in an undistorted and unconditioned way.

Krishnamurti rejected the traditional position of the authority that confidently answers the confused and dependent disciple. The new mode of "learning" that he proposed proved challenging for most people. Most of those who heard him speak could not grasp the significance of his insistence on providing no formulas and exhorting

164 Pupul Jayakar, *J. Krishnamurti: A Biography* (New Delhi: Penguin Books, 1986), 78.
165 Ibid., 83.

questioners to engage in self-reflection, yet many were deeply impressed by his unique personality and the deep silence that pervaded his being. The renowned American writer Henry Miller wrote:

> Krishnamurti has renounced more than any man I can think of except Christ … Hailed in his youth as the coming Saviour, Krishnamurti renounced the role that was prepared for him, spurned all disciples, rejected all mentors and preceptors. He initiated no new faith or dogma, questioned everything, cultivated doubt (especially in moments of exaltation), and, by dint of heroic struggle and perseverance, freed himself of illusion and enchantment, of pride, vanity, and every subtle form of dominion over other.[166]

A mind without a yesterday

What was the nature of the deep inner revolution that resulted in this exceptional renunciation? An initial answer to this question can be found in one of Krishnamurti's earliest speeches from 1928:

> I have long been in revolt from all things, from the authority of others, from the instruction of others, from the knowledge of others; I would not accept anything as truth until I found the truth myself. I never opposed the ideas of others but I would not accept their authority, their theory of life. Until I was in that state of revolt, until I became dissatisfied with everything, with every creed, with every dogma and belief, I was not able to find the truth … For long I have searched for that goal, and during my search I have watched people trapped in their desires, as a fly is caught in the web of a spider. Ever since I was able to think I have watched people absorbed in their own thoughts,

166 "Henry Miller on Krishnamurti," JKrishnamurti-sussex, June 18, 2009. http://jkrishnamurti-sussex.info/henry-miller-on-krishnamurti-2/.

suffocated by the futility of life ... I saw people who had all the comforts of this world, and yet their lives were in confusion, because they were enslaved by these things. I saw people who loved greatly and yet were bound by their love, for they had not found the way to give love and yet be free. I saw people who were wise in knowledge; and yet they were bound by their very learning. I saw people who were steeped in religion and yet they were bound by their traditions and by their fear of the unknown. I saw the wise withdraw from the world into their own seclusion, and the ignorant caught up in their own labours. Watching people thus, I have seen that they build for themselves walls of prejudice, walls of belief, walls of credulous thought, walls of great fear against which they fight, trying to escape from the very walls they themselves have built. Watching all people, I have seen how useless is their struggle if they are not free from the very gods they worship, from the interpreters who would guide them ... Ever since I was young I have observed these things, and I have never allowed myself to be caught up in any of these confusions ... I was in revolt also against theosophists with all their jargon, their theories, their meetings, and their explanations of life. When I went to a meeting, the lecturers repeated the same ideas which did not satisfy me or make me happy ... I walked about the streets, watching the faces of people who perhaps watched me with even greater interest. I went to theatres; I saw how people amused themselves, trying to forget their unhappiness, thinking that they were solving their problems by drugging their hearts and minds with superficial excitement ... I saw people satisfied with the stagnation which is unproductive, uncreative—the bourgeois type which never struggles to be above the surface or falls below it and so feels its weight. I read books on philosophy, on religion, biographies of great people and yet they could not give me what I wanted ... By observation of one type and another I gathered experience

> vicariously. Within everyone there was a latent volcano of unhappiness and discontentment. I passed from one pleasure to another, from one amusement to another, in search of happiness and found it not.[167]

This exalted text reveals Krishnamurti's structure of thinking to us. In his search for truth, he quietly observes every possible pattern of human thinking and behavior and negates it completely. Krishnamurti's "negation" was dissatisfaction with any conditioned view of life, any repetition of an old and familiar pattern of thinking. One might expect that such all-encompassing negativity would lead to a severe form of nihilism; however, for Krishnamurti, this was actually a key to total freedom and a direct perception of life's mystery. In fact, inner freedom and direct perception were the outcomes of a consistent state of negating thinking. According to his own testimony, it was his inherent negating thinking that kept him unconditioned. It is not surprising that, as an eternal outsider, he found it impossible to assume a role of great authority and thereby lead others to neglect their capacity to freely negate everything and anything.

The human mind is shaped by conditioning. Collective beliefs or values, national tendencies, and religious symbols all mold the mind from birth onwards. The mind becomes conditioned to react automatically to concepts that it has learned to cherish. Language itself, with its associations and connotations, is a powerful conditioning force. The word "God," for example, which makes the believer tremble with emotion and enrages the atheist, is merely a product of language. However, we tend to forget that, assuming that the word has somehow always been there. Hindus condition their children to react emotionally to the word "Shiva," while a Christian mind will react strongly to the word "Jesus." If our parents and environment tell us, "You're a Jew," we are quick to identify ourselves as Jews, with all the associated history and

167 Maya Nayanar, "The Serach J Krishnamurti 1927," April 5, 2020. https://archive.org/details/thesearchjkrishnamurti1927_202004_229_R/page/n5/mode/2up.

tradition. Our conditioning is strengthened by imitation and repetition. An essential part of Krishnamurti's negation was the refusal to be shaped by any form of conditioning. He sought to free himself from anything that was man-made, anything that was not original, in order to cultivate, in his words, a mind like pure water, like a mountain stream that has never been touched by human mind or hand. The tool with which one can attain such a freedom from external design is negative thinking, thinking that never accumulates but only unburdens itself.

In the mid-1940s, Krishnamurti made friends with the American author and philosopher Aldous Huxley. The two met often, going for long walks during which Huxley did most of the talking and Krishnamurti mainly listened. Huxley, an intellectual giant, was perplexed. His formidable intellect found it difficult to comprehend the pliant strength of a mind born of perception untainted by knowledge. Huxley listened and learned to be silent when Krishnamurti spoke of perception unburdened by accumulation and memory. On one of their walks, Huxley told his Indian friend that he would give everything for a moment of direct perception of the truth, but his mind was incapable of such perception—it was too filled with knowledge.[168] More than a meeting between two thinkers, their dialogue illustrated the abyss that separates two forms of thinking: negating thinking and accumulating thinking.

According to negating thinking, no valuable perception of truth—deeply seeing into life's mysteries—can be achieved through the gradual accumulation of knowledge or experience. Any positive construction of knowledge represents a burden for the mind that seeks truth. The deepest truths of life can be unveiled only through negative thinking, which seeks to wipe out past knowledge or experience. True knowledge of life eludes knowledge-laden, memory-based, step-by-step thinking. Only the mind that negated everything and attained perfect lightness and emptiness was genuinely capable of exploring the mysteries of life.

---

168 Jayakar, *J. Krishnamurti*, 91.

Consistent negating thinking results in the cultivation of a mind that is completely untainted by knowledge. It rejects anything that man has thought, said, or done in the hope of attaining perfect happiness or perfect wisdom. Boldly, it leaves the familiar, brightly illuminated, and well-paved human pathways and sets out on its lone journey, unguided by any known map. In Krishnamurti's mind, tradition—cautiously following in the footsteps of others—constituted nothing more than the fear of making mistakes. Thus, he avoided the use of traditional words that evoked automatic reactions of reassuring familiarity in his listeners. He would also tell religious recluses that they were never really alone since they retained their gathered knowledge and meditations. "That is not being alone," he would tell them. To be alone meant to renounce the burden of conditioning. "To renounce your heredity, your tradition, the burden of your condition, that demands enormous enquiry."[169]

To experience what this state would be like, we can try this short thought experiment: Imagine for a moment that the entire planet is bereft of humans and that all human knowledge and thinking has never existed. There have been no packed libraries, no scientific inquiry, no philosophical probing, and no religious contemplation. Not a single book has been written; none of the great traditions of knowledge have ever been conceived. You are the first human to walk this Earth and your mind is the first mind to ponder life's mysteries. There is only you and the mystery of life, in unmediated, direct communication. You are the first to explore a totally uncharted territory. You cannot rely on any received answers, knowledge, or mental formulae. No one but you can come up with answers. Inhabit your mind anew, without leaning on anything from the past, since there is no past. You are opening up to the experience of a life that is completely unknown. Do you find this exciting or frightening?

Whereas accumulating thinking relies on the past as its storehouse of ready-made knowledge, negating thinking rejects anything that is memory-based. Its relationship with the past is uncompromising: Since

169 Ibid., 221.

life's mystery can only be perceived with fresh eyes, unburdened by knowledge and past experience, anything that is already known to us, even if it seems magnificently wise, eventually becomes a hindrance. When we watch the morning dew on glimmering grass, we sense that life, as well as being billions of years old, can simultaneously be forever fresh and young. Our minds must likewise be in a state of constant renewal to correspond with the aliveness and renewal of the world around us. Negating thinking is like purging. It vehemently destroys a thousand yesterdays to make room for new perception.

Negative thinking becomes leaner, lighter, and quicker with time, whereas accumulating thinking gets fatter, heavier, and more inflexible. Accumulating thinking leads to mental obesity. It continuously ingests information, concepts, memories, and experiences. Consequently, it may feel more reassuring and solid; however, this comes at the cost of it being obscure and dull. The newness of life becomes inaccessible and one's mind feels old and worn. Negating thinking abhors the crystallization and stagnation of the mind, which occurs when it becomes clouded by so many yesterdays and the habitual patterns it has formed. Negating thinking locates mental habits that stifle the mind, negates them, and leaps to newness.

According to Krishnamurti, he never experienced a sense of mental "storing up"—accumulating more knowledge and experience with every day that passed—or "pouring out," forever repeating his own accumulated knowledge. This was a striking feature of his mind. Even at the age of 85, his inner youth, brought about by negating thinking, was still palpable. His way of thinking simply would not permit the experience of mental fullness and the consequent unwillingness to examine everything anew. "As one grows older," he once told an aging friend, "as the mind gets more set and more mechanical, it is very important to break down every pattern of thought and feeling—to be aware of every movement of thought, to watch ceaselessly."[170] The

170 Ibid., 246.

accumulation of that which one had discovered led to the cessation of discovery; thus, one had to "die to experience" every day, in the same way that scientific thinking must set aside past experience to attain new insights.

The art of pure seeing

For the most part, geniuses tend to direct their genius toward certain discoveries. Krishnamurti's mind was wholly devoted to looking into the mind itself in order to discover a certain "truth." Was our thinking, as it was, capable of truly listening or exploring? Were our minds free enough, unconditioned enough, to realize anything directly, with the freshness of morning dew? People tend to concern themselves with that which they are learning and forget that the quality of the learner is no less important than the object of learning. For Krishnamurti, the cultivation of a new mind was the only genuinely philosophical and spiritual act. A revolution of human perception had to take place and the endless repetition of traditional knowledge could only hinder this revolution. Only the intense intelligent awareness of an uncompromising all-negating approach could radically renew the aging human mind. This was an austere teaching in that it totally negated even the subtlest of anchors, crutches, and rituals. Meditation, for example, was rejected as a form of mesmerism, since intelligence could never be brought about by repetition or conditioning of any kind. Intelligence was to be found in the way in which one listened and paid attention to everyday phenomena. It arose from a tremendous, total vision of the actual contents of ones' inner and outer realities.

Seeing and listening to the actual contents of one's reality, without the slightest distortion, is no easy task. As soon as one experienced one's inner stream of thoughts and feelings—with all its selfishness, jealousies, conflicts, fears, loneliness, and so on—one would escape to the ideal, an image of oneself as a selfless, loving, peaceful, and respectable person.

Krishnamurti believed that people perceived "what should be" rather than "what is." Thus, people's desire to match their self-image resulted in their psychological reality remaining unchanged and untransformed as this positive thinking led them to avoid the actuality of their loneliness and pain.

Morality, religion, and spirituality greatly contributed to the notion of an ideal self by putting saints and the righteous on a pedestal. However, they failed to penetrate the human condition and change it fundamentally. Despite all human achievements and knowledge, the inner reality remained as it had been. Krishnamurti's negating thinking vehemently rejected all self-ideals, claiming that ideals not only constituted clouded self-observation but, worse, had, for thousands of years, prevented man from changing fundamentally. By cultivating the self-improvement approach—slowly and gradually transitioning from being a selfish person to being a selfless person—we merely evaded the direct reality of selfishness.

We cannot put an end to our suffering as long as we refuse to look it in the eye. It is for this reason that Krishnamurti negated even the subtlest forms of escape, forcing us to confront only the actual content of the mind. Indulging in metaphysics, then, represented man's wish to turn his back on this inner reality. Thus, Krishnamurti would always refuse to discuss abstract subjects like God or eternity as he recognized that the mind was a whirlpool of lust, hatred, and jealousy. Over and over again, he would return his listeners to the harsh facts of everyday life: the emptiness of the heart that we try to fill with restless doing. A true religion, he once said, would not be possible until the mind understood its own workings. One needs to know the self as it is, not as one wishes it to be. Understanding what one is—ugly, wicked, evil—without distortion was, for Krishnamurti, the beginning of virtue.

The only way of exploring the reality of the mind was by negating all possible reactions: all opinions, judgments, and conclusions. When we are confronted with the reality of our jealousy, for example, we tend to justify or condemn it. For Krishnamurti, one had to attain a state of pure seeing, observing the jealousy without the slightest movement away from it. "Watch your mind, let not a thought escape, however ugly, however brutal. Watch without choosing, weighing, judging."[171] One must never substitute or alter the content of the mind. On the contrary, one should observe the mind as if in a clear mirror. If one could achieve this, one's inner reality would finally unfold, "blossom," and be released of its own accord.

This is most difficult when it comes to strong emotions like anger, hatred, or lust. We have been taught to fight such emotions; however, according to Krishnamurti, our resistance just feeds these emotions. His solution to the problem of repression was a surprising one. One had to experience these states without trying to change or to strengthen them. Thus, they could blossom and, eventually, come to an end. One had to allow oneself to feel without thinking—riding a feeling without seeking to change it or labeling it as "good" or "bad." When dealing with a woman who had suffered three miscarriages and was no longer able to have children, he did not console her. Rather, he encouraged her to bring her yearning to the surface: She should not look away from women with babies on the streets, she should not feel ashamed of the feelings that arose in her, and she should not to be intellectual about the matter. When she said that she had accepted her lot, he responded: "Acceptance, rationalization are escapes. They have no place. Listen to your loneliness, frustrations, comparisons. If you so listen, something happens: the ache of the denial of personal motherhood dies."[172]

The hasty reactions of our mechanical thinking prevent us from truly seeing. When we do not react, this pure seeing has the power to transform. This way of thinking was unusual. Krishnamurti strongly believed that one could not change through self-modification and correction, as offered by psychological analysis or spiritual practice.

171 Ibid., 11.
172 Ibid., 234.

For him, seeing was the one true action of transformation. However, man was prevented from achieving this totality of seeing by one great hindrance. This was what Krishnamurti called "psychological time."

According to him, there were two types of time: functional time (i.e. the time of the watch) and psychological time. The former was essential for the functioning of life, such as the growth process of a tree or the organization of meetings. However, buried deep in the vast recesses of our mind was another illusory experience of time that made it impossible for us to change. Psychological time does not allow us to see the reality of the present as it traps our thinking in time: Either we move forward toward the future or backward toward yesterday, trapped in either "I was" or "I will be." Our thinking is never in the "now," so change only ever exists in some undefined "tomorrow." What would happen if we could not conceive of a "tomorrow" when we would change and we were not burdened by a thousand yesterdays? For Krishnamurti, such a negation could enable us to realize that change is not gradual. If you see clearly and fully, you can transform at once. In fact, the word "gradual" did not exist in Krishnamurti's dictionary—action was always immediate.

Krishnamurti claimed that our whole attitude is based on evolution—becoming, growing, achieving, and ultimately reaching. This assumption was, in his opinion, radically false. Total self-abandonment in the moment was always possible. This required "insight." Insight was instantaneous, a total perception that allowed us to shed an illusion and undergo a radical transformation. Insight depended on the intensity of our listening. Listening in a profound manner has the power of a storm; it can wipe everything away and erase all that is false. A profound insight required no techniques, processes, or psychological preparation. Indeed, the question "How? How can I change?" was a sophisticated evasion of true seeing. For example, if one deeply saw that tradition is motivated by nothing more than the fear of making mistakes or that nationality is merely a form of conditioning, would one drop these illusions on the spot? Or would one say, "I see it, but how can I be free of it? I now need a whole process to drop it"? The moment I ask "How?", I am lost. But if I truly see, I can change instantly.

The most powerful means of negation and insight that Krishnamurti developed involved a new way of using questions. While most philosophers seek answers to life's greatest questions, Krishnamurti never used questions to attain some final and satisfying conclusion. Instead, he would pose a fundamental question—such as, "What is love?" or "What is death?" or "What is the meaning of life?"—and would not let go of the tension created by the question in the mind, thereby refusing to allow the mind the cathartic release of an answer. According to him, the question was meant to reveal the failure of our structure of thinking: the conditioning that surfaced as a result, the automatic reactions, the reality of everyday life, which our thinking was trying to escape. The question was more like a giant spotlight, illuminating the conditioned processes of our thinking. "When a question is normally put," Krishnamurti's biographer Pupul Jayakar writes, "it is like grains of sugar being dropped on the ground—the ants from all over come toward it. It is the same with the mind; when a question is put, movements, responses are awakened that gravitate toward the question." If asked "Do you believe in God?" most people would immediately answer "yes" or "no." When presented with any fundamental question, the trivial mind produces the easy answer, arising from what it has already experienced. Comparing our brains to computers programmed to hold information, Krishnamurti said: "Our brains are trained that way, they have been programmed for thousands of years, and that brain replies immediately to a question. If the brain is not programmed, it is watching, looking … Can one have a mind that is capable of not reacting immediately to a question? Can there be a delaying reaction, perhaps holding the question indefinitely?"[173]

173 Ibid., 422.

Since, for him, there were no answers to life's greatest questions, the true role of such questions was to reveal the state and quality of the questioning mind. They were meant to make the listener rely only on his or her own mental faculties. If we kept holding the question, just as a cup holds water, without reacting or trying to find an answer, the answer would come out of that very holding. Negating all possible answers would lead to total freedom from conditioned thinking and, thanks to this freedom, a door would open. One would arrive at an answer in the form of a direct perception.

In 1948, Krishnamurti's use of questions to negate the process of thought led him to devise his major instrument of exploration: a unique form of dialogue in which participants pursue a fundamental question from their initial conditioned reactions to the end of ordinary thinking and the attainment of a shared insight. Previously, Krishnamurti had used the more traditional question-and-answer format. The dialogue, it seemed, was the final manifestation of the crumbling of the teacher–student relationship.

At first, these dialogues were confused and dispersed. A question was put to Krishnamurti. His fluid mind took in the question and reflected it back at the questioner, challenging him or her and the group to seek an answer on the basis of a direct perception. He spoke slowly, often pausing, bending forward as if he were making each response for the first time. He seemed to listen to his own responses with the same openness and receptivity with which he had listened to the questioner. His unwillingness to provide an authoritative answer was challenging to his interlocutors, who had been conditioned to respond from memory and to seek solutions from a higher authority. "We attempted to approximate, to reach beyond the word with the only instruments of inquiry available—memory and thought," Jayakar writes, "But these were the very instruments that were being challenged."[174] For Krishnamurti, any reaction to a question precluded truly probing the

174 Ibid., 117.

question. He demanded that his interlocutors see into and penetrate the question itself. To pause, to ponder, was to awaken the listening mind, which was not based on thought.

In the dialogue, Krishnamurti would push, block, retreat, and advance until the thought process slowed down. Then, in an instant, the participants would experience a direct perception that illuminated the question and the answer. Participants observed the movement of the mind as it became entangled in thought and recognized its inability to provide a truly "new" answer. Recognizing this inability of the thinking process led to the shattering of limitations. Krishnamurti would persist with his relentless questioning, refusing to let the energy aroused by the question dissipate in any reflexive response. When the dialogue became bogged down or the group engaged in sterile dialectics, he would take yet another leap, demonstrating to the participants that no fundamental question was really a philosophical question—rather, such questions always related to the actualities of love, death, fear, and sorrow.

A new methodology founded on seeing and listening was thus created, adding a new dimension to the field of intellectual and spiritual inquiry. In this methodology, negating thinking fully blossomed, blocking all positive thinking and all attempts to construct a new base of knowledge. After all, our thinking, despite its sophistication, had failed to lead us to the realization of love, freedom, and happiness. When the thinking mind let go, profound silence filled the mind and wiped away time and memory. Krishnamurti felt strongly that this state of total negation and the ending of thought had the power to renew brain cells. Having previously been conditioned by memory and reaction, the brain cells would transform when their automatic activity was forestalled by negation. Insight was, therefore, the replenishing force of the human brain.

The never-aging mind

In the spirit of Krishnamurti's methodology, we should ask at this stage: Is it possible to keep the mind forever young? Is it possible to attain a state in which the mind is not only prevented from deteriorating, but becomes even fresher with each passing day? Is it possible to reach old age with a feather-light mind that is not weighed down by a thousand yesterdays?

Consider your immediate reaction to these questions. Accumulating thinking, which is, by its very nature, a memory-based form of thinking, will answer no. How could it be possible when new layers of memory, experience, and knowledge are added to the mind each day? The truth is that accumulating thinking *is* the growing old of the mind; therefore, we cannot use such thinking to answer this question. To keep the mind forever young, Krishnamurti tells us, it is necessary to constantly negate accumulating thinking. In this very negation, there is renewal.

After all, what makes us think of someone as "old"? Surely, it is not the person's chronological age, since even certain adolescents may seem "old." An old mind is characterized by mental stiffness: The mind is rigid and refuses to accept anything outside its own restricted circle. It moves around within its circle, repeating the same habits of thinking, like a closed system that does not welcome the interference of external elements. This mind conveys a sense of "heaviness," for it weighs itself down. Does it really *refuse* to accept anything new? Or is it that it is *unable* to allow even the tiniest new thought to enter because it's so "full"?

We already mentioned that even at 85, Krishnamurti was willing to passionately look into a question as if for the first time. He never reacted by turning to the memory drawers and extricating some overused answer. Truth could never be a memory, nor could it be turned into a memory; it was to be found in the state of newness or nowness. Krishnamurti was living proof that it was possible to retain the youth of the mind. Could his negating thinking serve as a hitherto unknown key to the rejuvenation of our brain?

In a way, Krishnamurti's conviction that the mind and brain could be regenerated, which he expressed as early as the mid-twentieth century, anticipated the concept of neuroplasticity. During most of the twentieth century, the consensus among neuroscientists was that brain structure is relatively immutable after the critical period of early childhood. However, this notion of the brain as a physiologically static organ has been increasingly contradicted by growing evidence that many aspects of the brain remain plastic even into adulthood. Research has made it clear that the experiences a person has can change both his or her brain's physical structure and its functional organization. If the brain changes in response to stimuli, why wouldn't it transform in response to profound insight?

The celebrated physicist David Bohm, who engaged in profound dialogues with Krishnamurti and eventually developed his own method of dialogue, confirmed the philosopher's hypothesis:

> It is worth remarking that modern research into the brain and nervous system actually gives considerable support to Krishnamurti's statement that insight may change the brain cells … It is now well known that there are important substances in the body … that respond, from moment to moment, to what a person knows, to what he thinks, and to what this all means to him … In this way, the brain cells and their functioning are profoundly affected by knowledge and passions. It is thus quite possible that insight, which must arise in a state of mental energy and passion, could change the brain cells in an even more profound way.[175]

The closest thing to Krishnamurti's concept of "insight" is the state achieved through meditation. Several studies have proven that this state

175 Aryel Sanat, *The Inner Life of Krishnamurti* (Wheaton, IL: Quest Books, 1999), 71.

is capable of resulting in functional changes in the brain—affecting attention, anxiety, or even the body's ability to heal itself—probably as a result of changes to the physical structure of the brain. This also corresponds with Krishnamurti's belief that feeling that there was no yesterday and that there will be no tomorrow is the healthiest way of living, a state of mind that could prevent deterioration and heal the damage caused by years of wrong functioning.

Our brain seems to be flexible enough to transform at any time. Yet accumulating thinking creates the illusion that transformation is very difficult. From the point of view of such thinking, this is an understandable illusion. The prospect of discarding the past and the reactive mechanisms one has developed evokes a strong reaction, which one masks with the claim that it is simply impossible to do so. Accumulating thinking is made of the past; it is the outcome of many yesterdays, so how can it be discarded? We need to realize that accumulating thinking is just a habit of the mind, not a necessity. It is the habit of automatically measuring new things on the basis of our previous experience and knowledge. It is the habit of quickly responding to questions and rarely wondering where this instantly accessible knowledge comes from. It is the habit of ultimately holding onto only that which "worked" for us in the past and rejecting new possible responses and more creative actions. It is the habit of specializing and thereafter seeing and interpreting everything through the lens of our expertise. It is the habit of wrapping ourselves in a seemingly coherent narrative of the past, which becomes our "story."

Accumulating thinking results in an extremely thick and inflexible sense of oneself based on memories and experiences that have been gathered together to form a coherent story. Memories have been craftily woven together to create this final story, which we repeat to ourselves and to others whenever we have the chance. We become this story, which is the result of many past impressions. We see the world through it and react from within its restricted circle of experience and knowledge. We are "married" to it—till death do us part, it seems. The problem is that, psychologically and even neurologically speaking, it is only a story. In psychology, it is called a narrative: the construction of one's story using carefully selected and interpreted memories.

We don't really "remember." As in a sloppily written screenplay, our story is filled with holes that we try to cover up using special effects and over-dramatization. Moreover, we continually adjust our memories. Every time a memory is recollected, it is modified and redesigned. Trusting our "memories" is practically impossible. Cognitive psychologist and human memory expert Elizabeth Loftus has conducted extensive research that has demonstrated the malleability of human memory. Her groundbreaking work has demonstrated how we form false memories and how easily we can be influenced by others to form such memories due to the "misinformation effect"—that is, when memories are made less accurate by post-event information. This growing body of evidence seems to indicate that autobiographical memory is deeply unreliable and that there are no memories, but only stories about memories.[176]

The problem is not functional memory, which relates, for instance, to driving a car, but rather psychological memory: registering a moment in time and all of the emotional meaning we ascribe to it. This emotionally significant information builds up in our mind and we react quickly to any new experience on the basis of the old emotional data. So although gaining wisdom and experience may be a beautiful aspect of growing old, such wisdom and experience are perhaps given so much centrality that eventually very little room remains for anything "outside the box." We accumulate so many impressions, quotations, and ready-made statements that we become fixed in one static position from which we view the world, just as a computer whose memory is overloaded becomes annoyingly slow.

---

176 Elizabeth F. Loftus, "Creating False Memories," *Scientific American*, September 1997, vol. 277, no. 3, 70–75.

It seems obvious that we cannot eat continually without excreting. However, for some reason, we do not find it necessary to expel old thoughts to allow new ones to enter. "Waste" does not build up in our minds—or, at least, so we think. Perhaps we believe that our minds are infinite in their capacity to store or perhaps we do not think of thoughts as junk because they are invisible—if we turned totally pink, for example, when our minds were full, perhaps this would demonstrate to us the reality of our mind. Negating thinking is like the cleansing mechanism of the mind and brain; it disposes of the unnecessary burden of the past.

Through negation, we can regain some of the freshness that we see in the eyes of children. We have lost this freshness because of accumulating thinking, which leads us to approach life with over-familiarity—the sense that life is so familiar to us that we need only react automatically to whatever it brings. It is not life that has become old; it is us. Trying to feel who we are without our stories or searching for the part of our mind that has remained unaffected could be a good starting point. We would also benefit from delaying reactions to questions that are put to us, identifying ready-made responses before expressing them, and noticing automatic emotional reactions that we have in response to certain words. Letting our mind truly connect with the newness of the day when we wake up in the morning might also have a rejuvenating effect.

Hearing without the ear

"How do you receive a question which is put to you?" Biographer Pupul Jayakar asked this question of Krishnamurti when he turned 83. In response, Krishnamurti used the following analogy: "A pond is absolutely quiet. A question is dropped into the pond. The pond is pure water without all the pollution that man has put into it, which is the past. The pond is clear, clean water, and into that water a question is put as a pebble and the reply is the wave."[177]

In this intriguing dialogue, Krishnamurti revealed what happens to one's mind when one fully engages in negating thinking. The mind eventually turns from a thinking mind into a listening mind. He elaborates: "When a question is put, it is heard with the ear and there is also a state in which the hearing is not with the ear and out of that there is the answer."[178] Listening with the ear involves remembrance of past knowledge; experience answers the question. Listening without the ear has nothing to do with remembrance and does not retrieve a response to the question from memory. In the latter, there is no barrier separating inner and outer, no solidly existing "listener" made of a cluster of memories—only pure looking and seeing.

Krishnamurti's listening mind was the very opposite of the state of focused attention, which limits one's perception to a particular thing. This state of focused attention is the daily experience of most humans: shifting focus from a person to some piece of information to a certain emotion. In stark contrast, Krishnamurti's mind was more like a vast, all-inclusive attention that, for the most part, was not selective at all. It was a total awareness endowed with immense sensitivity to everything and anything. According to him, such awareness was possible only when the ordinary center of attention, the "me" that is watching and choosing what to pay attention to, was utterly absent.

In dialogues characterized by intense concentration, he would listen attentively, without reaction, to the others, but also to everything that was happening around him: a bird singing in a tree, a flower falling from a vase. In the midst of a talk, he might ask, "Did you see that flower fall?" He experienced a simultaneity of awareness, an inclusive seeing that did not shut out the outer or the inner, but let it flow through the mind, with the result that nothing was exclusive and nothing was a distraction. Interestingly, whereas religious and spiritual practices often

177 Jayakar, *J. Krishnamurti*, 329.
178 Ibid., 332.

instruct adherents to detach from their senses and withdraw from the world, for Krishnamurti, the listening mind was the total blossoming of the senses. Upon seeing a group of monks walking with their eyes focused on the ground before their feet, totally unaware of the beauty of nature around them, he commented that however silent their minds became, this silence would be a limited silence.[179] One must expand one's attention to such an extent that it includes the entire universe.

This was the culmination of negating thinking. Discarding memory, reaction, and the habit of naming and tagging everything was like doing away with the frontiers of the mind. A state of pure observation could then arise and it would be possible to listen to a thought or a twittering bird with the same quality of non-reactive attention. For Krishnamurti, this conscious but silent awareness was a different kind of intelligence. This extra-sensitive state is rare in this age, in which we struggle with overwhelming stimuli, inattention, and the need for quick reactions. Just think for a moment of the endless data with which we are inundated by our computers and cellular phones. We are kept so busy responding to this constant flow that eventually the quality of our attention becomes scattered, jumping from one piece of information to another. A silent awareness would necessitate that we put all that data aside from time to time.

Krishnamurti felt that the two different streams of the religious spirit and the scientific spirit converged in the listening mind. Science observes the small and the great, the ugly and the beautiful, the pure and the impure equally, without judging, rejecting, or discriminating. This state of listening also represents the attainment of pure observation without an interfering observer. Rather than immediately ascribing words and meanings to everything, the listening mind does not limit that which is revealed to it. Instead, it bathes it in its river of attention, which washes the dust off yesterday's memories and receives everything in its path indiscriminately.

179 Allan Anderson, *A Wholly Different Way of Living* (London: Victor Gollancz, 1991), 102–103.

When we experience life and ourselves through accumulating thinking, our attention becomes dull and over-focused. Over time, it limits itself to a restricted selection of automatic reactions and thoughts. Negating thinking, on the other hand, allows more space in the mind, space for new revelations, new insights. It has the power to instill in us the exciting feeling, perhaps experienced in our youth, that there is so much more to learn, internally as well as externally. There are vast unexplored regions within and without and it is only accumulating thinking that creates the tired sense that we have "been there, done that." We can test the aliveness of our mind by asking ourselves, at the end of each day: Have we discovered anything new? Have we learned something today that we didn't know yesterday? By never allowing a day to go by without discovering something new, we can rest assured in the knowledge that we are on the path to the never-aging mind.

CHAPTER 10

GIORDANO BRUNO

Thinking in context, *or* Why there is a universe in every hair[180]

On a cool day in the spring of 1548, Filippo Bruno was born near the small southern Italian town of Nola. If his parents had known that their baby would rip up the boundaries of the cosmos a few decades later under the name of Giordano, they would probably have been terrified. For them, the universe was still reassuringly ordered. There weren't any telescopes. One could only gaze at the starry sky with the naked eye. It seemed clear that the Earth was immobile, situated at the center of the universe. In general, people still believed in the Ptolemaic model of the cosmos: The moon, the sun, and the five planets that were visible to the naked eye revolved around the Earth as resplendent globes, their orbits describing concentric circles (or spheres). The fixed stars were part of the "eighth sphere," which marked the outer limit of the universe. Beyond that last sphere, there was only God and his angels. For the Vatican, the center of Western culture, this view of the universe was treated like a dogma as it was consistent with the central role of the world in the creation story and the idea that a god watched over everything from the kingdom of heaven.

180 Unless otherwise stated, all translations in this chapter are by David A. Brenner.

When the Polish astronomer Nicolaus Copernicus displaced the Earth from the center of the universe in his 1543 work *De revolutionibus orbium coelestium* [On the Revolutions of the Heavenly Spheres], claiming that it revolved around the sun and on its own axis, the established view of the world cracked. But it didn't fracture completely, as Copernicus could not yet provide conclusive evidence. Moreover, he had left the old model relatively intact. What we call "outer space" was still enclosed by an outermost sphere. The universe remained finite, with God outside it. Thus, the universe into which Bruno was born was rather small.

Today we live in a different universe. Within endlessly expansive space, the Earth and the sun are nothing but insignificant infinitesimally tiny dots. We know what the Earth looks like from outer space; photographs of the Milky Way are used as screensavers. We have such knowledge due to technological developments that have made it possible to look directly into space, not to mention countless measurements, research studies, and mathematical analyses. All of this makes it even more astonishing that the grown-up Bruno, in the sixteenth century, conceived of a vision of the cosmos that pretty much resembles our current understanding of the universe.

In his works, Bruno depicted a universe in which neither the Earth nor the sun were the epicenter, but in which countless solar systems filled a limitless space. His theses thus went a step beyond what his much more famous contemporaries, the Italian Galileo Galilei and the German Johannes Kepler, had to say about the universe. Both were better qualified as mathematicians and astronomers and were, at a certain point, even able to design and use telescopes. Their findings have, accordingly, achieved greater recognition in the history of science. In contrast, Bruno was a philosopher and a lapsed Dominican monk. His knowledge of mathematics was somewhat limited and he was notoriously impatient. Precise observation in the form of experiments—that is, the measuring and weighing of natural phenomena—was not among his research methods. His personality was, to say the least, rather unsuited to such precision. He was "less a scientist and more a poet, an artist painting with concepts."[181] Instead of using measuring equipment, Bruno worked with logical and metaphysical arguments, recording his ideas in allegories, passionate dialogues, and poems. He devoted himself to theology, magic, philosophy, and the natural sciences. For him, all were of a piece, a reflection on the same phenomenon—the universe.

Bruno's methodology may have been unscientific, but the content of his thought was highly progressive and made him a pioneer of modern astronomy. His approach was often intuitive, which is one of the reasons why he has never received the recognition he deserves. His accomplishment seems preposterous from today's point of view: How could this man grasp the structure of the universe merely by reflecting on it? To understand this, you have learn a little about his life story.

A rebellious star of memory

The house of the Bruno family was situated on the slopes of Mount Cicala, about 5 miles east of Naples. The family wasn't particularly well-off. The father was a soldier and rarely home; the mother was often on her own. Filippo was an only child and precocious. When a snake slithered into his cradle, he is said to have called for help in complete sentences—these were his very first words. Years later, his memory of the incident was so clear that his parents found it uncanny. It became apparent that Bruno had an excellent memory—indeed, it was so good that some of his contemporaries alleged that he had magical powers.

The young Filippo was an outsider who read a lot, observed nature, and liked to spend his time among the rosemary- and laurel-scented trees and shrubs of Mount Cicala. He had a special relationship to this mountain, which he wistfully recalled years later during his restless

181 Wolfgang Wildgen, *Das kosmische Gedächtnis. Kosmologie, Semiotik und Gedächtniskunst im Werk von Giordano Bruno* (Bern: Peter Lang, 1998), 10.

wanderings through Europe. When he looked eastward to the slopes of the Cicala, he could see the dark outlines of Vesuvius on the horizon. It was here that he thought for the first time that the world around him had no absolute center and no fixed borders. "Once upon a time, as a child, I remember, lovely Mount Cicala, caressing your holy lights [...]. In whatever field of earth I am, I see that west and east are equally spaced from me [...] and wherever I go, there is the same measure. [...] So the sky is not bounded by any particular border."[182]

At the age of 14, Bruno left his hometown, never to return. However, the town remained so dear to him throughout his life that he often referred to himself as "the Nolan" and his teachings as "Nolanic philosophy." In Naples, the capital of the then Spanish-dominated kingdom, the teenager began a comprehensive education, learning grammar, rhetoric, poetry, and logic. At the age of 17, he entered the Dominican Order and adopted the name Giordano. This was an unusual decision considering Bruno already had a well-developed rebellious spirit by then and was not likely to be able to conform to the rigid rules and regulations of monastic life. However, if he wished to continue learning, he had little choice: His parents could not afford to finance his studies. And he really did want to learn. Only the monastery could give him what he desired: access to its large library with its precious collection, which had once been used by his fellow Dominican Thomas Aquinas. Besides, as he later lamented when on the run from the Inquisition, the silence and concentration of monastic life were a good thing for a free intellect.

Life in the monastery was never going to turn out well in the long run. Bruno was expressing his thoughts aloud instead of quietly reading and reflecting. His superiors quickly realized that the young man from Nola was not a particularly obedient monk. Certainly, he plunged eagerly into his studies, acquiring Latin, Greek, and Hebrew, as well as reading reams of philosophy and literature. Yet, soon after entering

182 Paul Richard Blum, *Giordano Bruno* (Munich: Beck, 1999), 9.

San Domenico Maggiore, the prior of the monastery reprimanded the new monk for speaking out against the cult of Mary and removing the images of saints from the walls of his cell. Fortunately, Bruno was already a skilled rhetorician by then and talked himself out of trouble. Perhaps the prior was happy to drop the charges as Bruno was becoming the star of the monastery. It had become increasingly clear that he had a phenomenal memory. His immense natural talent for it was perfected through memory arts—also known as "mnemotechnics" or "mnemonics"—that he had cultivated himself. Word of his fame even reached Pope Pius V, who invited him to Rome. Bruno didn't disappoint during his audience with the Pope, reciting Psalm 86 in Hebrew—both forwards and backwards—and then explaining his technique to the Pope.

The pontiff and his cardinals were by no means unacquainted with mnemotechnics, also called "artificial memory." It was part of the standard curriculum of secondary schools and the Dominicans in Naples had accomplished a great deal with it. Aquinas had categorized his thoughts so well using mnemotechnics that he was able to dictate four books simultaneously. But Bruno wasn't satisfied with the traditional system. He had a unique structure of thinking that he systematized—and thus improved—using mnemotechnics. He asserted that the difference between his method and the old methods was as immense as that between the printing press and primitive carvings on bark.

The young monk wrote about several techniques he used. However, like a modern-day marketing expert, he only revealed enough to keep his readers interested. Without more detailed explanations, it is not possible for us to learn his technique. It is clear that he made use of two main sources. First, he utilized the mnemonics of the Romans, thanks to which Roman lawyers could speak for hours without notes. They visually constructed mental buildings, which they could later access: Specifically, they visualized rooms containing various objects and statues, each of which represented a particular idea or part of a speech. When delivering their speeches, they would walk through these mental constructions and retrieve their ideas. Memory artists today still use this method, usually in a simplified form. For example, they remember long series of numbers by linking the individual digits to images, on the basis of which they create a chronological storyline in their minds.

Bruno was also inspired by a Catalonian mystic named Ramon Llull. Llull created his own variant of the old mnemonics—a kind of thinking machine. He substituted the Roman buildings with concentric circles, each of which was divided into sections containing letters and concepts. By spinning these circles, he could endlessly generate new combinations and ideas.

Bruno made use of both Llull's circles and the Romans' symbolic images. The resulting system, which was highly complex, was made up of concentric circles on which encrypted information was stored in the form of letters, images, and symbols. Thus, words could be fed into memory as images, by turning the individual syllables into symbols and linking them together to form an image. The word *numero* [number], for instance, was stored as an image of the mythological Apis bull lying on a carpet. These images were then placed upon the imaginary memory discs, each of which was divided into dozens of compartments. "A speech stored in this way could contain the population of a small city,"[183] Bruno's biographer Ingrid D. Rowland writes. Was all the effort involved in such complex mental acrobatics worth it? However impressive it might be, did it justify the outcome? Natural memory operates in a much simpler manner than its "artificial" counterpart: You simply remember the things themselves, not complex interrelated patterns of symbols and characters. If Bruno's system merely related to memorizing information, he would not have merited a chapter of his own in this book. But there is much more to his "artificial memory":

183 Ingrid D. Rowland, *Giordano Bruno: Philosopher/Heretic* (Chicago: University of Chicago Press, 2009), 124.

Bruno's mnemotechnics indicates how his thinking operated and how he ultimately managed to grasp the infinitude of the universe.

Bruno deployed this art to continuously train his mind. In his view, normal memory was primitive, whereas mnemotechnics represented an evolution of the human mind, comparable to the ability to walk upright or learning to read. Artificial memory constituted a way of seeing the world and systematically processing one's impressions of it. Through the senses, human beings ceaselessly received impressions of the world, which streamed into them without any apparent meaning or order. The mind, however, could create and recognize order and harmony. Artificial memory involved using that faculty of the mind in an intentional way. It meant reflecting on the fundamental order of the world using one's own imagination, "to represent, by inward writing, as it were, what nature represents externally, as it were, by outward writing,"[184] as philosopher Georg Wilhelm Friedrich Hegel put it in his essay on Bruno. One could thus identify with the fundamental principle of nature's harmony through the ordering of the mind. For Bruno, the information he received from the world did not consist of scattered or disconnected fragments. Rather, every single thing was related to everything else, part of a larger category, which was itself part of an even larger category—like the concentric circles on which the memory artist would deposit his data. The individual parts were not randomly juxtaposed or superimposed; they were linked together by an internal logic. Bruno explained it thus: "[J]ust as a hand joined to an arm, a foot to a leg, or an eye to a head is more recognizable than when it is separated, likewise with parts and whole species."[185] Moreover, all things, both concrete and abstract, could be grasped by conceiving of them as part of a single large circle with an infinite amount of internal circles. In general, the ostensibly complex mental architecture of Bruno's mnemotechnics seemed intelligently simple and meaningfully ordered

184 D. Karl Ludwig Michele (ed.), *Georg Wilhelm Friedrich Hegel's Vorlesungen über die Geschichte der Philosophie*, Volume 3 (Berlin, 1836), 16.
185 Rowland, *Giordano Bruno*, 125.

in the "light" of the mind. With this argument, Bruno challenged those critics who regarded his artificial memory as too complicated. "Whereas those things that occur in Nature are different from one another, contrary, and diverse, [in the light] they are like, harmonious and single,"[186] Bruno affirmed. He proceeded to counsel his readers: "Try, therefore, if you are able with your powers, to identify, harmonize, and unite the phenomena you perceive—and you shall not exhaust your faculties, you shall not upset your mind."[187]

The human mind, Bruno knew, could hold a vast amount of information if it was perceived in the right order. The concentric discs of memory represented this principle visually in his imagination. The endless possible combinations of these discs gave Bruno a very real idea of infinity. The immeasurable was part of his daily experience, a natural part of how he saw the world, for he was a *contextualizing* thinker.

Normal thinking works differently—it is fragmented and gets lost in small, isolated details. The internal logic and links that Bruno saw everywhere are alien to this kind of *fragmented thinking*. You can observe this tendency in yourself when you look out the window: You probably see people, cars, trees, lights, dogs, and scraps of paper as disconnected fragments. Concentrating on a certain detail narrows your perception, which is like a camera that can only focus on a particular detail or area. Yet the moment a detail comes into focus, it loses its context. It is also possible to zoom out mentally and see the bigger picture. However, this will result in you losing sight of the details. In principle, there is nothing wrong with visually perceiving things in this way. The difference between fragmented and limitless thinking is the way the mind interprets the images. Fragmented thinking can be deceived by visual perception: When it *sees* a detail out of context because that is what it is concentrating on, it *thinks* of this detail out of context. Conversely, when looking at the overall picture, such thinking

186 Ibid., 127.
187 Ibid.

has no sense of the details of which the picture is composed. It only sees fragments, so it assumes that reality is fragmented. On the other hand, for Bruno, the details always represented the whole and the whole in turn represented another detail. No matter how large it was, there had to be something even larger that encompassed it. The innumerable small details of life, rather than confusing him, allowed him to conceive of infinite space. He was continuously training his perception through his mnemotechnics, which may even have influenced his visual perception.

Bruno's artificial memory was so effective that it became his main profession when his life at the monastery suddenly ended. After managing not to cause much trouble for 10 years, he attracted the attention of the provincial Fra Domenico Vita—likely because of heretical-sounding statements he had made in conversation with an older monk. While Brother Giordano was away in Rome, Fra Vita had his cell searched. When nothing untoward was found, they looked in the privy, where they found a text by Erasmus of Rotterdam that was on the Inquisition's index. Bruno came under suspicion of heresy, which ended his career as a Dominican. He could not return to Naples, fearing that he would be punished. The Inquisition was not to be trifled with. He left the monastic order and wandered throughout Europe for the rest of his life.

A universe without a center—and without limits

When Bruno turned 30, he had a vision that determined the course of the rest of his life. It is often said that his vision took the form of a dream. He supposedly dreamed that he awakened in a world and under a sky that corresponded to the prevailing image of the universe in his epoch. The starry sky formed a solid circle around the world. For a moment, he was afraid, but then he mustered his courage: "I spread confident wings to space and soared toward the infinite, leaving far behind me what others strained to see from a distance. Here, there was no up, no down, no edge, no center. I saw that the sun was just another star, and the stars were other suns, each escorted by other earths like our own."[188]

Later in life, Bruno frequently tried to describe the moment when he realized that the universe was infinite. Each attempt led to a poetic outpouring. The experience seemed to defy sober description—and Bruno was, in any case, an ecstatic type of person. However, he was also very astute and managed to justify his intuitive inspiration *post facto* in a logical manner. Nonetheless, it was not philosophical logic that led him to his insight, but rather the same kind of thinking that had produced his mnemotechnics. His unceasing work on his book *Ars Memoriae* had triggered an intuitive breakthrough: He had comprehended the architecture of space using the architecture of his imagination. Thanks to his ordering of his thoughts, he was able to illustrate a universal basic principle that he had recognized in the world. For he knew that everything we perceive—be it an object, an animal, or an idea—exists both individually and as part of a larger whole. Were Bruno alive today, he might have used the term *holon*, a philosophical term coined by the writer Arthur Koestler to designate an independent entity that nevertheless exists as part of a larger whole. A simple example is a cell in the body: It functions as an autonomous unit while at the same time being part of a larger organism. That organism—the body—is comprised of innumerable cells. The cell itself is in turn comprised of smaller units, such as DNA, RNA, and mitochondria.

But this image can also be extended to the macro level: Our solar system can be regarded as an element in itself. Yet, at the same time, it is part of the larger Milky Way, which in turn is one of the untold thousands of galaxies that make up the universe. Every aspect of our reality can be seen both as an individual component and as part of something larger. It seems that Bruno by nature had the ability to classify all his impressions

188 Ann Druyan and Steven Soter, *Cosmos: A Spacetime Odyssey* (2014). Episode 1 (20:28).

into this context; he was able to simultaneously perceive the part and the whole. As a result, when he looked at an object—be it abstract or concrete—he knew that he was not dealing with a disconnected part of a thing. The large things were composed of smaller things and the smaller things of even smaller things.

Bruno's contextualizing thinking is well illustrated by a text he composed about everyday life in his hometown of Nola:

> He [Jove] wishes that, at the same time thirty jujubes, perfectly ripe, be picked from the jujube tree which stands at the floor of Mount Cicala on the property of Gioan Bruno, thirty of them should be picked perfectly ripe, seventeen should fall to the ground unripe, and fifteen should be worm-eaten. He decreed that Vasta, the wife of Albenzio, while she tries to curl the hair on her temples, shall burn fifty-seven of them because she overheated her iron. [...] He decreed that two-hundred fifty-two maggots be born out of the dung of Albenzio's ox; that, of those, fourteen be trampled upon and killed by Albenzio's foot, that twenty-six of them die from being turned upside down, that twenty-two live in a cavern; that eighty wander about the courtyard, that forty-two go to live under the tree stump by the door, that sixteen turn their feelers wherever they see fit, and that the rest go in search of their fortune.[189]

The world as Bruno saw it consisted of innumerable details, all of them equally important. Each hair that is burned by a curling iron deserves our attention. Infinity is in everything.

Unlike us, Bruno never saw a picture of a solar system during his lifetime. But when he looked up in the sky at night, he knew that each star had to consist of parts, which themselves consisted of parts, while, at the same time, the star itself had to be part of a larger whole. Bruno

---

189 Giordiano Bruno, *The Expulsion of the Triumphant Beast*, trans. and ed. Arthur D. Imerti (Lincoln: Nebraska University Press, 1964), 132.

gradually came to believe that the universe was limitless, that is, that the spherical shells that enclosed the universe according to the old view of the world could not have been the outer limits of the universe. "From our sense of sight, we must therefore conclude that it's infinite, since there isn't anything that doesn't end in another and we can't see anything that ends in itself."[190]

Such reflections must have induced ecstatic states in Bruno for he "got drunk on space, or, to use his own metaphor, he felt as though he'd been liberated from prison."[191] This is understandable given the circumstances in which he had these insights. Today, at least on an intellectual level, we are accustomed to the notion that the universe we live in has no identifiable limits; however, we must imagine what this would have meant for a person living in a time when nothing seemed limitless (except, perhaps, the power of God). The universe of the sixteenth century was just as hierarchically structured as human society at that time. The Ptolemaic view of the world was like a cage from which there was no escaping. It is no wonder, then, that Bruno was beside himself. His insights were highly destructive to hierarchical thinking. His conception of an infinite space in which the Earth was not the center but rather one of countless celestial bodies was not merely a theoretical reinterpretation of the old worldview; it also fundamentally questioned the role of humanity and its relation to divinity.

In 1583, after spending time in Geneva, Toulouse, and Paris, Bruno went to London, where he found lodging at the French ambassador's home, thanks to a letter of recommendation from Henry III. He established contact with the university in Oxford. He was presumably hoping to obtain a permanent position there, having already taught in Paris as a professor. His lecture at Oxford, however, turned into a

---

190 Harro Heuser, *Unendlichkeiten: Nachrichten aus dem Grand Canyon des Geistes* (Wiesbaden: B.G. Teubner Verlag, 2008), 175. The original source is Bruno's Dialogues on the Infinite Universe and Worlds.
191 Vwadek P. Marciniak, *Towards a History of Consciousness: Space, Time, and Death* (New York: Peter Lang, 2006), 192.

disaster. On the one hand, Bruno was defending Copernicus' worldview, itself controversial, to his audience. On the other, he had to deal with his British audience making fun of his small stature, his strong accent, and his dramatic gestures. They hardly listened to him and frequently disrupted his talk. Some members of the audience even accused him of plagiarizing the work of others. The humiliated Bruno returned to the home of his host. The event had dealt him a tough personal blow. However, the setback proved good for his work. He returned to his writing. Not only did he transform his rage into verse; he also succeeded in clarifying his philosophical ideas. In the years following the Oxford episode, between 1584 and 1591, he penned his most important works, including *On the Infinite Universe and Worlds*, while also elaborating his ideas through philosophical argumentation. Contextualizing thinking allowed him to go on thinking about the Earth and the cosmos, as any number of people had done before him and as many still do. After he had dissolved the limits of the universe, he devoted himself to depriving it of its center.

Copernicus had done something outrageous by putting the sun, instead of the Earth, at the center of the universe. His heliocentric system must have been tantamount to an earthquake for his contemporaries. Most were unwilling to accept this new view of the universe and those who did had not grasped the full implications of such a view. Even Copernicus himself had not realized that his theory implied much more than he had described—perhaps he hadn't dared to explicitly state the full implications publicly. The Polish astronomer had tried to fit his new findings into the old, generally accepted view of the world. The Earth was no longer immobile at the center of the cosmos; the sun had taken its place. Further, the Earth no longer stood still, but revolved on its own axis, as well as revolving around the sun. Nonetheless, the old order remained largely intact because Copernicus upheld the idea of the spheres (or spherical shells), on the outermost of which the fixed stars were attached.

Bruno was a philosopher, so he did not think in terms of models and measurements. For him, life could never be fully grasped through calculations. He used calculations merely as starting points, a basis from which to speculate about reality. Thus, he was one of the only people in his time to accept Copernicus' system and he was one of the few who understood the full implications of doing so. It was not possible to change the epicenter of creation and then pretend that this was merely a minor correction to an otherwise coherent model. Once the center changed, everything else had to change, too. If the Earth wasn't the center of the universe, why should the sun be? Indeed, why should there be a center at all? As Bruno had already realized as a child when looking into the distance from Monte Cicala, the experience of the center was always relative. You couldn't understand the universe from a relative perspective. So Bruno did something that would have frightened even Copernicus: He dispensed with the center altogether, conceiving of an infinite sphere, whose center is everywhere and whose circumference is nowhere.

Bruno extended the principle of Copernicus' heliocentrism to all stars. There wasn't a single center in the universe around which all other celestial bodies moved; rather, each star in the universe was a sun, as well as being part of its own solar system. In addition, the discovery that the Earth revolved on its own axis and around the sun was taken a step further by Bruno: He explained that the sun must also revolve on its own axis—a supposition in which he was correct, as we now know. Bruno's vision of the universe was thus utterly different to the Ptolemaic view of the world. Instead of a static, well-defined model centered on the Earth, in which the fixed stars were affixed to the outer layer of the universe, Bruno's cosmos had no limits, no center, and was filled with motion. Bruno claimed that the universe was composed of innumerable stars and that these stars—like all matter—were composed of innumerable atoms. There wasn't one world, but innumerable worlds. The same principle applied to life on Earth: It consisted of an infinite number of parts and details. Everything that seemed static and solid was actually made up of innumerable parts. If you tried to imagine the smallest possible component, you would end up thinking in terms of infinity for everything that could be measured had to be comprised of still smaller parts.

Bruno was not the first person to claim that the universe had no limits, nor was he the first to conceive of atoms or of myriad other worlds or to acknowledge that the Earth wasn't at the center. But Bruno's contextualizing thinking joined these fragments together, for the first time, to provide a general picture of the cosmos—a rather modern one from today's perspective.

The egocentric cosmos

There is something odd about the way we experience the world. Our knowledge about the role of our planet in the universe does not accord with lived experience. Imagine that you are taking a walk one evening by the sea. You look out across the water. Waves stretch to the horizon and it seems as if there's nothing beyond that except water. It is for this reason that our ancestors thought that the Earth was flat and that the sky floated on the water. Nowadays, we know that this impression is deceptive: The surface of the water is curved because it follows the curvature of the Earth. If you watch the sunset, you will see the sun descend as a radiant disc and then appear to drop beneath the surface of the water on the horizon.

Isn't it odd that we continue to use the term "sunset"? It is a relic of a time when we thought the Earth was the center of the universe. We now realize that the sun doesn't really *set*; rather, it disappears from our field of vision because the Earth is turning. We know these things, but this knowledge does not correspond to our experience. As cosmologist Brian Swimme comments in *The Hidden Heart of The Cosmos*, most of us watching a sunset today still experience something similar to what people experienced in medieval times or even the Stone

Age. It is "just what any primate has experienced at any time since the very beginning of primate life seventy million years ago,"[192] Swimme contends. Our fundamental experience of what this glowing ball does on the horizon hasn't really changed over the past 70 million years. When we experience the Earth turning away from the sun and the sky turning red, we still feel that we're standing still, at a fixed point, and the sun is circling around us. Over 400 years after Copernicus, our everyday *experience* is that of a geocentric view of the world. In this sense, we haven't advanced much further than Giordano Bruno's contemporaries who resisted a heliocentric view of the world and the infinitude of the universe. We have accepted both of these views in theory because we have much more verified information about the cosmos than they had in the past and we have the technological capacity to look—and travel—far beyond the horizon. We can now see pictures from space. However, these developments have not led to a new vision of life, a consciousness that would redefine the daily lives of all human beings. In principle, the same way of thinking predominates: We still perceive the sun as *setting*, just like those in the sixteenth century who resisted a heliocentric universe and an Earth in motion.

If you were to walk up to someone on the street today and ask what he or she thinks about the universe, the true answer would most likely be, "I don't care" or "It doesn't matter in my life." This seems reasonable: How can we be expected to deal with the vast, incomprehensible universe when our own lives are difficult enough already? Yet, at the same time, this notion that the Earth somehow exists separately to the rest of the universe is absurd. Once again, it's a question of sense perception: We do not see outer space when we leave the house in the morning, pick up breakfast, and drive to work. Rather, we see life on Earth. For Bruno, in contrast, the Earth and space were no more separated than were a single human being and the cosmos. He is entirely right when we consider the overall picture. The notion of a completely

192 Brian Swimme, *The Hidden Heart of the Cosmos*, 2nd edn. (Maryknoll, NY: Orbis Books, 2000), 23.

discrete life is a fiction: Every human is involved in a myriad of contexts. In that sense, "cosmos" is just a word for the largest possible (and very real) context.

Isn't it interesting that we live in a time when every serious truth has to withstand scientific analysis and yet we still do not take science seriously enough to draw genuine conclusions from what it has discovered about our place in the universe? It is for this reason that our thinking about life and the world is distorted and our personal perceptions are at variance with the facts: When we are at the beach at night and see the sky ablaze, that sunset remains a personal experience. We forget that we are witnessing an incredible activity in an unfathomable realm. At this very moment, we're standing on a sphere rotating within a void. We forget that neither the Earth nor the sun are the center of the universe. Our basic experience of reality is still that our own ego is the center of all existence—an experience shared by the billions of other human beings on this planet. However, even this knowledge does not prevent us from feeling as if we play a central role. Everything we see exists only in relation to us. The world is a stage and we are playing the lead role; everyone else is playing a role in relation to us or populating the stage as extras.

In Germany, for example, when reporting a disaster, the news announcer will always mention how many of the victims were German. This ensures that the message has a more personal effect on the German viewer, despite the fact that he or she was equally unfamiliar with all of the victims—the Germans as well as the French or Chinese and so on. When a victim is stated to be German, a relation to the universe is established and the viewer senses that he or she is at the center of this universe. You may call this egocentric or narcissistic, but such judgments represent unnecessary moral evaluations. Irrespective of such evaluations, the simple facts illustrate that every center in life is relative. Rationally, this can be easily understood. But changing your perspective on the basis of rational knowledge is more difficult.

Our thinking is both fragmented and centralizing. Thus, we cannot imagine an existence in which there is no absolute center. It may be that we don't want to think about existence in this way, because it gives rise to an uncomfortable question: In a life with no center, what happens to our understanding of ourselves as individuals? It seems that we cling to *centralizing thinking* because we don't know where else to find support. In Douglas Adams' novel *The Restaurant at the End of the Universe*, the worst punishment that one can receive is being put into the "Total Perspective Vortex": "For when you are put into the Vortex you are given just one momentary glimpse of the entire unimaginable infinity of creation, and somewhere in it a tiny little marker, a microscopic dot on a microscopic dot, which says 'You are here.'"

Giordano Bruno was not afraid of such a "vortex." He could live in a universe without a center and without external limits because he did not need these to feel secure. In place of a fixed center, he had a wide-ranging context. Consequently, he did not shrink from the implications of Copernicus' discovery. Moreover, he profoundly mistrusted the explanatory power of mathematical calculations and astronomical models, as well as of the natural sciences more generally. It wasn't that he doubted the need for calculations and models; rather, he didn't believe that their creators were always in a position to grasp the significance of their own theories or discoveries. This was precisely his criticism of Copernicus, whom he deemed to be "confusing mathematical concepts and physical reality."[193] Understanding the meaning of such concepts was the task of the philosopher, not the scientist. This is where normal thinking still fails today: It considers research findings without applying them to lived experience. It is for this reason that we still think of the sun as "setting."

In his philosophy, Bruno did exactly what Brian Swimme called for: He did not relegate Copernicus' new view of the world to the realm

193 Hilary Gatti, *Giordano Bruno and Renaissance Science* (Ithaca, NY: Cornell University Press, 2002), 83.

of abstract theories, but rather accepted it as a reality of everyday life. Swimme advocates the development of a consciousness that does not merely incorporate our knowledge of the cosmos theoretically, but also integrates it, so that a new, more realistic perspective can emerge:

> It is not enough simply to learn more facts and knowledge about the universe. Something much deeper and more difficult is necessary [...]. Science arrives at truths that are not part of our genetic heritage, and thus they often appear strange and unnatural. But so long as these truths are left to dangle outside as abstractions, we are condemned to lead a split life. [...] What is needed here is a transformative process where one can learn to see and to feel the world in a way congruent with what is actually happening. Such a transformation would enable one to transcend the split modern condition of experiencing the world one way while knowing the truth about the world is otherwise.[194]

Even if you have no interest in astronomy and cosmology, it is important to realize that our direct experience of the world is an illusion. If you rely only on that which you can visualize directly, you will end up with a worldview that is consistent with that of our ancestors in the Stone Age. Like Bruno, though, we can apply our knowledge of the cosmos to experience life differently. "Sense perception suggests rather than denies infinity,"[195] Bruno concluded (apparently citing Lucretius). This perspective is liberating for it is exhausting always being the center of the world. You might say that Bruno's point of view was *cosmo*centric, rather than *ego*centric.

---

194 Swimme, *The Hidden Heart of the Cosmos*, 24.

195 Dorothea Waley Singer, *Giordano Bruno: His Life and Thought, With Annotated Translation of His Work On the Infinite Universe and Worlds* (New York: Schumann, 1950), 102.

How to ride a cosmic whale

Giordano Bruno's life came to a violent end. In 1600, he was burned at the stake in Campo de' Fiori square in Rome by the Inquisition. The Catholic Church had realized that Bruno's way of thinking did not accord with the view of the world and God that it wanted to impart. Moreover, Bruno had made disparaging remarks about Church teachings. Bruno is purported to have had his tongue tied on the day of his execution so he could not speak to the crowd. Two days later, on 19 February 1600, the Roman pamphlet *Avvisi di Roma* read, "He was an uncommonly obstinate heretic who [...] fabricated various dogmas against our beliefs" and "[t]he wretch was so stubborn that he was willing to die for it."[196] Indeed, Bruno had been given the opportunity to recant. After nearly eight years in terrible conditions, he was physically broken; nonetheless, he refused to renounce what he had said. He had probably known that, sooner or later, he would find himself in this position. In a poem written earlier in life, he had compared himself to Icarus: "Woe, woe! Repentance follows too daring a chariot / I do not fear the fall, I exclaim, from the heights, / Up and away, through the vault! And die happily / You were granted a gloriously noble death!"[197]

Throughout his life, Bruno contemplated the cosmos and the importance of scientific knowledge about the cosmos. His notion of space, in which there could be an infinite number of other worlds, was deemed heretical by the Catholic Church. The Church was characterized by *centralizing thinking* and everything it taught was consistent with this perspective: the central role of the Earth in the creation story, the special role of humanity, the omnipotence of a monotheistic God who existed somewhere beyond. Even as a monk, Bruno had had difficulties with these teachings. Later, as a wandering philosopher, he definitively

196 Klaus Franke, Ulrich Schwarz, and Peter Wensierski, "Gottes willige Vollstrecker," *Der Spiegel*, January 6, 1998. https://www.spiegel.de/spiegel/print/d-7897629.html.
197 Georg Weber, *Literar-historisches Lesebuch* (Leipzig, 1852), 334f.

rejected them. Bruno's rejection of the Catholic faith was an inevitable consequence of his understanding of the universe: If, as he claimed, our Earth was just one of an infinite number of other worlds, then the entire Christian story of creation, expulsion from paradise, and redemption—if there were such a thing—were simply one of the countless stories in the universe. A personalized God couldn't exist as a being outside of creation, as an "unmoved mover," to quote Aristotle. There was a gradual difference, but not a qualitative one, between plants, animals, and humans. Bruno also disputed the special roles of the saints and even Jesus Christ.

Whereas others, such as Johannes Kepler, carefully distinguished between an infinite God and his finite creation, for Bruno there was only infinite space. Thus, there could not be a son of God who was sent from heaven to Earth, for there was no otherworldly kingdom of heaven. Nor was there any essential difference between God and the world. Schopenhauer designated this kind of pantheistic attitude a form of "polite atheism."[198] However, Bruno was not particularly polite: He often satirized the stupidity of his fellow human beings and the Church in highly caustic terms. Nor was he an atheist. In the final years of his life, when he advocated that metaphysics be completely abolished, he did not call for a purely material or mechanistic universe. The dualism of matter and mind, of instinct and reason, simply did not exist for Bruno. For him, God was what would later be called the "laws of nature." In his essay *On the Immeasurable and Innumerable*, he explained that God "is not subject to any numerical law or to any law of measure or order. He himself is law, number, measure, limit without limit, end without end, act without form."[199] Thus, Bruno's universe had no need of a supernatural being.

198 Arthur Schopenhauer, *Schopenhauer-Lexikon. Ein philosophisches Wörterbuch, nach Arthur Schopenhauers sämmtlichen Schriften und handschriftlichem Nachlaß*, ed. Julius Frauenstädt, Vol. 2 (Leipzig, 1871), 198f.

199 Giordano Bruno, Das *Unermeßliche und Unzählbare*, I. und II. Buch (De Immense et Innuberabilibus), trans. Erika Rojas (Ahrensburg: Skorpion, 1999), 112.

In a sense, Bruno anticipated Nietzsche, who would, a few centuries later, proclaim the death of God. Although Bruno believed in a divine principle that was manifest in everything, both spirit and matter, he had rejected the idea of an external god and opposed religion. Like Nietzsche, Bruno realized that the death of the external God implied a new responsibility for humanity. If you renounce any possibility of outside help from an external power, you cannot leave the world to its own devices. Bruno saw "the good" as a divine quality that might permeate the universe, but that would not intervene in human lives. If a person wanted to see the good in this world, he or she would have to be a force of good him- or herself.

Here, we can observe a deeper level of Bruno's contextualizing thinking: A cosmos in which every hair and every maggot were just as important as people and planets would give rise to an ethical obligation to accept and respect all components of the universe. In his work *The Expulsion of the Triumphant Beast*, Bruno described a social ideal whereby the well-being of the individual is taken just as seriously as the common good. If the individual was not the center of his own personal universe and perceived his or her connection to the rest of the universe, on both the micro and macro levels, it would be clear to him or her that no one can live apart from everything else. A life of pursuing only one's own interest would thus not be "wrong" in the moral sense; rather, it would simply be unrealistic. Only fragmented thinking can accommodate the idea of an individual who exists without a context. Today, in the twenty-first century, it is only fragmented thinking that still seriously hopes to be rescued from beyond.

In this regard, we are still rather primitive and not so different from Bruno's believing contemporaries, although we certainly think of ourselves as infinitely more advanced. If we're honest, many of us still cling to the idea that we will be rescued from beyond. Even if we're not hoping for a god to effect change, most of us have faith in the ability of some outside power to fix things—even if that outside power is science.

There's obviously a certain irony in this: The rational person boasts that he or she does not depend on the consolation that religious people seek; ultimately, though, one could say that it is just as irrational to believe that science will solve all of our problems.

If you want to experience the cosmos not only theoretically, but also as a practical reality, you could try this thought experiment developed by cosmologist Brian Swimme. Leave your house some evening about half an hour before sunset. Call to mind a rough model of the solar system and then focus on the planet Venus, which should be low on the horizon at that hour. (Venus is often the brightest star in the sky, so it is easy to spot.) As you look at Venus keep the model of the solar system in mind. Venus is 65 million miles from the Sun, about a third closer than the Earth, which is 93 million miles from the Sun. Jupiter is 480 million miles from the sun. And all the three planets are moving on a single plane around the Sun. Use that model to help you comprehend the great distances involved in what you're seeing and experiencing. Swimme writes:

> Simply by focusing on the experience and viewing it through the theoretical model of the solar system's form, there comes a wonderful moment: you feel in an experiential, imaginative, and direct way the Earth slowly turning away from the Sun. You have a sense of the plane in which the planets move, and even a beginning recognition of the great distance to Venus. You'll also feel, and perhaps for the first time in your life, the immensity of the Earth as it rolls away from the great Sun. It happens in a flash. A single surprising shudder passes through you and you realize you are standing on the back of something like a cosmic whale, one that is slowly rotating its great bulk on the surface of an unseen ocean.[200]

200 Swimme, *The Hidden Heart of the Cosmos*, p. 27.

EPILOGUE

OUTLINES OF THE GENIUS MIND

We have delved deeply into the enormous minds of ten different thinkers and explored their unique processes of thought and insight. This has yielded various treasures, such as "paradoxical thinking," "organic thinking," and "excavating thinking." Each one of these ten explorations seemed, to us, to be more than enough individually, a world unto itself. As our journey comes to a close, the inevitable question arises: How different are these ten modes of thinking? Have we really considered ten exceptionally individual minds, each incomparable to all others? Perhaps these modes of thinking were all interconnected, sharing, or even springing from, a common source?

We might ask an even more daring question: Is it possible to speak of one genius mind, one essential structure of thinking that leads to all human breakthroughs in science and philosophy? If so, the differences we have detected are nuances, rather than clear distinctions separating one mind from another.

The more we explored the extraordinary mental capacities of the thinkers we chose, the more we found that we were unable to erect clear barriers between them. The various modes of thinking seemed to flow into each other and mix in a way that embarrassed us. We had to artificially prevent the various modes of thinking from bleeding into each other and often had to restrain the urge to refer to other chapters ("Like Einstein, McClintock demonstrates ..."). Indeed, it is likely that some of our readers suspected as much while reading. Nietzsche and

Darwin, Bruno and Einstein, McClintock and Socrates are clearly distinct only as long as you observe their biographies and discoveries from an external perspective. If you zoom in and explore their internal mental worlds, it quickly becomes difficult to distinguish them from one another.

To illuminate this point, let's play a little game. Try to identify the different thinkers to whom the following three statements refer. (The answers are given in a footnote at the end of this chapter.)

"You're an extremely clever boy/girl. But you have one great fault: You'll never let yourself be told anything."

"The role of vision in his/her experimental work provides the key to his/her understanding ... He/she cannot even say how he/she 'knows' what he/she knows."

"He/she was impressive to his/her schoolmates: While they chatted during school recesses, he/she marched around the schoolyard, hands clasped behind his/her back ... lost in solitary thought."

Our experience has led us to conclude that the 10 thinkers we have discussed share certain consistent features and qualities. You can think of these as a mental blueprint that gives rise to innovations in philosophy and science. Before bringing this book to a close, we wish to highlight the common qualities of the genius mind. All of the features we discuss are exhibited by at least seven of the ten figures in this book, as well as many of the thinkers who did not make our final list.

An outsider, observing mind

Probably the most obvious characteristic of all of the figures we have studied is their individuality. That is not to say merely that they were strong-minded and independent-thinking people; rather, they were people who, from childhood, refused to adopt the herd mentality, even when the mentality in question was that of their intellectual peers. They were loners who never felt that they belonged to any structure or framework. Their very thinking was aloof, solitary, and usually did not rely on any kind of teamwork or group involvement. They were reluctant to engage with anything that might threaten their uncontaminated observation. From childhood, they demonstrated a remarkable appreciation of solitude and intense contemplation. More often than not, this aloofness was criticized by others as unemotional and inhuman.

Their sense that they did not belong is often apparent in their disidentification with their heritage, religious background, and/or nationality. The majority of these figures expressed a universal experience; they were citizens of the world, rather than belonging to one group.

They were rebels, who did not feel committed to accepted conventions and authorities. Their only commitment was to their radical freedom of thought, which they cherished above all else. They felt that they had to do everything in their own way, reaching solutions only through their own creative process. They could not bear to feel limited or inhibited in their thinking and often struck others as pretentious and audacious. This audacity allowed them to withstand intense pressure and resistance and to persevere in pursuit of their goal of inquiry, even when others strongly doubted their chances of success.

This extreme individuality turned them into what we might call "eternal observers." Their minds seemed to be separate from the world and the human experience, silently and curiously observing from the outside. In many respects, they were strangers even in the eyes of their loved ones. This detachment from the world and human experience made it possible for them to objectivity discern patterns that ordinary minds, too immersed in the world, simply cannot see.

Non-attachment to knowledge and intellectual experimentalism

These figures maintained a dual relationship with conventional knowledge that had been gradually accumulated over the generations in their individual fields of expertise. They were usually extremely learned and possessed enormous amounts of necessary data in their minds; however, they were not attached to this data in a way that might limit their free inquiry.

They seemed to reject mechanical learning and often rebelled against it, denying any process of learning that threatened to condition and mold their minds. So although they were confident of their mastery of ordinary knowledge, they treated it as a platform for their innovative thinking and never as a reference point to which they could cling.

The great thinkers we discussed did not identify with the wisdom tradition of their fields. This allowed them the freedom to shrug off the past when necessary and bravely dismiss assertions that others would not even dream of doubting.

Their discontent with existing "truths" did not stop at rebelling against the wisdom tradition. These geniuses demonstrated a remarkable, even shocking, ability to rebel against their own erroneous assumptions, including doctrines that had been acclaimed by others. Their commitment to truth endowed them with the capacity to disregard their own research, including research that took many years to complete.

Equipped with the powerful weapon of non-attachment to knowledge, they felt safe inquiring even in the most unsafe, uncharted territories of the mind and life. Their thought experiments often pulled the rug out from under them, leaving them floating in the terrible space of uncertainty. However, their imagination and experimentalism led them to soar high above the safe ground of accepted knowledge.

They often intuited principles that they only took the trouble to prove logically later. They had a "top-down" way of thinking: first the vision, then the observation and proof.

Since they did not rely on fixed worldviews, they were capable of looking at things anew. They perceived that which was taken for granted by others in an almost childlike manner, with awe and curiosity. This enabled them to identify some detail, overlooked by others, and determine its potential revolutionary implications. This also allowed them to discern previously unknown patterns that ordinary thinking automatically rejects for not according with familiar knowledge.

Rapid and trans-verbal thinking

As well as transcending social structures and conventional knowledge, the outsider minds of the thinkers we have examined even transcended words. They do not seem to have relied on verbal thinking to attain their insights. They attained the insight first and only then would they articulate it in "human" language. In most cases, verbal thinking was preceded by either visual or sensory mental activity. It is as if they used a different faculty of the mind to perceive their object of study. Certainly, this mode of perception is different to our gradual, linear reasoning.

The majority of these thinkers even went so far as to describe these processes of thinking as "unconscious"—as if they take place in the unknown regions of their mind and ultimately emerge as a sudden insight. That unconscious process takes time, but the resulting insight surfaces in the conscious mind; it is experienced as an ecstatic, physical, emotional, and spiritual insight, rather than an ordinary instance of intellectual comprehension. Verbal thinking comes after the unconscious processing.

Consequently, such thinkers appear to be exceptionally quick-witted. Others find it difficult to keep up with them, as they seem to directly perceive the problem and its solution, immediately discerning the essence of the matter.

Impersonal, generalizing, and unifying thinking

Great thinkers seem to fix their gaze beyond the trivialities of everyday living. As suggested by the title of Hannah Arendt's book, *The Life of the Mind*, inner probing is, for such thinkers, so much more interesting than physical existence. Their real life unfolds in the rich environment of their mental world.

Their mind seldom troubles itself with small, mundane matters. It is, rather, oriented toward the greatest, most impersonal, and universal questions of life. One great thinker, Gautama the Buddha, demonstrated this 2,600 years ago when, instead of asking, "How can I be happy?", he determined to answer the far bigger question, "What is the source of human suffering?" Every small question is enlarged to include the whole of humanity or the whole of life or even the whole of existence. For such thinkers, life can be understood only as Life with a capital L and never as a solely personal phenomenon.

Unlike other scientists and discoverers, the thinkers we discussed were not mere specialists. They did not bury themselves in one particular area of study. Rather, they strived to gain a complete view of life. That is the difference between lower thinking and higher thinking. Lower thinking relates to one's personal existence in the world, whereas higher thinking relates to one's capacity to contemplate universal or general questions. The context in which the latter takes place is radically different.

Universal questions, with which ordinary minds usually do not trouble themselves, concern laws and fundamental principles of life and the cosmos. They aspire to identify patterns that embrace the totality of the phenomenon, rather than just expressing a fragment of it. Whether it is Freud's desire to comprehend the human psyche or Einstein's attempt to devise an all-inclusive equation, the underlying aspiration is always the attainment of a total picture of reality. Such thinkers longed for integration: making all of the pieces fit and reaching the perfect comprehension not of one element, but of everything. Two great thinkers who did not make our final list, physicist Stephen Hawking and philosopher Ken Wilber, called this the "Theory of Everything"—one system that explains it all.

An all-consuming and uncontrollable passion

Great thinkers' lives are ruled and dictated by one master: their unbridled passion for their subject of study. Indeed, they engage with this intense questioning much more than they engage with their actual lives. They would have been possessed by this passion regardless of whether they could earn their living from it, never mind becoming famous for their work. As Marie Curie described it, they are so preoccupied by their inquiry that they seem to enter a kind of dream state in which everything else fades away. They simply love what they do. They live for the questions they seek to answer and neglect their personal lives.

They cannot let go of their central question. Indeed, it often seems as if their central question, like a living entity, won't let go of them! This can last for many years and even decades, 24 hours a day, even if their pursuit ends in a failure—as in the case of Einstein, who could not realize his ambition to generalize an ultimate unified field theory. Only death can put an end to their inquiry.

This passion endows them with unimaginable powers of endurance. They undergo tremendous mental strain even in the harshest conditions, such as when afflicted by a deadly disease, experiencing personal turmoil, or living in a time of war. They fight to overcome any external obstacles to their mental task and always remain mentally alert and lively. They long for death only when they become mentally incapable. From Hawking to Freud to Einstein to Nietzsche, their unparalleled self-discipline is motivated by their passion for wisdom.

They dismiss their emotional lives as "the personal" and do not allow suffering in the emotional realm to cloud their intellectual life. It is the probing intellect that rules, not the emotions, and such thinkers seem to be capable of pushing aside emotions for the sake of their higher thinking.

Intimate relationship with nature and the cosmos

Psychoanalyst Phyllis Greenacre, who devoted a lifetime to studying the dynamics of artistic creativity, observed that the necessary condition for the blossoming of great talent or genius is the development in the young child of what she calls a "love affair with the world." She felt that this special sensitivity facilitated an early relationship with nature that resembled and could even serve as a substitute for the intimacy of personal relationships. This is congruent with our own observations. It is evident that great luminaries often have an exceptionally intense and intimate relationship with nature and the cosmos, which takes precedence over their relationships with people.

Six of the ten figures examined in this book have given mystical descriptions of the process of discovery. All six experienced a profound feeling of the wholeness of life, as well as a feeling that the answers they had come up with had derived from the depths of this wholeness. However, their relationship with this wholeness is highly individual, outside any known mystical or religious framework. Einstein captured this sentiment well when he referred to it as a "cosmic religious feeling."

Finally, six of the ten figures were characterized by a sense of mission or purpose. They seem to be relentlessly driven by this sense of purpose and feel that they can die only once they have realized their masterwork.

A touch of genius thinking

Let us return to the question with which we started our journey: Can we learn from such geniuses or are they unique figures whom we can only admire? We have made it clear from the beginning that we believe it is possible to learn from such thinkers. However, we must make two important reservations. Firstly, as illustrated in this epilogue, these thinkers' extreme demonstrations of passion and drive cannot be emulated by a simple act of wishing. Secondly, it seems that the main characteristic of the genius mind is its total autonomy and freedom. A truly free mind rejects any form of imitation and follows its original path faithfully. Therefore, no one can possibly copy this type of freedom.

Nevertheless, when we realize that we are not talking about specific and special minds, but rather about a more general type of thinking with different nuances, we may begin to see in such thinkers our own evolutionary potential. Perhaps our own minds can grow as theirs did. Perhaps such thinkers give us an early indication of how the brain of the future will function.

This may be a wild hypothesis, but geniuses do encourage us to experiment and use our imaginations, don't they? Perhaps these are qualities of thinking that we can intentionally adopt until our minds become accustomed to possessing them. Perhaps they are like pathways we can create in our minds and brains. After all, we now know for a fact that the human brain is elastic and can be continuously molded through different forms of intentional cultivation.

We can train our minds, for example, to sometimes keep us at a distance from that which is unfolding so we become mere observers, watching from the outside rather than immediately getting pulled into the drama of life. We can intentionally direct our thinking to focus on universal questions, to generalize our outlook, and to educate the brain to live with a great question for a certain period of time. We can learn to engage in daring thought experiments—boldly using our imaginative spirit—and to put aside conventional knowledge in order to obtain a fresh perspective on questions that have supposedly been completely resolved. We can even learn how to meditate on nature and the cosmos, encouraging the development of a "love affair with the world." Acquiring certain qualities, such as listening to and looking at everyday phenomena with fresh ears and eyes, not taking that which seems obvious for granted, forever staying open to new and challenging information and impressions, and freely questioning all fixed positions and dogmas, could help us to cultivate the ever-young quality of the genius mind.

Most importantly, we should feel that we are capable of doing all of these things, that the gateways to new ways of thinking are open to us. If there's one thing we can learn from geniuses, it is that our thought is an amazing tool with which we can become totally free to explore everything and anything.[201]

201 The statements at the beginning of the chapter respectively refer to Albert Einstein (Asis Kumar Chaudhuri, "Einstein in Love: Part-2 (Mileva Maric – Einstein's unfortunate wife)," *Cooking Cosmos*, May 4, 2018), Barbara McClintock (Keller, *A Feeling for the Organism*, xxii), and Hannah Arendt (Young-Bruehl, *Hannah Arendt*, 33).

BIBLIOGRAPHY

Preface

de Beauvoir, Simone. *The Second Sex.* Translated and edited by H.M. Parshley. New York: Vintage Books, 1974.

Timmermans, Maurice. "Myth: hardly anyone understands the general theory of relativity." *Observant.* January 10, 2018. https://www.observantonline.nl/English/Home/Articles/articleType/ArticleView/articleId/13192/Myth-hardly-anyone-understands-the-general-theory-of-relativity.

Chapter 1

ALBERT EINSTEIN

Thinking without words, *or*
The beetle that managed to see

Bartusiak, M. *The day we found the universe.* New York: Vintage Books, 2010.

Brenner, Richard. *Lepton and Photon Interactions at High Energies: Proceedings of the XXII International Symposium, Sweden 30 June–5 July 2005.* Hackensack, NJ: World Scientific, 2006.

Capria, Marco Mamone. *Physics before and after Einstein.* Amsterdam: IOS Press, 2005.

Condon, Edward U. "60 Years of Quantum Physics." In *Selected Popular Writings of EU Condon*, 262–278. New York: Springer, 1991.

Cunningham, D.S. *Vocation across the academy: A new vocabulary for higher education.* Oxford: Oxford University Press, 2017.

Dawkins, R., and L. Ward. *The God Delusion*. Boston, MA: Houghton Mifflin Company, 2006.

Diamond, Marian C., Arnold B. Scheibel, Greer M. Murphy, Jr., and Thomas Harvey. "On the brain of a scientist: Albert Einstein." *Experimental neurology* 88, no. 1 (1985), 198–204.

Einstein, Albert. "The Apparent Incompatibility of the Law of Propagation of Light with the Principle of Relativity." In *Relativity: The Special and the General Theory – 100th Anniversary Edition*. Princeton, NJ: Princeton University Press, 2015.

Galison, P., G.J. Holton, and S.S. Schweber. *Einstein for the 21st century: His legacy in science, art, and modern culture*. Princeton, NJ: Princeton University Press, 2018.

Galison, Peter, Gerald James Holton, and Silvan S. Schweber. *Einstein for the 21st Century: His Legacy in Science, Art, and Modern Culture*. Princeton, NJ: Princeton University Press, 2018.

Glickenstein, David. "A Bug's Eye View: The Riemannian Exponential Map on Polyhedral Surfaces." *The Mathematical Intelligencer* 40, no. 2 (2018), 1–9.

Howard, Don A., and Marco Giovanelli, "Einstein's Philosophy of Science," *The Stanford Encyclopedia of Philosophy* (Fall 2019 Edition), edited by Edward N. Zalta, https://plato.stanford.edu/archives/fall2019/entries/einstein-philscience/.

Isaacson, Walter. *Einstein: His Life and Universe*. New York: Simon & Schuster Paperbacks, 2017.

Modell, Arnold H. *Imagination and the Meaningful Brain*. Cambridge, MA: MIT Press, 2006.

Root-Bernstein, M., and R. Root-Bernstein. "Einstein on creative thinking: Music and the intuitive art of scientific imagination." *Psychology Today* 42 (2010), 1–7.

Root-Bernstein, R. "Multiple giftedness in adults: the case of polymaths." In *International handbook on giftedness*. New York: Springer, 2009.

Root-Bernstein, Robert Scott, and Michele Root-Bernstein. *Sparks of Genius: The 13 Thinking Tools of the World's Most Creative People*. Boston, MA: Houghton-Mifflin, 1999.

Suzuki, David, and Ian Hanington. *Everything under the Sun: Toward a Brighter Future on a Small Blue Planet*. Vancouver: Greystone Books, 2012.

Swimme, B. *Hidden heart of the cosmos: Humanity and the new story*. Maryknoll, NY: Orbis Books, 2019.

Treder-Wolff, Jude. *Possible Futures: Creative Thinking for the Speed of Life*. Smithtown, NY: Lifestage Productions, 2008.

Zhang, L., Sternberg, R.J., and Rayner, S. *Handbook of intellectual styles: Preferences in cognition, learning, and thinking*. New York, NY: Springer, 2012.

Chapter 2

FRIEDRICH NIETZSCHE

Thinking that seeks no comfort, *or*
Sailing the stormy sea of doubt

Hollingdale, R.J. *Nietzsche: The Man and his Philosophy*. New York: Cambridge University Press, 1999.

Kahneman, Daniel. *Thinking, Fast and Slow*. London: Penguin Books, 2012.

Kaufmann, Walter. *Freud, Adler, and Jung*. Piscataway, NJ: Transaction Publishers, 2009.

Nietzsche, Friedrich. "The Anti-Christ, Ecce Homo, Twilight of the Idols, and Other Writings – Edited by Aaron Ridley and Judith Norman." Cambridge University Press. http://assets.cambridge.org/052181/6599/excerpt/0521816599_excerpt.htm.

Nietzsche, Friedrich. *Beyond Good and Evil*. Translated by Helen Zimmern. Marxists.org, 2003. https://www.marxists.org/reference/archive/nietzsche/1886/beyond-good-evil/index.htm

The Nietzsche Channel. "Nietzsche Poems." The Nietzsche Channel, 26 November 2020. http://www.thenietzschechannel.com/poetry/poetry-dual.htm

Peery, Rebekah S.. *Nietzsche for the 21st Century*. New York: Algora Publishing, 2010.

Philosiblog. "Convictions are more dangerous foes of truth than lies." Philosiblog, May 20, 2013. https://philosiblog.com/2013/05/20/convictions-are-more-dangerous-foes-of-truth-than-lies/#:~:text=%E2%80%93%20Nietzsche,what%20a%20fight%20it%20was!.

Popova, Maria. "Friedrich Nietzsche on Why a Fulfilling Life Requires Embracing Rather than Running from Difficulty." Brainpickings, November 26, 2020. https://www.brainpickings.org/2014/10/15/nietzsche-on-difficulty/#:~:text=I%20have%20a%20terrible%20fear,anyone%20can%20confer%20upon%20himself.

Ratner-Rosenhagen, Jennifer. "American Nietzsche." *Nochrisis*, November 26, 2020. https://nochrisis.blog/american-nietzsche/#:~:text=Nietzsche%20never%20tired%20of%20contemplating,consolation%2C%20where%20would%20I%20be%3F.

Westacott, Emrys. "Nietzsche's Idea of Eternal Recurrence." ThoughtCo., February 12, 2020. https://www.thoughtco.com/nietzsches-idea-of-the-eternal-recurrence-2670659.

Westacott, Emrys. "What Does Nietzsche Mean When He Says That God Is Dead?" ThoughtCo., January 8, 2018. https://www.thoughtco.com/nietzsche-god-is-dead-2670670.

Young, Julian. *Friedrich Nietzsche: A Philosophical Biography*. New York: Cambridge University Press, 2010.

Chapter 3

BARBARA MCCLINTOCK

Organic thinking, *or*
The different kernel on the corn cob

"Colleagues: Barbara McClintock," Esther M. Zimmer Lederberg Memorial Website, retrieved March 2, 2013. http://www.estherlederberg.com/EImages/Cold%20Spring%20Harbor/McClintockB.html

Comfort, Nathaniel C. *The Tangled Field.* Cambridge, MA: Harvard University Press, 2003.

Keller, Evelyn Fox. *A Feeling for the Organism*. New York: Holt Paperbacks, 1983.

Mitchell, Juliet. "Introduction to Melanie Klein." In *Reading Melanie Klein*, edited by Lyndsey Stonebridge and John Phillips. New York: Routledge, 1998.

Soble, Alan. "Keller on Gender, Science, and McClintock," in Cassandra L. Pinnick, Noretta Koertge, and Robert F. Almeder, eds., *Scrutinizing Feminist Epistemology: An Examination of Gender in Science* (New Brunswick, NJ: Rutgers University Press, 2003), 65–101.

Todayinsci. "Science Quotes by Barbara McClintock." November 27, 2020. https://todayinsci.com/M/McClintock_Barbara/McClintockBarbara-Quotations.htm.

Chapter 4

SIGMUND FREUD

The excavator, *or*
The forgotten secret of the burnt pudding

Breger, Louis. *Freud: Darkness in the Midst of Vision*. New York: Wiley, 2000.

Cleantis, Tracey. "Freudian-Express: Dreams, The Royal Road to the Unconscious." *Psychology Today*, January 14, 2011. https://www.

psychologytoday.com/us/blog/freudian-sip/201101/freudian-express-dreams-the-royal-road-the-unconscious.

Freud, Sigmund. *The Interpretation of Dreams*. Translated by A. A. Brill. London: Wordsworth Editions, 1997.

Gay, Peter. *Freud: A Life for our Time*. New York: Norton, 1998.

Gresser, Moshe. *Dual Allegiance*. New York: State University of New York Press, 1994.

Rabate, Jean-Michel. *The Cambridge Introduction to Literature and Psychoanalysis*. New York: Cambridge University Press, 2014.

Robinson, Forrest, "Twain and Freud," in *The Jester and the Sages*. Edited by Forrest G. Robinson, Gabriel Noah Brahm Jr., and Catherine Carlstroem. Columbia: University of Missouri Press, 2011.

Scherer, Frank F. *Freud's Orient: Early Psychoanalysis, "Anti-Semitic Challenge", and the Vicissitudes of Orientalist Discourse*. A dissertation. York University Toronto, Ontario, 2010. https://central.bac-lac.gc.ca/.item?id=NR80539&op=pdf&app=Library&oclc_number=890511509.

Chapter 5

LEONARDO DA VINCI

Thinking from all perspectives, *or*
Life as an unfinished work of art

BBC Culture. "Leonardo da Vinci's groundbreaking anatomical sketches." October 11, 2014. https://www.bbc.com/culture/article/20130828-leonardo-da-vinci-the-anatomist.

Clark, Kenneth, and Martin Kemp. *Leonardo da Vinci*. Revised edn. London: Penguin, 2015.

Csíkszentmihályi, Mihály. *Creativity: Flow and the Psychology of Discovery and Invention*. New York: HarperCollins, 1996.

da Vinci, Leonardo. *The Notebooks of Leonard Da Vinci, Vol. 2.* New York: Dover Publications, 2012.

D'Epiro, Peter, and Mary Desmond Pinkowish. *Sprezzatura: 50 Ways Italian Genius Shaped the World.* New York: Anchor Books, 2001.

Hürter, Tobias. "Ich bin Zwei." Translated by D. Brenner. *Die Zeit*, no. 25, 2013.

Ladwein, Michael. *Leonardo da Vinci: The Last Supper. A Cosmic Drama and an Act of Redemption.* Forest Row: Temple Lodge, 2006.

McGilchrist, Ian. *The Master and his Emissary: The Divided Brain and the Making of the Western World.* New Haven, CT: Yale University Press, 2012

Pedretti, Carlo (ed.). *Leonardo da Vinci on Painting: A Lost Book (Libro A).* Berkeley: University of California Press, 1964.

Popova, Maria. "Leonardo's Brain: What a Posthumous Brain Scan Six Centuries Later Reveals about the Source of Da Vinci's Creativity." Brainpickings. http://www.brainpickings.org/2014/11/17/leonardos-brain-leonard-shlain/.

Shlain, Leonard. *Leonardo's Brain. Understanding Leonardo's Creative Genius.* Lanham, MD: Lyons Press, 2014.

Steinberg, Leo. *Leonardo's Incessant Last Supper.* New York: Zone Books, 2001.

Chapter 6

SOCRATES

The philosophical lover, *or*
Do not fear the nothingness

Beck, Sanderson. "The Socratic Problem." In *Confucius and Socrates: Teaching Wisdom.* http://www.san.beck.org/SocraticProblem.html.

Cicero, Marcus Tullius. *Cicero and the Natural Law*. Translated by Walter Nicgorski. http://www.nlnrac.org/classical/cicero.

Engelmann, J.B. (ed.). *Sokrates und seine Zeit. Eine historische Schilderung für Jünglinge und Jungfrauen*. Translated by D. Brenner. Frankfurt am Main: Andreä, 1812.

Helfer, Ariel. *Socrates and Alcibiades: Plato's Drama of Political Ambition and Philosophy*. Philadelphia: University of Pennsylvania Press, 2017.

Hughes, Bettany. *The Hemlock Cup: Socrates, Athens and the Search for the Good Life*. New York: Vintage Books, 2012.

Johnson, Paul. *Socrates: A Man for Our Times*. New York: Viking, 2011.

Nietzsche, Friedrich. *Werke in drei Bänden*. http://www.zeno.org/nid/20009241035.

Plato. *Apology*. In *Plato in Twelve Volumes, Vol. 1*. Translated by Harold North Fowler. Introduction by W.R.M. Lamb. Cambridge, MA: Harvard University Press, 1966. https://tinyurl.com/y6w2ntjh

Plato. *Phaedrus*. Translation quoted from Plato, *Complete Works*, edited by John Cooper. Indianapolis, IN: Hackett, 1997.

Plato. *Symposium*. In *Complete Works*, edited by John Cooper. Indianapolis, IN: Hackett, 1997.

Xenophon. *Memorabilia*, edited by E.C. Marchant. http://www.perseus.tufts.edu/hopper/text?doc=Xen.%20Mem.%203&lang=original.

Chapter 7

HANNAH ARENDT

Active thinking, *or*
Eichmann as a metaphor

Arendt, Hannah. *The Jew as Pariah*. New York: Grove Press, 1978.

Arendt, Hannah. "Martin Heidegger at Eighty." *New York Review of Books* 17/6 (October 21 1971), 50–54.

Arendt, Hannah. *Men in Dark Times*. New York: Harcourt Brace Jovanovich, 1968.

Arendt, Hannah. *Rahel Varnhagen*. Baltimore, MD: The Johns Hopkins University Press, 2000.

Arendt, Hannah. "What is Existenz Philosophy?" *Partisan Review* 8/1 (Winter 1946), 34–56.

Bernauer, James W. *Amor Mundi: Explorations in the Faith and Thought of Hannah Arendt*. Berlin: Springer, 2012.

Booth, Ken. *Theory of World Security*. Cambridge: Cambridge, University Press, 2007.

Goldoni, Marco, and Chris McCorkindale. *Hannah Arendt & the Law*. Oxford: Hart Publishing, 2012.

Stack Altoids. "Hanna Arendt 'Zur Person' full Interview." April 8, 2013. https://www.youtube.com/watch?v=dsoImQfVsO4

Voegelin, Eric. *Hitler and the Germans*. Colombia: University of Missouri Press, 1999.

Young-Bruehl, Elisabeth. *Hannah Arendt: For Love of the World*. New Haven, CT: Yale, 1982.

Chapter 8

CHARLES DARWIN

Dynamic thinking, *or*
A force like a hundred thousand wedges

Darwin, Charles. *The Autobiography of Charles Darwin, From the Life and Letters of Charles Darwin*, edited by his son Francis Darwin. http://www.gutenberg.org/files/2010/2010-h/2010-h.htm.

Darwin, Charles. *The Origin of Species by means of natural selection or the preservation of favored races in the struggle for life*, vol. 2 [1859]. https://oll.libertyfund.org/titles/darwin-the-origin-of-species-vol-2.

Darwin, Charles. *A Naturalist's Voyage Round the World: The Voyage of the Beagle*. http://www.gutenberg.org/files/3704/3704-h/3704-h.htm.

Darwin Correspondence Project. *The Correspondence of Charles Darwin, Volume 1: 1821–1836*. http://www.darwinproject.ac.uk/correspondence-volume-1.

Darwin Correspondence Project. *The Correspondence of Charles Darwin, Volume 2: 1837–1843*. http://www.darwinproject.ac.uk/correspondence-volume-2.

Engels, Eve-Marie. *Charles Darwin*. Munich: C.H. Beck, 2007.

Le Ker, Heike. "Darwins Selektionstheorie: Der zaudernde Evoluzzer." *Der Spiegel*. http://www.spiegel.de/wissenschaft/mensch/darwins-selektionstheorie-der-zaudernde-evoluzzer-a-601504.html.

Quammen, David. *The Reluctant Mr. Darwin: An Intimate Portrait of Charles Darwin and the Making of His Theory of Evolution*. Great Discoveries Series. New York: W. W. Norton, 2007.

Shapiro, Alison Bonds. "Getting out of the way. The Balance between Homeostasis and Growth." *Psychology Today*. https://www.psychologytoday.com/intl/blog/healing-possibility/201103/getting-out-the-way-the-balance-between-homeostasis-and-growth.

Stauffer, R.C. (ed.). *Charles Darwin's Natural Selection: Being the Second Part of His Big Species Book Written from 1856 to 1858*. http://darwin-online.org.uk/content/frameset?itemID=F1583&viewtype=text&pageseq=1.

Whewell, William. *History of the Inductive Sciences: From the Earliest Times to the Present*, vol. 3, 1837, quoted in David L. Hull, *Darwin and His Critics: The Reception of Darwin's Theory of Evolution by the Scientific Community*. Cambridge, MA: Harvard University Press, 1973.

Chapter 9

JIDDU KRISHNAMURTI

Negating thinking, *or*
A vessel with many holes

Anderson, Allan. *A Wholly Different Way of Living*. London: Victor Gollancz, 1991.

"Henry Miller on Krishnamurti." JKrishnamurti-sussex. June 18, 2009. http://jkrishnamurti-sussex.info/henry-miller-on-krishnamurti-2/.

Jayakar, Pupul. *J. Krishnamurti: A Biography*. New Delhi: Penguin Books, 1986.

Loftus, Elizabeth F. "Creating False Memories." *Scientific American*, September 1997, vol. 277, no. 3, 70–75. https://staff.washington.edu/eloftus/Articles/sciam.htm.

Lutyens, Mary. *Krishnamurti: The Years of Awakening*. New York: Farrar, Straus and Giroux, 1975.

Nayanar, Maya. "The Serach J Krishnamurti 1927." April 5, 2020. https://archive.org/details/thesearchjkrishnamurti1927_202004_229_R/page/n5/mode/2up.

Sanat, Aryel. *The Inner Life of Krishnamurti*. Wheaton, IL: Quest Books, 1999.

Chapter 10

GIORDANO BRUNO

Thinking in context, *or*
Why there is a universe in every hair

Blum, Paul Richard. *Giordano Bruno*. Munich: Beck, 1999.

Bruno, Giordano. *Das Unermeßliche und Unzählbare, Books 1 and 2 (De Immense and Innuberabilibus)*. Translation by Erika Rojas. Ahrensburg: Skorpion, 1999.

Bruno, Giordano. *De immenso*, quoted in Ramón G. Mendoza, *The Acentric Labyright: Giordano Bruno's Prelude to Contemporary Cosmology*. Rockport, MA: Element, 1995.

Bruno, Giordano. *Dialogues on the Infinite Universe and Worlds*, quoted in Dorothea Waley Singer, *Giordano Bruno: His Life and Thought: With Annotated Translation of his Work, "On the Infinite Universe and Worlds."* Westport, CT: Greenwood Press, 1968.

Bruno, Giordiano. *The Expulsion of the Triumphant Beast*. Translated and edited by Arthur D. Imerti. Lincoln: Nebraska University Press, 1964.

Druyan, Ann, and Steven Soter. *Cosmos: A Spacetime Odyssey* (2014). Episode 1.

Franke, Klaus, Ulrich Schwarz, and Peter Wensierski. "Gottes willige Vollstrecker." *Der Spiegel*, January 6, 1998. https://www.spiegel.de/spiegel/print/d-7897629.html.

Gatti, Hilary. *Giordano Bruno and Renaissance Science*. Ithaca, NY: Cornell University Press, 2002.

Heuser, Harro. *Unendlichkeiten: Nachrichten aus dem Grand Canyon des Geistes*. Wiesbaden: B.G. Teubner Verlag, 2008. The original source is Bruno's *Dialogues on the Infinite Universe and Worlds*.

Marciniak, Vwadek P. *Towards a History of Consciousness: Space, Time, and Death*. New York: Peter Lang, 2006.

Michele, D. Karl Ludwig (ed.). *Georg Wilhelm Friedrich Hegel's Vorlesungen* über *die Geschichte der Philosophie*. Volume 3. Berlin, 1836.

Rowland, Ingrid D. *Giordano Bruno: Philosopher/Heretic*. Chicago: University of Chicago Press, 2009.

Schopenhauer, Arthur. *Schopenhauer-Lexikon. Ein philosophisches Wörterbuch, nach Arthur Schopenhauers sämmtlichen Schriften und handschriftlichem Nachlaß*, edited by Julius Frauenstädt, Vol. 2. Leipzig, 1871.

Singer, Dorothea Waley. *Giordano Bruno: His Life and Thought, With Annotated Translation of His Work On the Infinite Universe and Worlds.* New York: Schumann, 1950.

Swimme, Brian. *The Hidden Heart of the Cosmos*, 2nd edn. Maryknoll, NY: Orbis Books, 2000.

Weber, Georg. *Literar-historisches Lesebuch.* Leipzig, 1852.

Wildgen, Wolfgang. *Das kosmische Gedächtnis. Kosmologie, Semiotik und Gedächtniskunst im Werk von Giordano Bruno.* Bern: Peter Lang, 1998.

Epilogue

Chaudhuri, Asis Kumar. "Einstein in Love: Part-2 (Mileva Maric – Einstein's unfortunate wife)." *Cooking Cosmos.* May 4, 2018. https://asischaudhuri.wordpress.com/2018/05/04/einstein-in-love-part-2-mileva-maric%E2%94%80-einsteins-unfortunate-wife/.

Keller, Evelyn Fox. *A Feeling for the Organism*. New York: Owl Books, 1983.

Young-Bruehl, Elisabeth. *Hannah Arendt: For Love of the World.* New Haven, CT: Yale, 1982.